This Land Is Not For Sale

INTEGRATION AND CONFLICT STUDIES

Published in association with the Max Planck Institute for Social Anthropology, Halle/Saale

Series Editor: Günther Schlee, Arba Minch University, Ethiopia, and Director Emeritus at the Max Planck Institute for Social Anthropology

Editorial Board: Brian Donahoe (Max Planck Institute for Social Anthropology), John Eidson (Max Planck Institute for Social Anthropology), Peter Finke (University of Zurich), Jacqueline Knörr (Max Planck Institute for Social Anthropology), Bettina Mann (Max Planck Institute for Social Anthropology), Ursula Rao (Leipzig University), Stephen Reyna (University of Manchester), Olaf Zenker (Martin Luther University, Halle-Wittenberg)

Assisted by: Viktoria Giehler-Zeng (Max Planck Institute for Social Anthropology)

The objective of the Max Planck Institute for Social Anthropology is to advance anthropological fieldwork and enhance theory building. 'Integration' and 'conflict', the central themes of this series, are major concerns of the contemporary social sciences and of significant interest to the general public. They have also been among the main research areas of the institute since its foundation. Bringing together international experts, *Integration and Conflict Studies* includes both monographs and edited volumes, and offers a forum for studies that contribute to a better understanding of processes of identification and inter-group relations.

Recent volumes:

Volume 27
This Land Is Not For Sale: Trust and Transitions in Northern Uganda
  Edited by Lotte Meinert and
  Susan Reynolds Whyte

Volume 26
African Political Systems Revisited: Changing Perspectives on Statehood and Power
  Edited by Aleksandar Bošković and
  Günther Schlee

Volume 25
Entrepreneurs of Identity: The Islamic State's Symbolic Repertoire
  Christoph Günther

Volume 24
After Corporate Paternalism: Material Renovation and Social Change in Times of Ruination
  Christian Straube

Volume 23
Lands of the Future: Anthropological Perspectives on Pastoralism, Land Deals and Tropes of Modernity in Eastern Africa
  Edited by Echi Christina Gabbert,
  Fana Gebresenbet, John G. Galaty and
  Günther Schlee

Volume 22
On Mediation: Historical, Legal, Anthropological and International Perspectives
  Edited by Karl Härter, Carolin Hillemanns
  and Günther Schlee

Volume 21
Space, Place and Identity: Wodaaɓe of Niger in the 21st Century
  Florian Köhler

Volume 20
Mobile Urbanity: Somali Presence in Urban East Africa
  Edited by Neil Carrier and Tabea Scharrer

Volume 19
Playing the Marginality Game: Identity Politics in West Africa
  Anita Schroven

Volume 18
The Wheel of Autonomy: Rhetoric and Ethnicity in the Omo Valley
  Felix Girke

For a full volume listing, please see the series page on our website: http://www.berghahnbooks.com/series/integration-and-conflict-studies

This Land Is Not For Sale
Trust and Transitions in Northern Uganda

Edited by Lotte Meinert and Susan Reynolds Whyte

berghahn
NEW YORK · OXFORD
www.berghahnbooks.com

First published in 2023 by
Berghahn Books
www.berghahnbooks.com

© 2023, 2025 Lotte Meinert and Susan Reynolds Whyte
First paperback edition published in 2025

All rights reserved. Except for the quotation of short passages
for the purposes of criticism and review, no part of this book
may be reproduced in any form or by any means, electronic or
mechanical, including photocopying, recording, or any information
storage and retrieval system now known or to be invented,
without written permission of the publisher.

Library of Congress Cataloging-in-Publication Data
Names: Meinert, Lotte, editor, author. | Whyte, Susan Reynolds, editor, author.
Title: This Land Is Not For Sale: Trust and Transitions in Northern Uganda / edited by Lotte Meinert and Susan Reynolds Whyte.
Description: New York: Berghahn Books, 2023. | Series: Integration and Conflict Studies; 27 | Includes bibliographical references and index.
Identifiers: LCCN 2022036407 (print) | LCCN 2022036408 (ebook) |
   ISBN 9781800736979 (hardback) | ISBN 9781805390473 (open access ebook)
Subjects: LCSH: Land tenure—Social aspects—Uganda. | Trust—Social aspects—Uganda.
Classification: LCC HD984 .T45 2023 (print) | LCC HD984 (ebook) |
   DDC 306.32096761—dc23/eng/20220801
LC record available at https://lccn.loc.gov/2022036407
LC ebook record available at https://lccn.loc.gov/2022036408

British Library Cataloguing in Publication Data
A catalogue record for this book is available from the British Library

ISBN 978-1-80073-697-9 hardback
ISBN 978-1-80539-742-7 paperback
ISBN 978-1-80073-698-6 epub
ISBN 978-1-80539-047-3 web pdf

https://doi.org/10.3167/9781800736979

The electronic open access publication of *This Land Is Not For Sale* has been made available under a CC BY-NC-ND 4.0 license as a part of the Berghahn Open Migration and Development Studies initiative.

This work is published subject to a Creative Commons Attribution Noncommercial No Derivatives 4.0 License. The terms of the license can be found at http://creativecommons.org/licenses/by-nc-nd/4.0/. For uses beyond those covered in the license contact Berghahn Books.

Contents

List of Illustrations	vii
Foreword *Sara Berry*	ix
Acknowledgements	xvi
Introduction. Trust and Transitions in Northern Uganda *Lotte Meinert and Susan Reynolds Whyte*	1

Part I. Claims to Land

Case I. A Disputed Land Sale *Mette Lind Kusk*	29
Chapter 1. Multiplicity *Stephen Langole, Susan Reynolds Whyte and Michael Whyte*	39
Chapter 2. Transactions *Lotte Meinert and Mette Lind Kusk*	57
Chapter 3. Conflicts *Irene Winnie Anying and Quentin Gausset*	73

Part II. Intimate Governance of Land

Case II. Disputed Land and Broken Graves   93
Sophie Seebach

Chapter 4. Generations   101
Esther Acio, Lioba Lenhart and Susan Reynolds Whyte

Chapter 5. Gender   120
Julaina A. Obika and Hanne O. Mogensen

Chapter 6. Belonging   138
Ben Adol Otto, Michael Whyte and Susan Reynolds Whyte

Part III. Imagining Development

Case III. Claiming 'Their' School: Land Dispute between Two Churches over a Primary School   157
Catrine Shroff

Chapter 7. Aspirations   165
Susan Reynolds Whyte and Catrine Shroff

Chapter 8. Inside-Outsiders   183
Marianne Mosebo and Lotte Meinert

Chapter 9. Conservation   203
Lioba Lenhart and Lotte Meinert

Afterword. Who Belongs Where, and What Belongs to Whom?   225
Christian Lund

Appendix. Land Legislation and Implementation in Uganda   231
Anne Mette Kjær

Index   233

Illustrations

Figures

0.1.	Building not for sale © Mette Lind Kusk.	xviii
CI.1.	In the office of the RDC © Mette Lind Kusk.	30
CI.2.	The RDC © Mette Lind Kusk.	30
CI.3.	Accusations © Mette Lind Kusk.	31
CI.4.	Accusations © Mette Lind Kusk.	31
CI.5.	Calculations © Mette Lind Kusk.	32
CI.6.	Calculations © Mette Lind Kusk.	33
CI.7.	Advice from the RDC © Mette Lind Kusk.	33
CI.8.	Enmity © Mette Lind Kusk.	34
CI.9.	'No road here' © Mette Lind Kusk.	36
CII.1.	Traditional grave © Mette Lind Kusk.	93
CII.2.	Cemented grave © Mette Lind Kusk.	93
CII.3.	Community meeting © Mette Lind Kusk.	94
CII.4.	In the office of the LC1 © Mette Lind Kusk.	95

CII.5.	Destroying graves at night © Mette Lind Kusk.	96
CII.6.	Shocked family members © Mette Lind Kusk.	97
CII.7.	Community meeting © Mette Lind Kusk.	98
CII.8.	Oyo leaves the community © Mette Lind Kusk.	99
4.1.	Daniel's family ties © Lioba Lenhart.	103
CIII.1.	The two churches and the school © Mette Lind Kusk.	157
CIII.2.	Wilderness © Mette Lind Kusk.	158
CIII.3.	Letter © Mette Lind Kusk.	158
CIII.4.	Meeting with the chief © Mette Lind Kusk.	159
CIII.5.	Catholic missionaries © Mette Lind Kusk.	160
CIII.6.	Police interrogation © Mette Lind Kusk.	161
CIII.7.	Community meeting © Mette Lind Kusk.	162
CIII.8.	A hindrance to development © Mette Lind Kusk.	163

Maps

0.1.	Subregions of Uganda with districts in Acholi, Karamoja and Lango regions. Map based on Uganda Bureau of Statistics. Graphics by Moesgaard Museum Graphics Department.	5
2.1.	Ik County bordering Turkana territory in Kenya, Dodoth Territory, Kidepo National Park and Timu Forest Reserve in Uganda. Map prepared by Nick Leffler.	61

Foreword

Sara Berry

For much of the twentieth century, both scholars and practitioners viewed Africa as a region endowed with abundant supplies of land. Unlike densely populated areas in Asia or areas of Latin America where a few people controlled large amounts of land, in Africa land was neither a constraint on economic growth or a major source of conflict, and hence of little concern to politicians, policymakers or students of development. Beginning in the 1980s, these assumptions came increasingly into question. As competition over land increased, land transactions became increasingly commercialized, land prices rose and conflicts multiplied. Rival claimants turned to government officials, adjudicators, NGOs, relatives and neighbours to mediate disputes or testify on their behalf. In the process, struggles over land restructured relations of kinship and authority as well as patterns of market exchange and the distribution of wealth – reinforcing or destabilizing established hierarchies and networks and sparking intense debates over value, entitlement and belonging.

Struggles over land took distinctive forms in northern Uganda, where decades of violent conflict gave way to relative security by 2010. In the Karamoja sub-region, disarmament and the decline of raiding opened possibilities of development, particularly projects by outside investors. The claims they asserted were very different from the claims and uses with which local people were familiar. In the Acholi sub-region, conflicts over land were delayed during the long insurgency of the Lord's Resistance Army, when the government forced much of the rural population into Internally Displaced Persons camps. Competition over access to and control of land re-emerged after 2006, when the camps were disbanded and people began to return to their former homes. While some chose to remain in the small urban centres that had hosted the camps, many returned to their villages, planning to reclaim their land, settle and resume cultivation. As they did so, however, frequent disputes broke out over who could legitimately claim which pieces of land. In many cases, returnees found that other people had occupied their land, or they faced challenges from their own relatives over who had the right to use family land. *This Land Is Not For Sale* presents a group of case studies that illuminate the complexity of post-conflict land-claiming processes and reflect on their implications for Ugandan society and economy.

The chapters in *This Land Is Not For Sale* are written by a group of Danish and Ugandan researchers who carried out field research in separate localities but conferred frequently through personal communications and in annual workshops to refine their field inquiries, compare findings and discuss the broader implications of their work. The result is a cohesive set of local studies that combine richly detailed ethnographic accounts of individuals' and families' struggles to claim and hold on to land, with broader reflections on their relevance not only for Uganda but also for social scientists' understanding of the way rising pressure on land is reshaping African economies and societies in the early twenty-first century. Through repeated sojourns in the localities they were studying, the authors were able not only to build long-term relationships with their local interlocutors, giving them access to information that was not shared on their first visits, but also to observe changes in people's attitudes towards the cases they were involved in and their relations with one another. The result is a series of studies that illuminate the dynamics of land-claiming processes by placing anthropological fieldwork in historical and comparative perspective.

In keeping with the collaborative character and multilevel aims of the authors' research, each chapter begins with a detailed narrative of a particular case; a specific theme is then highlighted – multiplicity, belonging, aspirations, etc. – that opens the way for broader discussions of policy and anthropological theory. In a further expression of the collaborative character of the study, each chapter is co-authored by two or three members of the research team. The group includes scholars of varying seniority – tenured professors, graduate students and recent Ph.D.s – who worked together throughout the research and writing process without regard to nationality or academic rank.

By carrying out their studies in conversation with one another, Lotte Meinert, Susan Reynolds Whyte and their colleagues address common themes from multiple perspectives, enriching both the local narratives and discussions of their conceptual significance. Nearly everyone involved in making, defending and adjudicating claims on land agrees on the importance of 'development' – a consensus made possible by the polyvalence of the term. By keeping their focus 'close to the ground and to people who use the ground', the authors interrogate the complexity of people's aspirations, seeking to provide a 'more nuanced understanding' of responses to development. By including studies of land conflicts in Karamoja and Ik as well as Acholi communities, they also go beyond the limitations of a single ethnographic case. Together, their studies support other recent analyses in arguing that many post-conflict land disputes are too varied and complex to be justly dealt with by a single act of legislation. In effect, *This Land Is Not For Sale* makes a case that to avoid arbitrary impoverishment or dispossession local disputes must be negotiated one case at a time at the local level.

In making their case that justice in land matters is local, the authors emphasize two major themes: 1) that making and defending claims on land is a process rather than a one-off event, and 2) that processes of making, defending and/or losing claims on land hinge on relations of trust. Trust (or the lack thereof) works to promote agreement (or conflict) among claimants and between claimants, NGOs, local authorities and state officials who seek to participate in and/or govern the claiming process.

Claims on land are regulated by law, but since Uganda, like many other African countries, recognizes both statutory and customary laws, reference to legal norms tends to promote multiple understandings of who owns the land and how it may be used. In many cases, disputed claims to land are carried out outside of official channels, through networks of interaction and understanding among acquaintances. In Chapter 2, Lotte Meinert and Mette Kusk describe the first sale of land in an Ik community in north-eastern Uganda. They argue that the sale itself *created* 'original owners'. Prior to the transaction, at least three families had been users of the land over time, and a clan leader had been the caretaker looking after the land. But because the buyer – a foreign company – needed a few specified sellers to sign the transaction papers, three 'owners' were established, and people who had previously used the land for different purposes were pushed aside.

Because they are 'embedded in social relationships', transactions in land often promote rather than quell disputes over who may do what with a piece of land. Access to and control over land hinge not only on 'bundles of rights' but also on bundles of obligations among the transactors, their relatives, neighbours and others. Their analysis echoes Shipton's observation apropos development agencies' frustration over farmers' unpaid debts, that rural Luo often failed to pay back institutional loans *not* because they did not understand the concept of repayment but because they had more important obligations to take care of first (Shipton 2007: 101–2). In a plural legal context, transactions may serve to reinforce claims as well as vice versa. In describing the growing number of land transactions in a cocoa farming area of southern Côte d'Ivoire, Jean-Pierre Dozon observed that the point was not 'I am an owner, therefore I sell' but 'I sell, therefore I am an owner' (Dozon 1985: 289).

Conflicts may also arise from different understandings of obligations, transactions or wealth. In the past, Shipton argued, Luo acquired livestock not to keep them but to give them away – as bridewealth, loans, collateral, funeral gifts, inheritance, etc. – transferring material wealth (in this case, animals) to other people in order to build and sustain social relationships (Shipton 2009). As population growth, urban expansion and commercialization changed the value of livestock in Kenya, the meaning of transactions changed too. Like transfers of land, transfers of livestock became increasingly commercialized, and livestock owners were more inclined to keep animals they acquired, treating them as a store of wealth to be sold only when needed to defray necessary expenses, rather than given away at the first opportunity. Yet social payments did not simply disappear. Land, cattle and other material goods – or their equivalent monetary values – continue to be transferred as wedding gifts, consumed in funerary rites or bequeathed to relatives of the deceased owners, reinforcing family ties even as they promote monetization.

The book's focus on tensions over land within close social relationships fits with developments in other African settings. In Ghana, many people now designate their heirs while they are still alive, rather than leaving their property to be held and managed collectively by their kin group as a whole. At the same time, however, individualized inheritance may coexist with older forms of family bequest rather than replacing them. Ghana's Law on Intestate Succession (PNDCL 111), passed in 1985, is a good example. Before the law was enacted, when a man died, his property passed to his matrilineal kin, leaving his widow to seek support from her own natal family or fend for herself. As cocoa farming became the economic mainstay of the Ghanaian economy, women who had worked on their husbands' farms for years without pay began to claim a share of the farm(s) they had helped create. By the 1980s, their plight caught the attention of J. J. Rawlings, head of Ghana's then military regime. To protect bereaved spouses and their children from dispossession, Rawlings' government enacted PNDCL 111, mandating that the bulk of a deceased person's property go to his (or her) surviving spouse, with minority shares reserved for surviving kin.[1] However, the law applies only to property the deceased person acquired for him/herself. 'Family property' in which the deceased held a beneficial interest by virtue of membership in his or her natal kin group remains family property forever. Upheld in repeated court judgments, individually held title deeds and collective customary property coexist (Berry 2022).

Land arrangements in Uganda also frequently involve combinations of statutory law, custom and social practice, often referred to as 'legal pluralism'. In Chapter 4, Esther Acio, Lioba Lenhart and Susan Reynolds Whyte show how the process of reclaiming land after disbanding the IDP camps fostered intergenerational tensions. Elders accused youth of being lazy and disrespectful, while young people complained that their elders were greedy, secretive and used witchcraft to secure family land for themselves. Mistrust did not sever the connections, however. Young men supported the restoration of patrilineal authority and control over land in order to claim access to family land through their elders. Those who were saving to buy land for themselves planned to do so in addition to sustaining their claims on family land. Ben Adol Otto, Michael Whyte and Susan Reynolds Whyte strike a similar note in Chapter 6 on 'Belonging'. Social membership, they argue, is not an ascribed fact but a process: 'belonging has to be practised'. People hold funerals and bury their relatives 'at home', they explain, to demonstrate that they belong to the land and the land belongs to them.

The authors share the view that land claims are best understood as social processes that play out over time as people assert their claims, challenge competing claimants, and appeal to a variety of authorities to help defend them. People with the knowledge and means to seek formal authorization of their claims may apply for titles or take land disputes to court hoping to settle them once and for all. But obtaining a title deed requires working through layers of bureaucracy – a long and expensive process that many people cannot afford and others prefer to avoid.

As the case studies in this volume make clear, probably a majority of land disputes are settled outside of official channels. This does not mean that 'settlements' are either straightforward or conclusive. Claimants may reach agreement on who may use a piece of land without settling the question of who owns it or attempting to consolidate multiple forms of land use in the hands of a single individual or social unit such as a household. Members of a household may cultivate a piece of land, individually or together, while allowing others to traverse the plot, hunt, gather naturally occurring plants or graze livestock on stubble left after crops have been harvested.

The variety of land uses and arrangements people have developed to enable or constrain them is vividly illustrated by Stephen Langole's 'autoethnographic' account in Chapter 1. At the time of writing, Langole claimed six different pieces of land – the plot at his residence in town, another urban plot and four rural parcels. Each plot was contested on a variety of grounds. Langole hoped to secure his claim by obtaining titles for his land but confronted many obstacles, social as well as bureaucratic. Access to land, the authors explain, requires 'a network of acquaintances' and continuing engagement with rival claimants, potential witnesses, adjudicators, authorities and others. 'Landholding', Langole concludes, 'is something that should constantly be negotiated and be accommodative of other interests'.

In all of these social processes, the authors of *This Land Is Not For Sale* emphasize the importance of trust. Trust and mistrust, they explain, are matters of affect as well as social interaction. Whether land transactions take place and on what terms depends, in part, on how land claimants feel about one another. Transactions between parties who do not know each other are mediated by 'inside-outsiders', who have some familiarity with each side (Chapter 8). As many of their cases show, trust and mistrust develop through interactions shaped by would-be transactors' behaviour and their experiences with one another. If a person is known to follow through on commitments, she/he is likely to gain access to land on more favourable terms than someone with a history of defaults. Mistrust grows where a party experiences lack of recognition and communication. Conflicts may arise over competing interests in land use, leading claimants to mistrust rival users, who cannot be relied on to respect others' needs. An example is the case of people not being allowed to collect water, firewood and wild plants within the boundaries of national parks and forest reserves (Chapter 9 on 'Conservation').

Throughout their essays, Meinert, Whyte and their colleagues use key themes – development, trust, and mistrust, and claiming and governing land, as socially embedded processes – to highlight commonalities among the cases without oversimplifying or reducing them to single issues. In doing so, they draw on richly detailed studies of local conflicts to address broader theoretical debates. Arguing that struggles over land are best understood as competing claims rather than 'rights' that are gained or lost, the book provides strong support for treating concepts such as ownership, kinship and belonging as social processes rather than social or legal facts. Maintaining a deft balance between ethnographic specificity and larger social trends, *This Land Is Not For Sale* elucidates both the importance and the difficulty of coping with land conflicts, not only in northern Uganda but across the continent. Comprised of richly detailed and insightful local studies, the book exceeds the sum of its parts.

Sara Berry is Professor Emeritus at the Department of History at Johns Hopkins University.

Note

1. The law applies to surviving spouses, male as well as female, but has been particularly influential in protecting widows, who often make contributions to conjugal property for years without any formal compensation (Kasanga and Kotey 2001).

References

Berry, Sara. 2022. 'Family Politics: Debt, Legal Pluralism and the Meaning of Wealth in Ghana', in Daivi Rodima-Taylor and Parker Shipton (eds), *Land and the Mortgage*. New York: Berghahn Books, pp. 95–118.

Dozon, Jean-Pierre. 1985. *La Société Bété: Histoires d'une 'Ethnie' de Côte d'Ivoire*. Bondy: Editions ORSTOM.

Kasanga, Kasim, and Nii Ashie Kotey. 2001. *Land Management in Ghana: Building on Tradition and Modernity*. London: IIED.

Shipton, Parker. 2007. *The Nature of Entrustment: Intimacy, Exchange and the Sacred in Africa*. New Haven, CT: Yale University Press.

———. 2009. *Mortgaging the Ancestors: Ideologies of Attachment in Africa*. New Haven, CT: Yale University Press.

Acknowledgements

This book is the outcome of a team project entitled 'Governing Transition in Northern Uganda: Trust and Land' (TrustLand) that ran from 2013 to 2018. It was funded by the Consultative Committee for Development Research under the Danish Ministry of Foreign Affairs, to which we are grateful – not only for the money but for the opportunity to carry on earlier collaboration between Gulu University in Uganda and the Universities of Aarhus and Copenhagen in Denmark. We are also thankful to Aarhus University, which funded the two Danish PhD students on the team, Mette Lind Kusk and Sophie Hooge Seebach. Lotte Meinert is grateful for the support from the Carlsberg Foundation for allowing time for writing and editing.

Mia Korsbæk, at the Department of Anthropology, Aarhus University, provided wonderfully efficient and always friendly support with administrative matters. *Tak*, Mia, for keeping things working smoothly right the way through. *Tak* also to Mikkel Honoré Thuesen at the Department of Anthropology in Copenhagen for help with budget matters. Anton Baaré was a much-valued discussion partner who made connections to World Bank officials working with land issues and also solved many technical problems and supported the project overall. We thank Clara Rose Sandbye too for stepping in quickly to check references.

On the Ugandan side, we wish to thank the Uganda National Council for Science and Technology, which gave permission (No. SS 3303) for the research. We appreciate the officials in the districts where we worked. From the village level Local Council 1 up to the elected and administrative officers at district level, they were not only supportive but also interested. The same goes for officials from Uganda Wildlife Authority and National Forest Authorities. These include Walter Odokorwot, Babu Bakhit Olanya, Gertrude Kirabo and Patrick Nyeko.

Officers from various NGOs and CBOs working with land issues assisted us and collaborated with us. The Danish Embassy in Kampala took keen interest in our project, and we would like to extend our thanks to Majbrit Holm Jakobsen, who was Deputy Head at the Embassy at the time. GIZ the German Corporation for International Cooperation supported a workshop about parks and people for which we are grateful.

At Gulu University, the project was hosted at the Institute of Peace and Strategic Studies; the director at the time, Stephen Langole, was the co-Principal Investigator. We are grateful to him and IPSS for facilitating the project. We also thank Sebastian Oguti for the management of the TrustLand project.

The project held annual workshops in Gulu to which we invited guests who discussed our work and inspired us with their questions and knowledge. For Ph.D. defences and contributions at the workshops and elsewhere along the way, we would like to thank: Sara Berry, Christian Lund, Daivi Rodima-Taylor, Opobo George, Julian Hopwood, Ron Atkinson, Catherine Boone, Michael Oloya Tebere, Zeru Abukha, Matthew Otto, Alex Ojera, David Martin Aliker, Otika Sanon, Andrew P'angom Ochola, Parker Shipton, Clemens Greiner, Ben Jones, Martin Mennecke, Jane Guyer, Sverker Finnström, Ruth Prince, Finn Stepputat, Heike Berend, Bjarke Oxlund, Peter Henriques, Ton Otto, and Maria Louw. John Oloya and Christian Gade joined the team for part of the time; we are grateful for their inputs and for the photo Christian took, which is on the cover of this book.

We want to thank the two anonymous reviewers who gave constructive support to our book project and who saw the special value in our long-term collaborative efforts. Many thanks to the book series editors, who provided good and helpful comments and gave a home and family to this book. We are grateful to our editors at Berghahn Books, Tom Bonnington and Anthony Mason, and their colleagues for their splendid work.

Many members of the TrustLand team enjoyed support from research assistants, who also became friends. We gratefully acknowledge Alice Adongpiny, the late John Mark Lomeri, Hillary Lokwang, Lilly Nakiru, Daniel Komol, Daniel Raphael Kerali, Samuel Odong, Alice Amwony, Kenneth Oyet Odong, Oluma Denis, Tamar Jakline, Oryem Simon, Obwola Samuel.

Our greatest debt is to our interlocutors – the individuals and families who shared their concerns and stories as we sat in their homes and walked on their land.

Figure 0.1. Building not for sale © Mette Lind Kusk.

Introduction

Trust and Transitions in Northern Uganda

Lotte Meinert and Susan Reynolds Whyte

In 2014, Omony painted the words 'NOT FOR SALE' on a building in the trading centre near his family home. His father was going away for training for a whole year, and he had heard rumours that his father's brothers had designs on the building and plot belonging to his parents. Omony's family did not stay in the building but rented it out to others, who used it for doing business. Omony painted the words to signal to the brothers: 'we heard what you want to do, so don't try to sell our property'. Of course, it was also to scare off potential buyers; that is the main point, Omony said. The sign appeared to be effective. Omony heard no more rumours about his father's brothers' plans, and he felt confident that the land was protected. As he said: 'Our family is very stable, and we are well-known in the trading centre, which safeguards the land against any sales.' In this case, the sign created a kind of presence in the absence of Omony's father. Of course, the presence of a sign was different from the presence of a person, but it conveyed a clear message to the brothers as well as to the people in the community and potential buyers: this place is not for sale no matter what you might have been told.

As part of our collective research project on land issues in northern Uganda, Mette Lind Kusk collected material about the signs in and around Gulu town stating 'Land not for Sale'. There were different versions of these signs, sometimes even including a telephone number, roughly painted on the side of a building, or simply stuck on a stake in the ground. We found it puzzling that people would advertise something that was *not* for sale. Soon we discovered that the signs usually pointed to tensions (Kusk and Meinert 2022). These signs of trouble flag a central theme of this book: the problem of trust and mistrust that permeates land matters in northern Uganda. Often, as in Omony's case, there was mistrust among family members. Concerns revolved around land that several actors were claiming – individually and collectively. Some signs were about land that was considered clan land with communal access rights, which some individual family members were trying to sell secretly for their own advantage. Such covert sales, where the seller's authority to sell is questionable, have been reported from West Africa as well (Colin and Woodhouse 2010: 8). But whether land issues involved relatives, neighbours, external 'developers', or government, questions of trust and mistrust were pervasive.

There is an impressive and growing literature on land conflict: large-scale land-grabbing by wealthy and powerful institutions (Cotula 2013; Ansoms and Hilhorst 2014; Batterbury and Ndi 2018); land concentration and transfers (Schlee 2021); enclosure (Galaty 2021); expropriation and dispossession (Hendricks, Ntsebeza and Helliker 2013; Ashami and Lydall 2021). Much less scholarly attention has been paid to small-scale land disputes among people with roughly similar amounts of power. Yet these small scale-disputes often play a central role in everyday lives: they disrupt fundamental social relationships and livelihoods; they are personal and experiential. Even in cases of powerful actors enforcing claims, there is always an element of personal interaction – with middlemen, with government authorities, even with wild animals. In this book, we pay close attention to small-scale disputes and the play of social connections in interventions by powerful parties – all in the context of historical transitions after violent conflict. We claim that questions of trust and mistrust are central to understanding the dynamics of land disputes and their connections to societal changes. We explore these matters within three topical areas: claims and transactions; intimate governing of land; and imagining development.

We see in Omony's case an attempt to confirm a *claim* to a plot of land and to prevent *transactions* in the form of sale. As would also be the case for agricultural land, he thinks the plot should not be alienated but kept in trust for the family and himself. Entrustment of land for the next generations is a fundamental ideal in much of northern Uganda, but suspicion and mistrust often flavour practices of entrustment.

The signs about land not for sale strongly reflect the second topical area of the book: *intimate governing*. Land is governed not only through official institutions and according to legislation but also, and mainly, through intimate and familial relationships. In this sense, Omony's sign was not only a sign to potential buyers but equally an intimate governing tool that signalled to his uncles that they had no authority to sell the land. Cases in our book highlight how land rights were almost always negotiated in interpersonal relationships, often of kinship and marriage. Inevitably, family and neighbour conflicts over land were also conflicts about other issues, which further complicated resolution.

The third topical area of the book, *imagining development*, is also pertinent to Omony's sign because the sign indicates that these are times of transition when land has new potential for generating money and some kind of development. The sign confirms that there IS a market in land in these places – land is being sold both to locals and to outsiders with disagreements to follow. Not only people disagreed about land use and development. Animals and humans also came into conflict over access to land. National parks and forest reserves were meant to conserve nature by separating humans and wildlife. Yet elephants, buffalos and baboons do not read human signs or respect human fences. Nor do people neighbouring these lands always share government values of developing tourism and maintaining forests for national purposes.

The big picture of historical transformation in landholding is a mixed one. Some land is NOT for sale; at least there is a strong ideal that ancestral land should not be sold but kept within the patrilineal descent group in trust for future generations. But land IS for sale, and as we shall see, there are many people who wish to buy a piece of land to call 'mine' rather than 'ours'. In the parts of Acholiland where much of our research took place, fragmentation and individualization of land were stronger tendencies than concentration of large areas in fewer hands.

Land and Conflict in Northern Uganda

At the national level, Uganda has seen a series of shifts in land legislation. Batungi (2008) recognizes six different land reforms: from the colonial period, when land formally belonged to the Crown, to the present era, when the Constitution of 1995 and the Land Act of 1997 declared that land belongs to the citizens under four different forms of tenure (see the appendix on land legislation). Importantly, however, Batungi also notes that throughout these legal changes the fundamental characteristics of land tenure have not changed since colonial times: ' . . . all customary land tenure systems, which account for 85 per cent of the total land mass of Uganda are still unregulated and completely outside the statutory framework of the country' (Batungi 2008: 79). We will argue that they are indeed regulated, or governed, even though they are outside the national statutory framework. But we appreciate Batungi's point that changes in land legislation that sound immensely significant are not necessarily felt on the ground by ordinary people dealing with land issues.

Customary tenure is even more prevalent in northern Uganda than the national average – in 2007 one estimate put it at 95 per cent (Foley 2007: 33). By its nature, it is flexible and varied, subject to informal arrangements. Customary land is a default category; it is land that is not officially registered. In contrast, freehold land is transacted in writing; it should be recorded in the National Lands Registry and confirmed by a title deed. Most land sales are not formalized in this way. Rather they are part of the vernacular land market, witnessed by neighbours or local officials, often noted on a piece of paper, but never subjected to the cadastral requirements of the District Land Board and National Lands Registry.

The parts of northern Uganda where our research took place are distant from the centre of Uganda, both geographically and politically. The Acholi and Karamoja sub-regions are closer to Kenya and South Sudan than to Kampala. As border areas, they have been subject to raids and influxes of refugees, both of which have implications for land use. Since colonial times, Karamoja has been neglected by central government as remote and inhabited by 'warlike pastoralists who refused to be governed' like the rest of the nation (Mamdani 1982). Like pastoralists in other parts of eastern Africa, they were labelled backward and incapable of using their land productively (Gabbert 2021). The people of the Acholi sub-region have felt themselves largely excluded from the political life of the nation, especially since 1986 with the accession to power of the National Resistance Movement. Like the people of Karamoja, they are sensitive to being exploited by the centre – for their underground resources of oil and minerals or for the land itself.

Two fundamental characteristics of these areas have a bearing on land issues. The first is that they have long been less densely populated than many other parts of the country (Hopwood and Atkinson 2013). In the late colonial period, the Acholi sub-region was characterized as 'under-populated'; indeed Girling (1960: 183) wrote that the low population density was one of the factors inhibiting social and economic change. Although Acholi people have long been wary of outsiders (the British, the Langi) having designs on their territory (Lagace 2016), many of our interlocutors spoke of earlier times when their forefathers had plenty of land and welcomed in-laws and friends to settle with them. This assumption of abundant land that could be given away to strengthen social relations has disappeared today. Land is no longer seen as a collective resource that is only valuable together with labour; today it is potentially an individual resource (Kusk 2018).

The Karamoja sub-region is even less densely populated in part because of geography; unlike the Acholi and Langi areas, much of the land is not well suited for cultivation. Pastoralism, which does not support a heavy population, has played a predominant role. This more mobile form of land use entails a different relation to land and territory and different kinds of conflicts, often over water and grazing. Even the indigenous Ik community, who inhabit the mountains in Kaabong District of Karamoja and pursue agriculture as well as hunting and gathering, move their villages frequently. Their area is not densely populated either, but they have seasonal tensions with pastoralists from the surrounding plains, who bring their animals to Ik territory in times of drought.

The existence of vast areas of unsettled or lightly settled land in these parts of northern Uganda is reinforced by the presence of two major national parks, Kidepo and Murchison Falls, and large forest reserves. Together with the impor-

First published in 2023 by
Berghahn Books
www.berghahnbooks.com

© 2023, 2025 Lotte Meinert and Susan Reynolds Whyte
First paperback edition published in 2025

All rights reserved. Except for the quotation of short passages
for the purposes of criticism and review, no part of this book
may be reproduced in any form or by any means, electronic or
mechanical, including photocopying, recording, or any information
storage and retrieval system now known or to be invented,
without written permission of the publisher.

Library of Congress Cataloging-in-Publication Data
Names: Meinert, Lotte, editor, author. | Whyte, Susan Reynolds, editor, author.
Title: This Land Is Not For Sale: Trust and Transitions in Northern Uganda / edited by Lotte Meinert and Susan Reynolds Whyte.
Description: New York: Berghahn Books, 2023. | Series: Integration and Conflict Studies; 27 | Includes bibliographical references and index.
Identifiers: LCCN 2022036407 (print) | LCCN 2022036408 (ebook) | ISBN 9781800736979 (hardback) | ISBN 9781805390473 (open access ebook)
Subjects: LCSH: Land tenure—Social aspects—Uganda. | Trust—Social aspects—Uganda.
Classification: LCC HD984 .T45 2023 (print) | LCC HD984 (ebook) | DDC 306.32096761—dc23/eng/20220801
LC record available at https://lccn.loc.gov/2022036407
LC ebook record available at https://lccn.loc.gov/2022036408

British Library Cataloguing in Publication Data
A catalogue record for this book is available from the British Library

ISBN 978-1-80073-697-9 hardback
ISBN 978-1-80539-742-7 paperback
ISBN 978-1-80073-698-6 epub
ISBN 978-1-80539-047-3 web pdf

https://doi.org/10.3167/9781800736979

An electronic version of this book is freely available thanks to the support of libraries working with Knowledge Unlatched. KU is a collaborative initiative designed to make high-quality books Open Access for the public good. More information about the inititative and links to the Open Access version can be found at knowledgeunlatched.org.

This work is published subject to a Creative Commons Attribution Noncommercial No Derivatives 4.0 License. The terms of the license can be found at http://creativecommons.org/licenses/by-nc-nd/4.0/. For uses beyond those covered in the license contact Berghahn Books.

Forces) and the Lord's Resistance Army (LRA) was pursued at varying intensities from 1986. Over 90 per cent of the population were forcibly interned in Internally Displaced Persons (IDP) camps and not allowed to use their land. The families upon whose land the IDP camps were located likewise lost control of their land for the duration of the war. With the ceasefire in 2006, the vast majority of those interned began to return to their rural homes. Many became embroiled in conflicts over land in the places where they went back to resume their livelihoods. Elders who knew the old boundaries had died; some women who had formed relationships in the camps were not welcomed to their partners' homes; their children did not have socially recognized fathers, so the sons had weak claims on paternal land (Whyte et al. 2013). During the war and encampment, people lost all their livestock and other property; they had not been able to generate income. Their only remaining asset was the land, and they were repeatedly warned to care for it and not to sell it.

In the Karamoja sub-region, which had long been ransacked by mutual raids between armed groups from Karamoja, Kenya and South Sudan, disarmament efforts had been ongoing. The latest initiative, the Karamoja Integrated Disarmament and Development Programme 2007/2008–2009/2010, was quite successful in some ways, so armed conflict had declined noticeably. Yet the effect of disarmament included increased sedentarization, shifts away from pastoral livelihoods and changing gender roles (Stites and Akabwai 2010). Although few people in Karamoja had been formally displaced from their land, all had been through an extended period of insecurity that involved great uncertainty about access to and safety in territories.

In both sub-regions, the relatively marked and concentrated transition from violent conflict to comparative peace ushered in an era of development expectations. While development is an ideal all over Uganda, the rhythm of efforts and activities has been different in those parts of the country where it seems to have been put on hold by protracted conflict and then made possible at a turning point when new horizons opened. Both the people who had lived through the hard times and outside donors and investors saw opportunities and needs that had implications for land use. There was thus a relatively sharp change in the significance of land as new economic possibilities arose and land was increasingly commodified.

These historical conditions were very effective in fostering mistrust (Meinert 2012; Gade, Willerslev and Meinert 2015). During the prolonged periods of violence, people felt they could not trust either government authorities or those who were attacking them. They could not rely on government institutions. Particularly in the Acholi sub-region, apprehension focused on land; rumours circulated about plots to grab the land over which people had lost control (Dolan 2009; Hopwood and Atkinson 2013; Lenhart 2013; Whyte et al. 2014). As peace and security were established, mistrust accompanied attempts to re-secure land rights. Individuals, families and kin groups vied with one another amid suspicions and doubt about belonging and boundaries. Development interventions evoked mistrust as well; in situations where most people were impoverished, an influx of resources available to some and not others brought suspicion. When development initiatives required land, who could be trusted to represent local landholders?

Ethnographic Journeys

It was in this setting of recent conflict, transition, development initiatives and heightened tensions over land that we undertook a set of related ethnographic journeys. 'We' are a team of researchers from Gulu University in Uganda and Aarhus and Copenhagen universities in Denmark. From 2013 to 2018 we cooperated on a project we called 'Governing Transition in Northern Uganda: Trust and Land',[2] in which we followed land conflicts and tensions as they evolved over time. Ethnographic approaches predominated, since the majority of us were anthropologists. However, there were scholars of law, philosophy and political science among our number as well.

In our research, we have followed the principles of multisitedness and multisightedness. We worked with various related topics at different locations in the Acholi, Lango and Karamoja sub-regions of northern Uganda, some in rural areas and some in towns. And we consciously tried to make use of the different perspectives we brought as men and women, older and younger, senior scholars and PhD students, from Uganda and Denmark. This book is conceived as a 'polygraph', on the model developed in an earlier project (Whyte 2014). That is, it has multiple writers addressing roughly similar material and common themes about which they have maintained a dialogue over several years. All of the chapters are co-authored, and all of the cases have been discussed jointly. Mette Lind Kusk made drawings of the cases introducing each part of the book, and these facilitated our analyses by pointing us towards key issues.

The researchers reviewed policy documents on land administration and litigation; some followed how land was used in political campaigning during the 2016 national and district elections (Meinert and Kjær 2017). Parts of the data collection were participatory in the sense that researchers asked respondents to draw maps, make timelines and do transect walks. We explored the semantics of land use and landholding in the relevant local languages. During our annual workshops, we invited policymakers and practitioners to participate and discuss our material as well as land issues they found pertinent. Based on our cases and these discussions and analyses, we developed and disseminated a set of policy briefs on various land issues (see www.Trustland.me).

One method predominated over all others: assembling extended cases. Every researcher followed a few selected land conflicts closely. We talked to a primary interlocutor and wherever possible to others involved in the tensions or open conflicts over a specific piece of land. We returned regularly in the mode of episodic fieldwork (M. Whyte 2013) to update ourselves on what had happened since the last visit. Staying for longer or shorter periods in the locality, we tried to get a sense of the immediate context in which the land struggle was taking place. Thus, rather than simply mapping governance structures and kinds of land conflicts and adjudication institutions at one point in time, we have followed transactions and disputes as they unfolded. This processual approach has allowed us to see how cases change over time, how they often get stuck or escalate, how they sometimes dissolve or are given up, and how they are occasionally resolved through a variety of social and legal processes.

Our case approach has yielded a personal and interpersonal perspective on land issues. Even when we are dealing with large-scale issues such as conservation or mineral extraction, we tell the story through the experiences of positioned actors, individual persons interacting with other positioned persons. In this way, we offer a complement to the research on land conflicts in Africa that focuses on more general patterns – for example, the displacement of pastoralists from their territories (Gabbert et al. 2021), the role of the state (Lund 2016; Van Leeuwen 2017; Kandal 2018) and land grabbing for investment (Cotula 2013). We show how these macro forces impinge on people's lives and how they are dealt with as people try to secure their livelihoods.

In organizing this book, we have selected a set of cases as springboards – one to open each of the three parts and one to open each chapter. We present them in detail, as the researchers learned about them. They are close-up and personal, providing a more intimate view than most descriptions of land conflicts in Africa. The strongest example is the frank autoethnographic case provided by Stephen Langole in Chapter 1 on Multiplicity. This case-based approach is part of the reason why mistrust emerged so clearly in our material. People talked about their experiences of claims and conflicts and what they thought about the others with whom they were interacting around land. They complained about secretiveness and wondered about intentions. They told us about tentative plans and doubts. We are conscious of the fact that their stories are about conflicts; by their nature they are likely to reflect mistrust. Still, we think they also reveal something about trust. Partly by negative implication, the suspicions and assessments of unreliability suggest which ideals of trust have been betrayed. Partly by the positive attempts to mediate and enhance trust, the practices of building confidence show what it involves.

After the cases that introduce each chapter, we begin by briefly answering the question 'of what is this a case?' With inspiration from Christian Lund (2014), we consider the general pattern of which the case is a specific example, and we suggest what concepts the case may be taken to instantiate concretely. This allows us to progressively contextualize the case while at the same time focus in on particular analytical themes. Of course, rich cases can be mined for many analytical points, and we refer to them back and forth across chapters.

Trust and Mistrust

'Fiduciary culture' (from Latin *fiducia* – trust) is the concept Parker Shipton (2007) introduced to capture the importance of trust among the Luo of western Kenya – and by extension in many African societies. Delayed reciprocity and generalized exchange involve trust; people give things, blessings, knowledge and rights to dependents with the assurance that others also give to them. They should care for what they have been given and pass things on. Entrustment is the keeping of something in care for further transmission in the future. The primary example of entrustment is the stewardship of land. Received from previous generations, it should be preserved for children and grandchildren to use. Shipton contrasts the notion of landholding through entrustment with 'ownership' in the sense of complete rights, including the right to alienate land for good. In entrustment, rights to land are embedded in social relations such that the belonging or attachment of people and land are intertwined. The entrustment view does not place the significance of land primarily in terms of its economic value but in the context of other values: social identity, belonging and generational succession. Trust in access to land involves trust in other people. Precisely because trust is such an important ideal, mistrust is ever present, especially under the historical conditions prevailing in northern Uganda. The kinds of trust and mistrust entailed in the entrustment of land constitute one major focus of our studies. However, our considerations encompass the play of trust in other kinds of land governing as well. In addition to bonds of reciprocity with intimate others, organizations and state hierarchy are governance mechanisms (Hydén 2006; Rhodes 2007). People's past experiences with these forms of governance are likely to affect trust relationships (Rothstein and Stolle 2008). Ruling elites may affect trust by the way in which they enforce existing rules; impartial enforcement of the rule of law is likely to enhance trust in the legal system, whereas favouring certain groups undermines trust (Evans 1996; Hydén 2006). Trust is normally regarded as an essential element of state legitimacy and a prerequisite for social interaction. Trust in institutions is also argued to have an important bearing on the outlook people have on livelihood investments (Fukuyama 1995). There is a common understanding that if only rules are set and enacted in an impartial and fair manner, trust will tend to increase, and if rules are twisted or enacted in ways that favour some over others, mistrust will grow (Rothstein and Stolle 2008; Hydén 2006). But what if there are multiple sets of rules? What if people do not agree about impartiality and fairness?

The plural legal situation in northern Uganda includes a variety of entities, from clan elders to high court and civil society organizations, and here people compare institutions, rules and possibilities in terms of competence, fairness, transparency and probity. It is sometimes argued that plurality of legal systems undermines confidence in each. Yet, cases in this book point to possible mutual recognition and collaboration between the legal systems. Customary fora sometimes refer to the statutory system when clan or family negotiations have come to a standstill and vice versa. Rather than describing a situation where plural legal systems undermine each other, we see a situation of legal pluralism, where actors from different systems often recognize and refer to each other – not in total agreement and support – but with some level of both trust and mistrust, and with an understanding that some cases are a better fit for other systems.

While much scholarly focus has been on the political, social and existential dimensions of trust (Løgstrup 1956; Luhmann 1979; Giddens 1990), less attention has been devoted to the role of scepticism and mistrust in governance. Yet there is a tradition in anthropology that explores widespread examples of mistrust, suspicion, scepticism, ambiguity, opacity, deception and doubt as assumptions and ontologies in social life (Douglas 1992; Geshiere 1997; Whyte 1997; Meinert 2012; Bubandt 2014; Gade, Willerslev and Meinert 2015; Carey 2017). These 'systems of mistrust' might be more complicated than systems of trust, as argued by Luhmann (1979). They play important roles in governance and development and do not only undermine efforts at cooperation and change. Sometimes mistrust and suspicion are warranted as forms of sanction against antisocial or corrupt behaviour.

Following this scholarly tradition, we recognize that in northern Uganda both trust and mistrust are defining features – sometimes even cosmological principles – that guide social action with respect to land and resources. Entrustment of land is the traditional and guiding principle for most land transmissions, but mistrust is also a traditional and normal part of these transmissions and of social life. New forms of trust and mistrust are appearing with the commercialization of land, and they do not simply lead to amelioration of relations – they create new complications. Trust and mistrust differ in regard to abstract and formal institutions and rules, and concrete face-to-face relations (Giddens 1990). In this book, we attend to the significance of social position for trust and mistrust in institutions and social relations between men and women, youth and elders, insiders and outsiders, elites and ordinary people. We examine the trust and mistrust that people and various systems have in different kinds of evidence about land rights (such as graves, oral accounts, or paper titles). We assume that casting doubt on the fairness, honesty, reliability and effectiveness of persons and institutions can be a first step towards demanding justice and rights. Lack of confidence in poorly functioning and inequitable institutions is merited. The problem in northern Uganda today is one of balance between, on the one hand, excessive mistrust accumulated during decades of insecurity and stirred up by certain politicians, and, on the other, exaggerated trust in leaders and institutions that neglect the human rights of some categories of people. Doubt and suspicion may be necessary first steps to making institutions trustworthy because they can set in motion processes by which governance is challenged and potentially improved.

Claims and Transactions

Claims to customary land are primarily based on descent and marriage. The transaction of such land is not usually recorded on paper. Parents show their children and daughters-in-law where to make their gardens. Brothers agree to let their sisters use some land if they have left their husbands. In contrast, freehold land is transacted in writing, recorded at the National Lands Registry and certified by a title deed. That requires a survey and the placement of mark stones – a complicated and costly process. Many think of land that is purchased in the presence of witnesses and with an improvised paper document as freehold land. Formally, it is not, although such a transaction has a certain validity, and the paper and witnesses can be mobilized as evidence. Most purchases of land are of this type and are increasingly common in the Acholi and Lango sub-regions.

Claims are made explicit when disputes erupt. The conflicts we encountered were mainly concerned with questions of belonging and boundaries. Although boundary disputes were very common, questions of belonging were the most serious: to whom does the land belong and who belongs to the land? They were considered in various fora; some were statutory like the Magistrates' Court and the Local Council Courts, and some were de facto like traditional authorities and NGOs. This composite set of possible ways to resolve land conflicts allowed parties to choose a forum that was convenient and in which they had some modicum of trust. Of course, it was often only one of the parties to a conflict who made a choice, after which the other party would be called for a hearing. Since the possibility of actually enforcing a decision was small, chances for resolution were greatest when both parties accepted it. This meant talking it through and involving other relatives and neighbours. Therefore, it was very common for conflicts to be referred back to the immediate local level. Even the Magistrates' Court sometimes sent cases back for resolution by local councils or traditional authorities. Conflicts often dragged on for years and sometimes never found a resolution. Or if a decision was reached, it might never be implemented. But no matter what forum deliberated, certain kinds of evidence were used in arguing a claim. Formal title deeds and mark stones, generated bureaucratically at considerable expense, were rare; even the Magistrates' Court was concerned with evidence of a more personal and informal kind.

The most important was the spoken word: of the claimant and of other knowledgeable people. The words of the elderly carried special weight; they were reckoned to be familiar with genealogical connections and to have witnessed how land was used in the past. In a statutory forum, the statements of the parties involved, and their witnesses, might be transcribed to create a paper record. In addition to words, material indications of use formed evidence. Most important was the presence of graves on the land. The assumption was that people were buried on their own land. This is one of the reasons why so many of the dead buried in the IDP camps were exhumed and reburied at home after the camps were closed (Meinert and Whyte 2013). A cemented grave incised with the names of the dead was reckoned to be even stronger evidence of belonging than an ordinary grave with its mound of earth and stones. The spirits of the dead that might linger about burials gave graves a special status as markers of belonging. Other material evidence of use that might be adduced included the remains of a house foundation and trees that a named person had planted. Even old gardens left evidence in the form of trenches and raised rows where weeds had been piled.

The kinds of claims that people make to land and their assumptions about landholding are revealed when transactions are made and when conflicts are negotiated. Not only are transactions and conflicts illuminating; they are often also transformative. This is evident in 'A Disputed Land Sale', which opens Claims to Land, Part I of our book. The case was brought by Elisabeth against her own daughter to be settled in the office of the Resident District Commissioner. The daughter had sold the land without her mother's permission. There seemed little disagreement about the facts of the case: Elisabeth had inherited the plot from her husband and allowed a grandson to stay on it. No evidence was adduced, even though the plot was freehold and had been transacted with the approval of the Local Council chairman. The dispute revolved around what was to be done. In the year following the meeting in the RDC's office, Elisabeth received payment but cut off her relationship to her daughter, who had betrayed her trust.

The disputed land concerned a plot in an urban area on which neither Elisabeth nor her daughter were actually residing. This kind of situation is analysed in a broader perspective in Chapter 1 on Multiplicity. In his extraordinary personal essay, our colleague Stephen Langole reviews the status of his six landholdings in and around Gulu and reflects on the mistrust that colours all of them. His autoethnography allows us to consider the variety that is often glossed over in writings about land in Africa. We discuss three kinds of multiplicity evident in Stephen's land claims: multiple forms of tenure and modes of access; multiple locations and uses; and multiple relational positions. The single category 'customary tenure' covers a multiplicity of arrangements involving different combinations of entitlements. The ways in which land is used are fundamental for how it is perceived and claimed. In towns and small urban centres, land is divided into plots; some buildings are for businesses, some for accommodation. In rural areas, there is land for farming, of course, but also for houses, graves, grazing and hunting. Having land claims in different locations for different purposes allows diversification of livelihood strategies and some security in case of problems with one of the claims. Because of the embeddedness of land in social relations, plural land claims mean a multiplicity of relational positions – to parents and siblings, maternal relatives, in-laws, neighbours and friends. Even in relation to one claim, a person may be dealing with several different stakeholders, as indeed was evident in 'A Disputed Land Sale'.

The multiplicity of stakeholders was marked in the case of 'Selling Land to Foreigners for a Wind Turbine', which forms a prologue to Chapter 2 on Transactions. In Ik County in the Karamoja sub-region, foreign investors had to identify 'original owners' in order to buy a piece of land for erecting a wind turbine. The transaction dragged on and had to be repeated. Using the case as a point of departure, we discuss the nature of transactions, comparing the vernacular to the formal land market. Whether they are informal sales or other transmissions of land access, most transactions are grounded and embodied in the sense that they take place on the land in question. The parties walk on the land, look at trees and stones, and are in bodily contact with one another. This contrasts with the abstract, disembodied and sometimes distant dealings with representations of land in the form of maps and deeds. The actors involved in transactions are crucial; the question is always who has authority to decide about the transaction and who can represent the various stakeholders involved.[3] Mistrust arises easily around this question. The formal sale of land assumes a temporality of finality; once the transaction is completed, the land belongs to another party in perpetuity. In contrast, most everyday transmissions of land keep open the possibility of adjustment. Contrasting perceptions of the temporality of transactions and failure to communicate clearly on this point can also be a source of mistrust.

Conflicts over land were rife during the time of our fieldwork. Most were among intimates, who had to find ways of managing disputes with people they knew well. Chapter 3 on Conflicts starts with the case of 'Navigating Legal Pluralism', which pits a widow, Sylvia, against her dead husband's brother, who is her immediate neighbour. The authors provide an overview of legal pluralism on two dimensions: normative pluralism, which consists of the fora mandated by law to resolve conflicts; and empirical pluralism, the instances that are actually used in practice, which include officials like the Resident District Commissioner and NGOs working with land issues. The District Magistrates' Court has an enormous backlog of cases, litigation is expensive, and few cases are actually resolved there. Sylvia navigates this pluralism in revealing ways, stating explicitly which fora are more trustworthy in her eyes. While emphasis is often on the competition between different institutions in a pluralistic system, the chapter shows how they supplement and sometimes support one another. The most local forum for dispute resolution is often the most effective because it takes account of the preceding social conflicts that so often underlie a land wrangle.

Intimate Governing of Land

Governance may be defined as the way in which 'rules of the game' are managed by particular actors (Kjær 2004). Governance usually refers to the processes by which political, social, economic and judicial rules evolve and are affected by individuals and groups. In this sense, governance always happens through relations. A common understanding of governance is that it is carried out by elected governments and implemented through formal institutions. We expand this understanding of governance to include the management of 'rules of the game' by informal actors and institutions such as families and clans because these entities are the most common fora through which land is managed. We highlight this as a *process* by using the verbal form 'governing'. Because most land issues involve intimate others, their governing takes place among relatives and neighbours.

Considering conflicts between groups over land, Schlee (2008) suggests that it is important to focus not only on the object of conflict, often an economic asset, but on the sociology of conflict. Who is set in opposition to whom? What are the criteria of identification with the opposing groups? Ethnicity? Religion? Class? Descent? In a sense, the opposition between economic and sociological approaches to land conflict was obviated by the scholars of African land tenure, who emphasized that claims to land were embedded in social relations (Granovetter 1985; Hann 1998; Shipton 2009; Chauveau and Colin 2010). Yet the questions remain about which social relations are mobilized in land issues and how. This is not only a matter of identifying lineage membership. As Schlee (2008: 59) points out, social formations in conflicts are about action and agency as well as structure and categories.

Where access to land is through people, land disputes are interpersonal conflicts, and interpersonal tensions can turn into land conflicts. Through pursuing and sometimes mediating land conflicts, people are revising social relations. Land conflicts are often about the nature of relationships. It is generally accepted that men have claims through their fathers and women have use rights through their husbands and residual rights to use the land of their fathers and brothers. This simple formula can be highly complicated in practice. Who is a father? The man who begot you, the man who claimed you through making payments to your mother's family, or the man who stands in for your dead biological or social father? Abstract principles are often ignored, and disagreements arise about their interpretation. Women have rights to remain on their fathers' land and to return there to use it if they divorce. Otherwise, they use their husbands' land, even after his death. But what if they are not formally married? Or what if, as widows, they form new partnerships with men not of their dead husbands' kin group? Children who have not been claimed by their genitors are considered to belong to their mothers' kin group. Still, if they are boys, they are considered nephews rather than sons and are seen as belonging properly to another clan.

Claims through people are not simply claims based on formal principles of genealogy and marriage ceremonies. They also depend on relatedness in the sense of how relationships have been practised through time – agency and action in Schlee's (2008) terms. The quality of a relationship (to a brother, to a husband's mother) depends on time spent together, familiarity, sharing of resources, respect and other things. Presence or absence is one important dimension of claims through people. 'Missing links', where a connecting person has died or lives elsewhere, may render a relationship weaker; the classic case is the widow, who must relate to her husband's brothers and parents in the absence of the man who was her link to his family (Whyte et al. 2014). But the inside-outsider (or outside-insider) is also a person whose relationship to the family and family land is strongly affected by having been away. A brother who is well educated, has a job in town and spent time away from the family land may not be welcome if he returns to claim his share.

Intimate governing is characterized by virtue and intimidation. The virtue may be broadly referred to in the Acholi region as *ber bedo*, a concept that implies living in harmony with neighbours, kin, friends, patrons or just playing by the rules or norms of the society (Porter 2012). There are other tactics that may be used to win; for example, a person may use his/her good character, reputation or generosity to win support or popularity. This may be through attending to community problems – for example, through burial support – and attending community functions or offering material support and services to the community. Such a person of good character may be easily accommodated in the society and entitled to land. A widow who keeps her dignity and sticks to the upbringing of her children in the clan would have a good reputation, but one who has questionable male relationships, is lazy, drinks too much, or is considered antisocial may not get enough support to continue using the clan land. The morality question goes for men as well, but more attention tends to be placed on the conduct of women. Virtue may also be linked to suspicion of witchcraft. If a person is suspected to be a witch, then he or she may be excluded from the community. Equally, those related or linked to people thought to practice witchcraft are treated with suspicion and not well accommodated in the society. Access to land therefore tends to be connected to virtue but also to several other things.

Through use of threats, a person may hold on to land. When people feel threatened about land, they may choose to leave it, sell it, buy land elsewhere or simply migrate. In some cases, the threat may translate into physical violence. Mere suspicion that something bad will happen to them may cause a person to lose land. Avoidance of conflict to a large extent determines access to land. To avoid conflict, people may simply choose to leave land. In all these games, of course, there are losers and winners. These are the dynamics in intimate governing that are less talked about, but they matter and need to be understood, and that is what this book sets out to do.

Part II of the book on intimate governing begins with the case of 'Disputed Land and Broken Graves', about a man, Edward, who offered land to a younger man, Oyo, treating him almost like a son. But the young man transgressed all the morals of intergenerational relations by destroying the graves of Edward's ancestors. Relations between generations are fundamental in access to land. The ideal of entrustment together with the principle of patrilineal devolution of land provide the general assumptions about generational transmission of land rights. However, the years of conflict and changes in marriage have complicated these assumptions (to which there were always exceptions anyway). Chapter 4 on Generations sets off with 'The Insecure Nephew', about Daniel and his brothers, who stay with their mother on the land of her brother. They do not count on being able to use his land in the future; it should go to his sons, not his nephews. In considering generations, we distinguish between three different understandings of the term. The first is genealogical and points to filiation to parents and the link to previous generations through descent. The significance of graves, which appear in many of the cases we followed, is testimony to the connection between genealogical generations and land claims. While patrilineal claims on land are normal and normative, filiation to mothers and their families plays an increasingly important part in land issues. The reasons for this lie in changes in political economy, captured in the idea of historical generations, the second understanding of the term. Conflict, internment and impoverishment have led to the weakening of the patrilineal ideal or at least to the necessity of alternative modes of accessing land for the generation that came of age during war. This leads us to a third understanding of generation – as the production of new social forms. Despite the general acclamation of patrilineally held ancestral land, many people struggle to obtain 'my land' in addition to, or instead of, 'our land'.

Patriliny and filiation are inextricably entwined with gender, the topic of Chapter 5. It begins with the case of two sisters, Atim and Awor, who live first in harmony and later in bitterness on the land of their father, having left their husbands. They are involved in intimate governing, working out the 'rules of the game' in a situation where it is not quite clear what rules should apply. Historical changes in the Acholi sub-region have affected gender relations just as they have transformed relations between generations. The war and encampment weakened the situation of many men, and women are taking on more responsibility for household livelihoods even though their claims to land are less clear cut. Despite, or because of, the inequities in patriliny and virilocality, women are finding diverse ways of accessing land. Since land access is so thoroughly embedded in social relations, they must cultivate relationships as well as cultivate the land itself. This may mean showing generosity by letting others use land. Or remaining on good terms with lineage elders who can defend your claims. Governing processes among intimates are also matters of morality and character; when the sisters Atim and Awor could no longer live in harmony, the male elders dropped support of their land claims. Navigating access through other people constantly raises questions of trust and mistrust. Suspicion is expressed in allegations of witchcraft, not uncommon in conflicts over land.

Because land access is embedded in social relations, it raises questions of attachments to persons and groups. We think of these attachments in terms of belonging rather than identification: identification suggests a more structural or cognitive approach (Schlee 2008: 15); belonging implies the emotional component in identifying with people or place. It also points more towards the continuing practice of affinity, the ongoing effort to maintain an attachment. Chapter 6 on Belonging begins with 'The Land Conflict at Ogul', a clash between Acholi and Langi over an area where people had long farmed side by side in harmony. With the intervention of a respected high court judge, who has roots in the area, ethnic belonging was countered by neighbourhood belonging. We consider the meanings of belonging as membership, (being a part of) and property, as in rights over something. And we discuss the ways this distinction tends to break down when land belongs to people, and people belong to land. Belonging is exclusive as well as inclusive, and in some situations, emphasis is put on one dimension of belonging in order to exclude others with possible claims to land. 'Patrilineal fundamentalism' is one example, where daughters' children or 'previously welcomed people' from other clans are excluded. Belonging can be stated categorically, but in connection with land, it must be practised – through use, cultivating relationships, and burial on the land.

Imagining Development

'Not for sale' notices are signs of trouble within families, as we have suggested above. They indicate suspicion and mistrust of intimate others, who might try to sell property without the consent of other stakeholders. But the idea that land should not be sold is broader. When the LRA war ended, people in the Acholi sub-region were advised to move back to care for their customary land; leaders held meetings and went on radio to give the message that customary land, especially ancestral land, must not be sold. Here too, the warning 'not for sale' or 'don't sell' was a sign of worry about the opposite – that land was increasingly being bought and sold. The commodification of land was given a push by encampment in the Acholi sub-region and gathered momentum with the end of violent conflict there and in Karamoja. During the time of our research, land was assuming new potential as a source of cash through sale or rent. It had exchange as well as use value; it could generate money as well as subsistence and a sense of connection to generations past and future.

A market for renting land emerged around the IDP camps, where interned people were willing to pay customary landholders to grow some crops on the periphery of the camp (Hopwood and Atkinson 2013). Those who fled to towns had to rent accommodation and sometimes a bit of land to farm. When the camps were closed, the owners of the land where they had been located could charge rent to displaced people who wanted to remain. As the former IDP camps grew into small urban centres with ambitions to become Town Boards and Town Councils, the value of plots along the roads became apparent to all. Most important, people who wanted to rebuild their lives, send children to school or establish a business had no assets except the land. Many were interested in selling, and there were buyers with cash.

Small urban centres planned streets and markets and divided up plots for building commercial and residential buildings. Families holding land in such areas were encouraged to sell off some plots to generate funds for putting up proper structures on their remaining plots. Land in the new Town Boards and Town Councils was definitely for sale; development there required the commodification of customary land. As several of our cases testify, locations in towns and trading centres, even locations along roads, were often the object of dispute. What was development for one party appeared a lost opportunity for another.

Some of these conflicts were between individuals or families and institutions such as schools and churches. Land that had once been given to institutions was being claimed by the descendants of the original donors. Those men, and they were always men, had seen schools and churches and health facilities as incarnations of development for their clans and communities. Their descendants saw the institutions as occupying land that should have been kept in trust for them. Or at least that is what they claimed. Others thought they were merely greedy and opportunistic.

In colonial times, large areas of northern Uganda had been gazetted as forest and game reserves and national parks. In a sense, these reserves were also a kind of entrustment in that they were meant to protect natural resources for future generations. The national parks were also a source of revenue and are increasingly so, as tourism has become an important source of income for Uganda. As the human population grows and people are farming close to the boundaries of parks, there are more problems with animals destroying gardens. This has been exacerbated in the case of Murchison Falls National Park, where oil exploration and its infrastructure have disturbed the movements of elephants. Conflicts between local residents and the Uganda Wildlife Authority reflect differing ideals of stewardship and development.

Oil is not the only natural resource whose exploitation leads to land conflicts. In the Karamoja sub-region, gold has long been mined; cement enterprises have been extracting limestone for nearly two decades. Now marble is being mined, and there are deposits of silver, iron ore, copper and other minerals as well. The national government has rights over underground resources and grants exploration licences to businesses wishing to survey mining potential. These enterprises do not have to negotiate with the customary owners of the land unless they get a mining lease.

There is an enormous gap between the local people and the outsiders, both foreigners and nationals, who wish to engage in extraction – for their own profit and for the development of Karamoja. Into this gap, development brokers insert themselves. Some are inside-outsiders, educated Karamojong who speak both local and international languages, literally and figuratively. While they do not live as pastoralists, they identify with local communities. The locals see some as a kind of foreigner, elites who might be out to enrich themselves at the expense of uneducated locals. Other inside-outsiders are seen as helpful allies in dealing with high-powered outsiders.

Here as in other development situations, uncertainty and opacity characterize relations between local landholders and those who come with development initiatives. Communication is a key issue. Who speaks for the local community? Who should be involved in negotiations? Where land is held communally, or where extended families hold use rights 'in perpetuity', such questions may not have clear answers. In any case, mistrust flourishes. A common remark is to the effect that 'we are not against development, but we want to be consulted'.

Signposts are emblematic of the era and idea of development in Uganda, and particular parts of northern Uganda are heavily 'forested' by signposts from NGOs, donors and development projects imagining and implementing particular ideas about development. The informal land signposts, like Omony's, mark conflicting imaginations of development. Often these signs are indications that individuals, families and institutions disagree about the development of land. Far from all disagreements and disputes over land are 'signposted'; many conflicts are hidden, silent, long-lasting and never resolved.

'Development cannot stand on air; it must stand on land.' This commonly heard statement underlines the need for land if development projects are to go ahead. It also implies that development is imagined as physical infrastructure in the form of buildings, roads, markets, mines, masts, electricity poles and perhaps bounded areas for commercial farms and game parks. Since early on, institutional buildings have been iconic images of development. The case that opens Part III of the book, 'Claiming "Their" School', describes land struggles around a kind of institution that is eminently 'developmental'. Two churches claim the same school and the land upon which it was built. As an ideal, development is almost universally appreciated; this was the case after independence, and it has been even more intensely desired since the end of hostilities made striving after progressive change possible. Development is an almost unassailable argument for initiatives that involve land. The problems arise in the implementation. Development for whom? Who wins and who loses?

Development as an ideal and reality is the topic of Chapter 7 on Aspirations. It begins with the case of 'Plotting Development', about the efforts of a small urban centre to achieve the formal status of Town Board. This entailed dividing up land owned by the sub-county and selling off plots to buyers who could develop them by building shops or rectangular permanent houses. But efforts were hindered by a man who claimed that part of the sub-county land being sold still belonged to his family. The pattern of reclaiming land or disputing the boundaries of land given to an institution by a forefather with visions of development is common. Partly this type of conflict reflects different views of the temporality of transactions. Descendants of the original donor feel they have continuing claims on the land.

It is striking that many of the land conflicts we followed occurred in small urban centres or Gulu town. In these locations, land *is* for sale, and there is a general perception that development happens there, where there are health facilities, shops and markets, and transport, electricity and other services. Whereas rural ancestral land is linked to the forefathers who entrusted it to the present holders, land in or near urban centres, even small ones, is infused with anticipation about the future. In practice, future development plans that involved land were pervaded with mistrust. A major complaint was that development actors were secretive; they did not communicate their plans, consult or discuss, much less listen to the views and wishes of others whose land claims were at stake.

While most of the land tensions we studied involved people who knew each other, large-scale conflicts tended to concern developers from outside – whether government officials or private investors. In order to gain access to land, they needed a broker, someone who could ask for permission and manage relations to local landholders. Development initiatives sometimes evoked engagement by NGOs, which took on the task of advocacy or mediation between the developers and the locals. Brokers were usually inside-outsiders – that is, people with local connections who spoke the local language and knew the local situation. At the same time, they had education, experience outside the local context, spoke international languages and had a degree of sophistication that made them 'elite' within the local context. Chapter 8, Inside-Outsiders, opens with the case of 'Middlemen for Marble Miners' in Karamoja. While the state owns underground minerals in Uganda, the holders of the land's surface must allow access to those who would exploit what is beneath. Local people are often hired to work in mineral extraction as well. A variety of inside-outsiders act as middlemen between mineral companies and locals.

At the outset, elites with local connections are at the forefront in imagining the potentials that the land may hold. In other settings, the potential could be timber, oil, agro-business or tourism. It is not unusual for politicians and other elites to take initiatives to exploit potential in their home areas. The middlemen are needed to create connections between insiders and outsiders and to establish some form of trust so that interaction can happen. Yet, whether facilitating development enterprises or trying to protect local people from being cheated, inside-outsiders carve out a place for themselves between the local and the national or international. In doing so, they are commonly the objects of mistrust. Their negotiations with the investors are invisible to landholders, and there is suspicion that they are acting for their own benefit rather than that of the local community. The middle position places the inside-outsiders in dilemmas frequently related to the mistrust with which they are viewed. They speak for the locals, but which locals? The problem of representation is amplified when a broker decides whom to contact.

Just as the state holds ownership rights to underground resources, it also has rights to the wildlife within national parks and the resources within national forests. Two kinds of justification underpin state ownership of these resources. One concerns a kind of entrustment at a national and international scale; animals, plants and their biodiversity should be reserved, kept in stewardship for future generations. The other is that parks and forests promote development; wildlife tourism is important for the Ugandan economy, and forest concessions bring income to the state. Chapter 9 on Conservation discusses the consequences of these policies for those who were displaced by them and now live nearby. It opens with the case of 'Human-Wildlife Conflicts over Land', in which Christopher and his family return to their ancestral land after internment in an IDP camp only to be forced off by the wild animals from the park that destroy their crops. His story and the experiences of many others in the area were that rights to use the land were seriously curtailed, not only by animals but also by the park rangers. The state treated ownership as exclusive monopoly on all rights to resources, while the local residents understood landholding as a bundle of rights including entitlement to hunt and collect water, firewood and wild plants.

The original transactions that established national parks and forests were abstract, remote and disembedded from interaction in the local community. They were cadastral in the sense that the state mapped, delineated boundaries and registered its claims. They concerned whole territories that had been used in various ways by local groups of people. The conflicts that emerged later were more about usage of the land than actual territory: the elephants trampling gardens of maize; tree planting and coffee projects that destroyed gardens people had made in the forest. Local people were not reclaiming former territories now converted to national parks and forests. Rather they were in conflict with wildlife and state agents about use of the land within and outside the boundaries. As with other development projects, failure to consult different parties and disappointment with management by the authorities have brought mistrust. The people of Lawaca, including Christopher, finally took matters into their own hands and found a way of again using the land to which they belonged.

Conclusion: Trust and Transitions

In this book, we offer accounts of land issues from northern Uganda during a particular passage of its history. In the aftermath of violent conflict and displacement, people were trying to establish continuity with earlier times when land was less problematic and also to realize divergent imaginations of development as land was becoming more commercialized. Widespread experiences of both neglect and aggressive interventions by government, together with a kind of paranoia about land, relatively abrupt opening of development opportunities, and pre-existing tendency to doubt the reliability of others have promoted mistrust during these times of transition.

By documenting the experiences of individuals and families around land, we show how and why and where mistrust emerges. The same cases reveal how attempts to increase trust are made through discussion, mediation and everyday recognition and confirmation of belonging. We concentrate mainly on the personal interactions within which most land issues play out. Thus, our book is not so much about large-scale land grabs and dealings with anonymous institutions and actors. Rather we stay close to the ground and to people who use the ground.

Where land is embedded in social relations, governing of land, to a large extent, is also a matter of social interactions. In most cases, land is only one aspect of social relations so that land use and land conflict are unavoidably entangled with other dimensions of relationship to kin and neighbours. Even responses to development enterprises initiated at a distance inspire varying degrees of trust and mistrust among intimate others. We hope that this book will contribute to a more nuanced understanding of how these processes unfold.

Lotte Meinert, Ph.D., is Professor at the Department of Anthropology, Aarhus University.

Susan Reynolds Whyte, Ph.D., is Professor at the Department of Anthropology, University of Copenhagen.

Notes

1. When areas that had been gazetted as forest or game reserves are de-gazetted and not claimed as customary land, the land devolves to the District Land Board, which can lease it to generate income. Leasehold was involved in the two large-scale land conflicts for which Acholiland is (in)famous: the Apaa dispute on the border between Adjumani and Amuru districts (Lenhart 2013; Sjögren 2015; Kobusingye et al. 2017; Serwajja 2018), and the Madhvani case in Amuru District (Serwajja 2012; Mariniello 2015). In both instances, areas that had been evacuated in the colonial period because of tsetse fly were later gazetted as game reserves and then de-gazetted. When the District Land Boards tried to lease them out, locals claimed them as customary land.
2. The project was funded under a grant from the Committee for Development Research under the Danish Foreign Ministry, for which we are immensely grateful.
3. During the period of our fieldwork, it was possible to apply for a Certificate of Customary Tenure, which was a simpler process than obtaining freehold on a piece of land. It did not necessitate a survey, but the certification required that members of the Area Land Commit-

tee inspect the land, draw a map, and that neighbours sign an agreement that there were not outstanding boundary disputes. The issue was: whose name(s) to put on the certificate? It could be an individual or the members of a lineage, family or household. There has been criticism of this procedure as having the inherent possibility that one or a few individuals might obtain legal rights to customary land to the exclusion of others, especially since such a Certificate could be converted to freehold at a later time.

References

Ansoms, An, and Thea Hilhorst. 2014. *Losing Your Land: Dispossession in the Great Lakes.* Woodbridge: James Currey.
Ashami, Maknun, and Jean Lydall. 2021. 'Persistent Expropriation of Pastoral Lands: The Afar Case', in Echi Christina Gabbert, Fana Gebresenbet, John G. Galaty and Günther Schlee (eds), *Lands of the Future: Anthropological Perspectives on Pastoralism, Land Deals and Tropes of Modernity in Eastern Africa.* New York, NY: Berghahn Books, pp. 144–166.
Batterbury, Simon, and Frankline Ndi. 2018. 'Land-Grabbing in Africa', in Tony Binns, Kenneth Lunch, and Etienne Nel (eds), *The Routledge Handbook of African Development.* London: Routledge, pp. 573–82.
Batungi, Nasani. 2008. *Land Reform in Uganda: Towards a Harmonised Tenure System.* Kampala: Fountain Publishers.
Bubandt, Nils. 2014. *The Empty Seashell: Witchcraft and Doubt on an Indonesian Island.* Ithaca, NY: Cornell University Press.
Carey, Matthew. 2017. *Mistrust: An Ethnographic Theory.* Chicago: HAU Books.
Chauveau, Jean-Pierre, and Jean-Philippe Colin. 2010. 'Customary Transfers and Land Sales in Côte d'Ivoire: Revisiting the Embeddedness Issue', *Africa* 80(1): 81–103.
Colin, Jean-Philippe, and Philip Woodhouse. 2010. 'Introduction: Interpreting land markets in Africa', *Africa* 80(1): 1–13.
Cotula, Lorenzo. 2013. *The Great African Land Grab? Agricultural Investments and the Global Food System.* London: Zed Books.
Dolan, Chris. 2009. *Social Torture: The Case of Northern Uganda, 1986–2006.* New York: Berghahn Books.
Douglas, Mary. 1992. *Risk and Blame: Essays in Cultural Theory.* London and New York: Routledge.
Evans, Peter, 1996. 'Government Action, Social Capital and Development: Reviewing the Evidence on Synergy', *World Development* 24(6): 1119–32.
Foley, Conor. 2007. *A Guide to Property Law in Uganda.* Nairobi: United Nations Human Settlements Programme.
Fukuyama, Francis. 1995. *Trust: The Social Virtues and the Creation of Prosperity.* New York: The Free Press.
Gabbert, Echi Christina. 2021. 'Introduction: Futuremaking with Pastoralists', in Echi Christina Gabbert, Fana Gebresenbet, John G. Galaty and Günther Schlee (eds), *Lands of the Future: Anthropological Perspectives on Pastoralism, Land Deals and Tropes of Modernity in Eastern Africa.* New York, NY: Berghahn Books, pp. 1–38.
Gabbert, Echi Christina, Fana Gebresenbet, John G. Galaty and Günther Schlee (eds). 2021. *Lands of the Future: Anthropological Perspectives on Pastoralism, Land Deals and Tropes of Modernity in Eastern Africa.* New York: Berghahn Books.
Gade, Christian B. N., Rane Willerslev and Lotte Meinert. 2015. 'Half-Trust and Enmity in Ikland, Northern Uganda', *Common Knowledge* 21(3): 406–19.

Galaty, John G. 2021. 'Modern Mobility in East Africa: Pastoral Responses to Rangeland Fragmentation, Enclosure and Settlement', in Echi Christina Gabbert, Fana Gebresenbet, John G. Galaty and Günther Schlee (eds), *Lands of the Future: Anthropological Perspectives on Pastoralism, Land Deals and Tropes of Modernity in Eastern Africa*. New York, NY: Berghahn Books, pp. 41–58.

Geshiere, Peter. 1997. *The Modernity of Witchcraft: Politics and the Occult in Postcolonial Africa*. Charlottesville and London: University Press of Virginia.

Giddens, Anthony. 1990. *The Consequences of Modernity*. Stanford, CA: Stanford University Press.

Girling, Frank Knowles. 1960. *The Acholi of Uganda*. London: Her Majesty's Stationery Office.

Granovetter, Mark. 1985. 'Economic Action and Social Structure: The Problem of Embeddedness', *American Journal of Sociology* 91(3): 481–510.

Hann, Chris M. 1998. 'Introduction: The Embeddedness of Property', in Chris M. Hann (ed.), *Property Relations: Renewing the Anthropological Tradition*. Cambridge: Cambridge University Press, pp. 1–47.

Hendricks, Fred, Lungisile Ntsebeza and Kirk Helliker. 2013. *The Promise of Land: Undoing a Century of Dispossession in South Africa*. Johannesburg: Jacana.

Hopwood, Julian, and Ronald Atkinson. 2013. *Land Conflict Monitoring and Mapping Tool for the Acholi Sub-region*. Kampala: United Nations Peacebuilding Programme in Uganda by Human Rights Focus.

Hydén, Göran. 2006. 'Beyond Governance: Bringing Power into Policy Analysis', *Forum for Development Studies* 33(2): 215–36.

Kandal, Matt. 2018. 'State Formation and the Politics of Land in North-Eastern Uganda', *African Affairs* 117(467): 261–85.

Kjær, Anne Mette. 2004. *Governance: Key Concepts*. Cambridge: Polity Press.

Kobusingye, Doreen Nancy, Mathijs van Leeuwen and Han van Dijk. 2017. 'The Multifaceted Relationship Between Land and Violent Conflict: The Case of Apaa Evictions in Amuru District, Northern Uganda', *Journal of Modern African Studies* 55(3): 455–77.

Kusk, Mette Lind. 2018. 'On Uncertain Ground: Intimate Wrangles over Land and Belonging in Northern Uganda', Ph.D. dissertation. Aarhus: Aarhus University.

Kusk, Mette Lind, and Lotte Meinert. 2022. 'Signs of Trouble: Land, Loans, and Investments in Post-conflict Northern Uganda', in Daivi Rodima-Taylor and Parker Shipton (eds), *Land and the Mortgage: History, Culture, Belonging*. New York: Berghahn Books, pp. 144–60.

Lagace, Martha. 2016. 'Paula Hirsch Foster: Anthropology and Land Tensions in Acholiland, 1954–58', *Journal of Peace and Security Studies* 2(1): 75–83.

Lenhart, Lioba. 2013. 'Alleged Land Grabs and Governance: Exploring Mistrust and Trust in Northern Uganda – The Case of the Apaa Land Conflict', *Journal of Peace and Security Studies* 1: 64–85.

Løgstrup, Knud E. 1956. *The Ethical Demand*. Notre Dame, IN: University of Notre Dame Press.

Luhmann, Niklas. 1979. *Trust and Power: Two Works*. Chichester: John Wiley and Sons.

Lund, Christian. 2014. 'Of What Is This a Case? Analytical Movements in Qualitative Social Science Research', *Human Organization* 73(3): 224–34.

———. 2016. 'Rule and Rupture: State Formation through the Production of Property and Citizenship', *Development and Change* 47(6): 1199–228.

Mamdani, Mahmood. 1982. 'Karamoja: Colonial Roots of Famine in North-East Uganda', *Review of African Political Economy* 9(25): 66–73.

———. 2013. 'The Contemporary Ugandan Discourse on Customary Tenure: Some Theoretical Considerations', *MISR Working Paper* 13. Kampala: Makerere University.
Mariniello, Giuliano. 2015. 'Social Struggles in Uganda's Acholiland: Understanding Responses and Resistance to Amuru Sugar Works', *The Journal of Peasant Studies* 42(3–4): 653–69.
Meinert, Lotte. 2012. 'Tricky Trust: Distrust as Ontology and Trust as a Social Achievement in Uganda', in Anne Line Dalsgård, Sune Liisberg and Esther Oluffa Pedersen (eds), *Anthropology and Philosophy: Dialogues on Trust and Hope*. New York: Berghahn, pp. 118–36.
Meinert, Lotte, and Anne Mette Kjær. 2017. '"Land Belongs to the People of Uganda": Politicians' use of Land Issues in the 2016 Election Campaigns', *Journal of Eastern African Studies* 10(4): 769–88.
Meinert, Lotte, and Susan Reynolds Whyte. 2013. 'Creating the New Times: Reburials after War in Northern Uganda', in Dorthe Refslund Pedersen and Rane Willerslev (eds), *Taming Time, Timing Death: Social Technologies and Ritual*. Farnham: Ashgate, pp. 175–93.
Porter, Holly E. 2012. 'Justice and Rape on the Periphery: The Supremacy of Social Harmony in the Space Between Local Solutions and Formal Judicial Systems in Northern Uganda', *Journal of Eastern African Studies* 6(1): 81–97.
Rhodes, R. A. W. 2007. 'Understanding Governance: Ten Years On', *Organization Studies* 28: 1243–1264.
Rothstein, Bo, and Dietlind Stolle. 2008. 'The State and Social Capital: An Institutional Theory of Generalized Trust', *Comparative Politics* 40(4): 441–459.
Schlee, Günther. 2008. *How Enemies are Made: Towards a Theory of Ethnic and Religious Conflicts*. New York: Berghahn Books.
———. 2021. 'Unequal Citizenship and One-Sided Communication: Anthropological Perspectives on Collective Identification in the Context of Large-Scale Land Transfers in Ethiopia', in Echi Christina Gabbert, Fana Gebresenbet, John G. Galaty and Günther Schlee (eds), *Lands of the Future: Anthropological Perspectives on Pastoralism, Land Deals and Tropes of Modernity in Eastern Africa*. New York, NY: Berghahn, pp. 59–77.
Serwajja, Eria. 2012. 'The Quest for Development Through Dispossession: Examining Amuru Sugar Works in Lakang-Amuru District of Northern Uganda', *International Academic Conference on Global Land Grabbing II, October 17–19, 2012*. Cornell University, Ithaca, New York.
———. 2018. 'The "Green Land Grab" in Apaa Village of Amuru District, Northern Uganda: Poer, Complexities and Consequences', *Mambo!* XV(2): 1–6.
Shipton, Parker. 2007. *The Nature of Entrustment: Intimacy, Exchange, and the Sacred in Africa*.
———. 2009. *Mortgaging the Ancestors: Ideologies of Attachment in Africa*. New Haven: Yale University Press.
Sjögren, Anders. 2015. 'Battles over Boundaries: The Politics of Territory, Identity and Authority in Three Ugandan Regions', *Journal of Contemporary African Studies* 33(2): 268–84.
Stites, Elizabeth, and Darlington Akabwai. 2010. '"We Are Now Reduced to Women": Impacts of Forced Disarmament in Karamoja, Uganda', *Nomadic peoples* 14(2): 24–43.
Van Leeuwen, Mathijs. 2017. 'Localizing Land Governance, Strengthening the State: Decentralization and Land Tenure Security in Uganda', *Journal of Agrarian Change* 17: 208–27.
Whyte, Michael. 2013. 'Episodic Fieldwork, Updating and Sociability', *Social Analysis* 57(1): 110–21.
Whyte, Susan Reynolds. 1997. *Questioning Misfortune: The Pragmatics of Uncertainty in Eastern Uganda*. Cambridge: Cambridge University Press.

Whyte, Susan Reynolds (ed.). 2014. *Second Chances: Surviving AIDS in Uganda*. Durham: Duke University Press.

Whyte, S. R. et al. 2013. 'Remaining Internally Displaced: Missing Links to Security in Northern Uganda', *Journal of Refugee Studies* 26(2): 283–301.

Whyte, S. R. et al. 2014. 'Urbanization by Subtraction: The Afterlife of Camps in Northern Uganda', *Journal of Modern African Studies* 52(4): 597–622.

Part I
Claims to Land

Case I
A Disputed Land Sale
Mette Lind Kusk

Mama Elisabeth has come with her fourth-born daughter Maria, Maria's son Ogen and Elisabeth's orphaned grandson, Ocan, to the Resident District Commissioner's (RDC) office in Gulu. She wants help from a powerful government representative to claim back the land she inherited from her late husband many years back after Grace, Elisabeth's fist-born daughter, sold it without her permission. Grace has also come to the office with her two sons Kilama and Otim. The RDC assistant is listening to music on his laptop while we are waiting for the meeting to begin. At his desk, there is a pillow with a picture of the president and a small Ugandan flag, underscoring his close connection to the government. After prayers and a short introduction of the people present, he begins to ask questions. Grace claims that it was Ocan, who was taking care of the land in Elisabeth's absence, who took the initiative to sell the land.

We go through several calculations to work out how much was paid for the land, how much had been spent or lost and what Elisabeth is owed. Numbers fly across the room, and I try to follow what is being claimed. There are no receipts or other documents supporting these relatively high sums. Despite the confusion, the RDC assistant manages to sum up and present a surprisingly precise number and ends the meeting instructing them to solve the matter from home. He asks them all to come back and report a week later. Grace leaves with her sons. She and Elisabeth do not look at each other, but they shout something to one another in agitated voices.

Figure CI.1. In the office of the RDC © Mette Lind Kusk.

Figure CI.2. The RDC © Mette Lind Kusk.

Figure CI.3. Accusations © Mette Lind Kusk.

Figure CI.4. Accusations © Mette Lind Kusk.

Figure CI.5. Calculations © Mette Lind Kusk.

Elisabeth inherited the plot of freehold land on the outskirts of Gulu town when her husband died many years ago. The land is 54 meters long on one side, 26 meters wide at one end, 62 meters long on the other side and 30 meters wide at the other end. In February 2014, she realized that most of her land had been sold in her absence and that the new owner was in the process of having it formally registered in his name. He was actually about to put down mark stones, but Elisabeth managed to stop him and report the incident to the RDC office. Elisabeth's decision to engage the RDC in this matter was a choice among many other options such as approaching an authoritative family member or a local leader. The first meeting in the RDC office transpired as described above.

Elisabeth was living in Kitgum, a district north-east of Gulu, with Maria. Elisabeth had given Ocan the task of taking care of the land in Gulu in her absence. Despite this, Grace – who lives in the peri-urban area on the outskirts of Gulu town – still managed to sell the land. Grace also lost her husband and has four living children. According to Elisabeth, Grace lied to Ocan and convinced him that Elisabeth had approved the sale to make him sign the sales agreement. Elisabeth does not blame him – rather, she feels sorry for him because he needed the land for the future or at least the money from it to pay bridewealth. While they are trying to resolve the conflict, Elisabeth and Maria stay in two simple huts on a small corner of the land in Gulu, which Elisabeth has left.

Figure CI.6. Calculations © Mette Lind Kusk.

Figure CI.7. Advice from the RDC © Mette Lind Kusk.

Figure CI.8. Enmity © Mette Lind Kusk.

Grace had the sale approved by the LC2 (Local Council 2), the local administrative-political leader at parish level, who claimed he had to approve any land transactions made within his jurisdiction. When Grace approached him to witness and approve the sale, he accepted without query. He might have viewed Grace as the rightful owner because she had been staying near the land for 27 years while Elisabeth has been in Kitgum.

Ideally, Elisabeth wants the land back. There are many orphans in their family, as the recently ended war took many lives. The land was a way of securing the futures of the grandsons who had been orphaned, to at least provide them with a place to reside. Especially boys have a problem if they do not have land to stay on. It leads to insults and shame: *gangwu peke*! 'you have no home!' is a common verbal insult. Boys need a place to belong to, where they can stay with their future wife and family.

The following week, everyone reconvenes in the RDC assistant's office. This time, the buyer of the land, George, and the local leader at village level, the LC1, also attend the meeting. Elisabeth and Grace did not have a meeting at home, so the matter is still unresolved. The whole process of calculating the huge sum of money that Grace owes Elisabeth repeats. The tone between Grace and Elisabeth is harsh. When the RDC assistant asserts that Grace owes Elisabeth 6.55 million Uganda shillings, Elisabeth shouts that she did not come here to get her money back; she came to get her land back. 'But your child sold the land; you can't get it back. You should forgive your child if you get the balance back. Grace should ask for forgiveness and pay . . . ' the assistant explains. Otherwise, Elisabeth has to go to the police to make a statement and then go through the courts, he continues. This will block everybody from using the land until the case is solved. George, the buyer, seems to get nervous. He fumbles for his papers in his bag. At no point in the process has he been asked to present any sales agreement, and at no point has Grace or Elisabeth been asked to show any papers documenting their claimed ownership of the land.

Elisabeth is uncertain about what to do. She talks with Maria, her fourth-born daughter, with me, and with a local leader, who tries to sketch out the consequences of each choice; if she takes the case to court, the land will be blocked. If she accepts the money, she must allow Grace some time to save up, as apart from a motorbike that Grace purchased for Ocan, the money from the sale has been spent on constructing a house and school fees. A central concern is how the courts often delay. People are often called to show up again and again without any progress in their case, and they spend a lot of money on lawyers and fees. Regardless of whether a person is in the right, in a legal sense, there is always a risk of losing because of bribery. Often people give up. Then they are left in a worse situation than the one they were in before they opened a case file. Clearly, in this instance, it was not working out as Elisabeth had hoped, and she was under pressure to make a decision.

The LC1 also speaks; she advises Elisabeth to forgive Grace: 'Here we can even forgive each other for murder, through *mato oput* [an Acholi reconciliation ritual carried out in case of murder].' My field assistant, Sam, is also asked to give advice, and he agrees with the LC1 that the family should reunite, as that possibility is already there, built into the Acholi culture.

In the end, Elisabeth decides to agree on getting a share of the money back. They ask Sam to help write an agreement, as the RDC assistant has left. Presumably, they ask him because they want somebody to formulate the agreement who does not have a part in the matter. The handwritten paper document is two pages long. Elisabeth, Grace and witnesses all sign the agreement as does the LC1 and a representative from the RDC office. In the agreement, it is described how Grace must pay back the balance of 6,550,000 million shillings in instalments over six months to Elisabeth. Grace has to give the money to the RDC assistant, and Elisabeth can pick it up from his office. He will make receipts to document the payment.

This was not what she wanted, Elisabeth says, when I meet her a month later on the small corner left of her land. She sits outside her hut on the veranda with her daughter Maria, who has just been working in the garden. They have met George, the buyer, a couple of times. He wants them to remove one of the huts and also organize a reburial for those buried on the land. But they are not Elisabeth's relatives; they are people who stayed here during the war, and she does not want to rebury them at her home in Kitgum. George has also previously brought people with him to look around. Elisabeth thinks he is trying to sell the land on because of all the trouble between her and Grace. Elisabeth and Maria do not talk to Grace. They hardly ever meet, and when they do, they do not greet each other. Elisabeth has not received any of the money yet and doubts if she ever will, though she has asked at the RDC office.

When I visit them again on the land in Gulu, it has been four months since the meeting in the RDC office, and Elisabeth has got all the money. It was not Grace who paid her but George, the buyer. The land Grace sold to George is gone for good now, as are the good relations between her and Grace, she tells me. They will be forever separated.

A barbed wire fence now surrounds the land. It separates Elisabeth's two huts from each other: one is on the land sold by Grace; the other is on the small piece remaining. A sign has been put next to the path that connects Elisabeth's hut to the neighbouring homes. *Yoo peke kany*, it says, 'no road here', and then there is a drawing of a watchdog biting a leg and a warning of a fine if one does not stay away. There is now no use in dwelling on the land they lost, Maria and Elisabeth state; they are tired of thinking and talking about it. Elisabeth and Maria also tell the sad news that Grace's son committed suicide the previous week. They do not know why the young man took his life. However, with Grace having sold off most of the land that was meant for the grandsons, Maria wonders if there is a connection. Both Elisabeth and Maria went to the burial.

Figure CI.9. 'No road here' © Mette Lind Kusk.

When I returned six months later to look for the women, Elisabeth and Maria had moved back to Kitgum. I obtained directions to Grace's place, as I wanted to hear her version of the conflict in more detail. Grace and a daughter-in-law were seated outside her home, which had several huts and a permanent construction with three sections. Grace told me in a tired voice that she was sick; she had high blood pressure. She explained how she had had to repay George but was so relieved that Elisabeth got her money. There was now no problem of money being owed to Elisabeth, but Elisabeth still did not phone. I asked her what she thought about the conflict more generally – if it could have been avoided. It had caused Grace a lot of stress; the pressure was huge, and she thought it was this that had made her so sick. She now had diabetes too. Elisabeth was still in contact with Grace's remaining children. Grace thought Elisabeth had been persuaded by others to get into the conflict but did not know who these people were.

Grace confirmed that after settling the money she had lost her son Kilama, but did not go into detail. She did not want to travel to Kitgum to see Elisabeth; if she was living closer, she would visit her. The shame was now on Elisabeth's side. Grace was not very eager to talk more about the conflict, her relations and her losses, so my visit was brief.

Mette Lind Kusk, Ph.D., is Assistant Professor at Via University College.

Chapter 1
Multiplicity

Stephen Langole, Susan Reynolds Whyte
and Michael Whyte

An Autoethnographic Account of Stephen's Multiple Land Claims

My experience, based on the way people who are intimately connected to me contest my ownership and control of land, demonstrates the difficulty in trusting anybody on matters of land. My interest is to get private land (*ngom ma alone iye kena*) in different locations, where I can claim ownership and full rights as a kind of insurance given the land greed that I think is unfolding in Acholiland. If I lose some land, some will still remain. Private land, to me, is land that I have rights over as an individual, am free to sell, transfer or mortgage without interference from any other person. I hope to acquire freehold titles for all my land, but I am put off by the bureaucratic challenges.

This autoethnographic account is based on personal reflections about my quest to possess private land free from any other claims, even from people who are intimately close to me like my wife and children. The personal narrative illuminates the challenges associated with land ownership in post-war northern Uganda. These challenges stem from complex negotiations involving multiple stakeholders and changing cultural traditions. I engage in Systematic Sociological Introspection (SSI), whereby I rely on data from personal diary entries, records of periodic informal encounters, 'land sales' agreements and other land transaction documents to recall personal sentiments that inform my narrative. The purpose of autoethnographic research and personal narrative is to identify issues through personal engagement with the data. Through an examination of my own case, I seek to develop a deeper understanding of conflict relating to land ownership in northern Uganda.

I currently lay claim to six pieces of land dotted around the countryside, but none of these are secure or free from conflict or encumbrances.

Land 1 is my current residence in town, about a quarter of an acre that I acquired from four different owners between 1991 and 2001. This is the only plot for which I applied to secure a title. I followed all the required procedures, beginning with a survey and placement of mark stones, inspection by the Area Land Committees in the presence of neighbours, payment of fees to the Division, and approval by the District Land Board. However, in the final stage at the Central Land Registry, an error was detected: the same Plot number (Plot 7) was allocated to two other plots in the area, and one of the applicants already had a title to Plot 7. The application was returned to the District Cartographer for correction. The Cartographer acknowledged the error and wrote to the Commissioner of Surveys and Mapping to draw a fresh Deed Plan with a new plot number allocated to me. This took a month and required additional fees. The struggle to get the land title continued three years on.

Before I surveyed this land, I planted some flowery thorny shrubs to mark the boundary, which borders a blind lady's land. The lady contested the boundary and did not accept the Local Council ruling that favoured me. When I surveyed the land, I left a portion to the lady to avoid the conflict. Additionally, I am concerned that a richer neighbour who requested to purchase the land may cause me some harm because I refused his request.

My brother and sister-in-law also claim a stake in the house that I built here in 1991, based on the premise that she cooked for the builders and her husband supervised the building process. They 'temporarily' settled on the land during the war but now refuse to leave. In yet another case, my cousin's daughter, who lost her parents and was supported through her education by my sister, has made a request to erect a small building on Land 1 for my sister. I acquiesced and the building is halfway finished.

Land 2 is five acres of farmland, where I built a one-room house. It is about 23 kms from Gulu Town. This land was originally given to my father by an uncle of his in the 1960s and passed on to me. I grew some crops on this land in 2009–2010 but gave up because I could not find labour to continue farming. I made a contract with a man that stated he could live here on the condition that he grows some crops for me, for which I will pay him. He decided to dig only for himself, but I have allowed him to stay on the land for the purpose of securing the land boundaries.

My late father left Land 2 in the 1970s, allowing his cousin-brother (his father's brother's son) to temporarily live there with the understanding that the land still belonged to his family. However, when I claimed the land after the end of the civil war in 2006, my father's cousin-brother claimed ownership. The clansmen, the traditional land mediator (*Rwot Kweri*) and Local Council levels all ruled it is my land. My father's cousin-brother vows to appeal the case. In 2010, my door was split and later a mysterious fire burnt down my hut.

To the south of this land, a neighbour refused to recognize a vitex tree as the previous boundary; an elderly neighbour to the east accepted the boundary, but her children contested it despite clear boundary markers.

Land 3 is only 20 by 30 metres in Gulu town. I bought it for UGX 3,600,000 in 2009 after a brother-in-law convinced me that it was a good investment. I built a small one-room temporary structure that I hire out for UGX 40,000 monthly. In addition to the temporary building, there are two huts. To keep the plot, I allowed a nephew who had taken refuge in Kigumba 120 kms away during the war to temporarily settle in the huts upon his return in 2010. Three years later, when I asked my nephew to leave as I prepared to develop the land, he flatly refused, saying he resented 'being sent away like a dog'. His bicycle repair business in the premises was doing well. He traced a grave in the compound with a stick and told me: 'You should know that your real land is this size. If you insist on sending away nephews, then you should stop producing girl-children.' I had to involve the *Rwot Kweri* to make the nephew vacate.

This land is adjacent to Gulu Railways Station, where Uganda Railways Corporation (URC) is plotting re-development. In 2015, URC sent their officials to re-survey the land. The officials organized a meeting with the 'landowners' in the area, and part of the land was marked for a road passage. The Corporation promised compensation but is yet to deliver.

The portion that remains free of URC interest is still big enough for some business. A neighbour who admired the plot came and negotiated with me to put up a small metal fabrication workshop in the plot. I thought it was a good idea to team up together, and we started erecting a structure for the workshop. We could neither agree on the building design nor the contractors, but the breaking point was when the neighbour fixed a kiosk in the plot without informing me. I told him to remove his share of infrastructure and the kiosk from the plot. He removed them but took my metallic frames as well.

I bought Land 4 through the connection of a cousin in 2010. It is located about 40 kms from Gulu Town and, at 40 acres, it is my largest claim. So far, I have paid UGX 10,000,000 for 20 acres. Later, the land seller informed me that if I wanted to secure the land, I should pay an additional UGX 15m because the rate had been revised in their family meeting.

In addition to my own 20 cattle, 8 goats and 13 sheep, I also take care of an additional 20 cattle, 10 goats and 3 sheep for my relatives. When I bought it, it was in an area sparsely settled, quite free from livestock farmer/crop cultivator conflict. This land initially had distant neighbours, but as fate would have it, a neighbour was allocated land where I had hoped to expand my ranch. Within a short while, two of my cows were cut in the tail. The suspect was the new neighbour. The cows were treated by a veterinary officer and survived.

My relatives feel entitled to keep their livestock on my farm, but they neither contribute to the regular treatment of the animals or contribute much to the salary of the herdsman. My wife has advised me to begin thinking of buying alternative cattle-keeping land, but I am afraid that no land seems free of encumbrances or conflict.

Land 5 is two acres located about 10 kms from Gulu Town. I do some farming here. It is ideal because it is easily accessible from my residence in town and casual labourers are easier to come by near the town. I bought it for UGX 4,600,000 from two brothers in 2014. A rich neighbour came and bought adjacent land. He surveyed his land and put mark stones at the edge of my garden without consulting me, as he should. The rich man left the land for his relatives in the neighbourhood to grow their crops. They created a footpath across my garden and even trampled my groundnut crops. When I complained, one of them mockingly said I am 'a poor man who cannot afford to survey his land.' At the western boundary, another neighbour who is a tipper lorry driver, created a way through a portion of my land to reach his own land. My complaints to him fell on deaf ears.

Land 6, my ancestral land, is 10 acres and located 30 kms from Gulu Town. I lay claim to this land along with my siblings. None of my siblings is currently settled there. This is where my grandfather and father were buried, and it will hopefully be my long home too. My mother died in 2010 at a time I was in Denmark. My people saw that the village land with no structures could not support the funeral that would attract multitudes and decided to temporarily bury her on my residential land in Gulu. Her remains will eventually be taken to our ancestral land, together with those from four other graves on Land 1. It becomes even more urgent now that Gulu is becoming a city. The good news is that now there is a house being painted on Land 6 (the long home), and I will spend a good percentage of my time in that house.

I have been interested in farming Land 6 but the only available labourers are my kin, who are unwilling to work the land even for pay. I built a small two-roomed house on this land for labourers, and in 2014 I met a man who was interested in keeping the place on the condition he was allowed to farm it. I planted some 200 pine trees on this land and assigned him to guard them from bush fires. The trees got burnt, and in 2015 the man locked the house and vanished along with the keys.

The boundaries to Land 6 are being contested on all four sides. A cousin-brother to my father (a lineage father to me) is contesting the boundaries to the east and south of the land. He asserts that when I was young my aunt adjusted the boundary to the land and encroached into his western boundary. He dug his garden extending westwards to within a few meters of the graves of my father and grandfather, which were originally located in the middle of the compound before war displaced residents. Where we had a hut in what was the eastern part of our land had been turned into parts of the garden, and the hut's marks remain in evidence. To the south of what was our land, the lineage father had shifted his home, encroaching a few more meters into what we thought belonged to us. The case was heard when the clan met in 2015 but remains unresolved.

On the northern boundary of the land, another lineage father built a makeshift church on what was our farmland. During the meeting of 2015, he agreed to remove the church and hand back the portion of land, but to date the church is intact. He had also sold off about three acres of the land. He brazenly told me that since I am educated and have good income, I can afford to buy land elsewhere.

To the west, a neighbour planted a banana plant and claimed that was the boundary. All my siblings remember we used to have a garden beyond this banana plant without any contestation. My siblings have not been very useful in pressing for this claim, which incidentally ties us to our legitimate lineage and identities. I am on the verge of giving up on this land altogether.

I can conclude that my land claims are intertwined with relationship issues (*ber bedo* – staying well with intimates and neighbours); *ber bedo*, I believe, is the principle that guides customary landholdings, yet I intend to convert these lands attached to customary norms into private freeholdings. The stories, therefore, demonstrate the complexity of converting customary landholdings (which are more communal) into private (individual) freeholdings. No one has expressed this complexity more clearly than the Nwoya District Land Board chairman, whom I quote here:

> Customary land is more a communal land, to be passed to the future generation, so how do you certify communal interest even for those who are not yet born, and those in the diaspora, and you do not know that that is their interest in the first place? How do you gain consensus of all stakeholders? How do you accommodate the interests of nephews, nieces and sisters? How do you include all of them in the application form for the certificate? You exclude some of them, yet they could be included in the customary sense.

Going by the customary landholding mindset, it would be 'illegal' to buy the lands that I purport to have bought unless people begin to accept the principle of commodity land. As it is, it appears that landholding is something that is to be constantly negotiated and accommodative of other interests. My attempts to buy and privatize land, therefore, amount to attempts to create outsiders who feel they are insiders. It is, in fact, a deception that I can acquire 'private' land that

I can pass on to my children – free of encumbrances. My nephew may be quite correct in stating that my 'real land' is the size of the grave that he traced.

Of What Is This a Case?

Stephen Langole's unusual and thought-provoking autoethnography of land claims counters the usual image of landholding in northern Uganda: that a person or a family has but one piece of land or one claim. Stephen has six and makes the point that having land in different locations provides insurance in the face of the land greed that is widespread in Acholiland. We may ask, in Christian Lund's (2014) words: 'Of what is this a case?' Part of the answer is that we have found this to be a specific case of a general pattern of multiple claims. Persons and families often have land claims in several places, even if they only have rights to use the land for a season or two. Shipton (2009: 118–20) found a similar pattern of multiple plot landholding among Luo people of western Kenya. He argued that this should not be seen as inefficient 'fragmentation' but rather as a deliberate strategy of diversification for ecological and social reasons.

Aside from empirical generalizability, Stephen's case raises another more conceptual issue that is another part of the answer. All his land claims were contested. As Shipton (2009: 120) also noted, the disadvantage of the strategy of multiplicity is that dispersed landholdings mean 'increased likelihood of boundary disagreements with neighbours (since there are more boundaries with more neighbours)'. In detailing the conflicts, Stephen shows how each concrete dispute involves different relationships. Moreover, these relations change over time. He takes different positions vis-à-vis the contenders but always sticks to the same position with regard to the land – that it is his alone, except for Land 6 where he admits his siblings have stakes. More abstractly, we can say that people with several land claims take a multiplicity of relational positions, each grounded in a given context. They are multiply embedded in social relationships. It follows from the notion of relational positions that the parties involved might have different perceptions of the situation. Stephen makes it very clear that his neighbours and relatives feel they have claims and that he should not press them because he has more resources than they do.

Recent research on land issues in Africa points to the variety within what is glossed as 'customary tenure'. Summing up this research, Peters (2013: 547) writes of 'overlapping and multiple rights and uses of land' . . . and of 'the rise of multiple forms of land transfers (rentals, leasing, sales)'. In this chapter, we address multiplicity of three different kinds: of acquisition and tenure; of location and use; and of relational positions. It is not merely our point that landholding is complex. By attending to multiplicity within this threefold framework, we attempt to make it more manageable and more amenable to analysis. In some instances, multiplicity refers to diversity, as when a variety of landholdings serves different uses. In other instances, multiplicity simply means plurality, as when the same land is embedded in many relationships.

Multiple Tenures and Modes of Access

Stephen's hope is to acquire freehold titles for all of the land he claims, but so far, he has only set this process in motion for the land where he resides in Gulu town. Freehold would give him the greatest legal individual control over the land. As stated in the Land Act, freehold tenure:

> (a) involves the holding of registered land in perpetuity or for a period less than perpetuity which may be fixed by a condition;
> (b) enables the holder to exercise, subject to the law, full powers of ownership of land, including but not necessarily limited to –
>   (i) Using and developing the land for any lawful purpose;
>   (ii) taking and using any and all produce from the land;
>   (iii) entering into any transaction in connection with the land, including but not limited to selling, leasing, mortgaging or pledging, subdividing creating rights and interests for other people in the land and creating trusts of the land;
>   (iv) disposing of the land to any person either as a gift inter vivos or by will.
> (The Land Act 1998 with amendments in 2001, 2004, 2010, Part II, section 3)

In other words, the freehold owner is free to do what he likes with the land. He (the male pronoun is intentional, since far fewer women hold freehold title) is not encumbered by obligations to others.

Individual registered ownership under freehold title was promoted by colonial governments from the 1930s as a way of strengthening agricultural efficiency and economic development through providing security of tenure. In many African states, land reform policies of the 1960s and 1970s were based on the same logic. Since the late 1980s, the rhetoric of donor agencies, including the World Bank, has changed somewhat, with more emphasis on pro-poor land security and other forms of registration including communal rights (Peters 2009: 1318). De Soto's (2000) trumpet call for individual titling has been criticized on the basis of empirical evidence and concerns for equity (Musembi 2007; Shipton 2009). Yet despite the shift of rhetoric and the differences in land reform policies across Africa, independent states have generally pursued policies that liberalize land tenure to allow individual rather than communal landholding (Manji 2006: 46).

Uganda is no exception. The Constitution of 1995 and the Land Act of 1998 favour freehold, especially with provisions for converting customary tenure to freehold (Manji 2006; Okuku 2006; Joireman 2007; Batungi 2008). However, in most parts of the country, freehold title is rare. As Joireman suggests, changing the law on property rights makes little immediate difference if institutions for implementation and enforcement are neglected. Impediments to the implementation of freehold include bureaucratic obstructionism, underfunding and understaffing of Land Boards, and corruption.

In Uganda, the government bureaucracy is infamous for its corruption and the additional 'fees' that are necessary to obtain proper documentation of landownership or land transfer, unless one is willing to wait years for access to a certificate of title. There are multiple instances of citizen complaints regarding delays of up to five years in the titling of land or requests for bribes from bureaucrats responsible for filing the title (Joireman 2007: 473). Against this background, it is understandable that Stephen's first attempt to obtain freehold title has still not borne fruit after three years.

Another hindrance that Joireman does not mention is the cost of the survey that is necessary in order to obtain title. One of Stephen's antagonists derided him as too poor to afford mark stones. Indeed, surveys and the placement of mark stones are expensive, a fact that contradicts the claim that individual titling is pro-poor. Moreover, they arouse suspicion in some quarters. They seem to indicate a lack of trust, and ambitions to acquire land for investment. The Nwoya District Land Board Chairman explained:

> In the past, giving was without documents. It was giving in an Acholi way. There was a certain guy in Koro who was given land by an old man. The guy called a surveyor. The giver asks why. People who bring surveyors are the ones who will take other people's land. The guy said I'm only going to survey the portion you gave me. The old guy said now you are becoming greedy. I don't trust you. They don't understand what surveying means. They think a survey will always include more land. You can put a permanent building, but don't survey. People who are illiterate know that surveying is for 500 acres, or 1000, for big farms. And yet he has only given one acre. You cannot survey that. They don't understand what you will do with the survey and that the survey has excluded theirs. They fear that much more land will be included than the piece given.

Surveying is sensitive; Stephen remarks that his rich neighbour at Land 5 surveyed his land and put mark stones at the edge of Stephen's land without consulting him as he should.

All of Stephen's holdings fall legally under the category of Customary Tenure, which means that they are regulated according to local practice. This includes land considered to belong to individuals or households as well as land held collectively by lineages or clans. The Land Act states that customary tenure includes:

applying local customary regulation and management to individual and household ownership, use and occupation of, and transactions in, land; providing for communal ownership and use of land in which parcels of land may be recognised as subdivisions belonging to a person, a family or a traditional institution.

In terms of legal tenure, Stephen has only one kind of land. But within the statutory category Customary Tenure, multiplicity reigns. Customary regulation rests largely on what is considered valid as a claim, whether it be inheritance, purchase, borrowing, hiring, bestowal, marriage or sustained use. Stephen obtained land through inheritance from his father, who in turn had been given Land 2; his claim to Land 6 was through membership in a patrilineage that held ancestral land. However, most of his land was purchased. In his autoethnography, Stephen initially puts 'land sales' in scare quotes to mark that such transactions are not formally recognized in the land registry even though they are usually witnessed and recorded on paper. Given that this 'sold' land does not fall within any of the other three categories of land tenure, it must be considered 'customary land' subject to local recognition and regulation.

It is striking that the broad category 'Customary Tenure' although statutory in that it is recognized in the Constitution is seldom certified by government. Attempts to introduce Certificates of Customary Ownership have not as yet been widely accepted in northern Uganda. That would be a kind of state authorization of ownership over a delineated piece of land. But as the Nwoya District Land Board Chairman said, it is difficult to reconcile such certification with the many potential stakeholders. Some organizations have spoken very critically of Certificates of Customary Ownership (Adoko 2017).

The 'sale' and lease of customary land is not a new phenomenon, but it is increasing rapidly across Africa, as documented in a special issue of the journal *Africa* on 'Interpreting Land Markets'. The editors review the literature on what is variously called 'vernacular', 'informal' or 'clandestine' markets and point out that there is often recourse to 'informal formalization', where witnesses and written records mimic formal procedures for land sale registration (Colin and Woodhouse 2010: 7). 'These "informal" documents and other means of recording land transfers ... depart from the oral methods prevalent among customary systems, and represent more definite signs of boundaries and exclusion' (Peters 2013: 552). While much of the research on vernacular markets concerns pioneer areas of newly opened land or parts of West Africa where migrants from outside are acquiring property, it is evident that informal sales of customary land are also common in Uganda, in areas where these conditions do not obtain.

Two other modes of acquiring land – borrowing and renting – are very common but seldom documented.[1] According to Stephen, he had lent ('temporarily') parts of Lands 1 and 3 to relatives, who later refused to leave. He was also hiring out a building on Land 3. Other examples from our TrustLand research showed that women and young people who had difficulty accessing family land borrowed or rented elsewhere (Chapters 4 and 5). Families forced to leave their ancestral land because of ravaging elephants rented places in a nearby trading centre (Chapter 9). In most of these cases, people did not give up their claims to one piece of land in favour of another. They maintained multiple land claims (Obika et al. 2018).

Again, this pattern is increasingly widespread across Africa. Colin and Woodhouse (2010: 4–5) draw attention to the variety of rental and sharecropping arrangements and note that this temporary transfer of rights may offer better prospects for improved efficiency in land use than freehold title. It is flexible and avoids the sensitive move of selling land. However, this very flexibility allows problems of interpretation (Peters 2013: 552). Different parties may have different perceptions of the conditions of an arrangement, especially in northern Uganda, where borrowing land is common as well as renting and sharecropping. Are gifts of produce after harvest payment or appreciation? What happens, as in the case of Stephen's Land 2, when a man allowed to cultivate the land does not grow crops for the owner as stipulated in the agreement? The flexibility of such arrangements is beneficial and sometimes problematic in the parts of northern Uganda hosting refugee settlements. Members of the host community lend or rent agricultural land to the refugees but sometimes withdraw it after one season so that the refugees do not continue to profit from the labour they invested to clear it. Some members of the Adjumani Elders Forum suggest making written agreements about the nature and duration of refugee rights to use the land (Paulino Vusso, personal communication, 2019).

If landholding and access are thought of in terms of 'bundles of rights', then freehold would entail having virtually the entire bundle. Under customary tenure, the multiple rights are disaggregated. The right to use, to sell, to give away, to harvest tree crops or to gather firewood are not necessarily held by the same party (Shipton and Goheen 1992; Doss, Meinzen-Dick and Bomuhangi 2014). Nor do the parties always agree on who has which right and for how long.

Multiple Locations and Uses

In describing his six pieces of land, Stephen states where each plot is located and what it is used for. His land claims are spread out geographically, in part because he wants land for different purposes, and he has the resources to pursue both rural and urban projects. He mentions land for residence, business, and rental in town, and for agriculture, grazing, a pine plantation and burial in various country locations. But having land for different purposes turns out to be not uncommon even for rural people.

Distinguishing kinds of land according to use is well established in Acholi discourse and practice.

> *Ngom kwaro*, which relates to patrilineal descent, may be contrasted with a family of Acholi terms for different kinds of land-in-use. Words such as *tim dwar* (hunting grounds) and *olet* (grazing land) point towards use as a fundamental characteristic of an area. While hunting and grazing are traditionally male occupations, two terms are particularly important for understanding women's land use. 'Garden' (*poto*, pl. *poti*) is used by Acholi when speaking English to indicate a field used for cultivation in one season or over years. ... women have a strong attachment to the gardens where they invest their labour and grow food. *Okang*, on the other hand, refers to garden use-history and denotes a garden opened by a particular woman on virgin land. Creating a new garden out of bush is demanding, and when people speak of a piece of land as the *okang* of their mother or grandmother, they implicitly recognize the work she did to establish a new garden. (Obika et al. 2018: 208)

Use is a more dynamic, processual criterion than ownership, which suggests continuity until an intentional transfer occurs. Maintaining multiple land claims involves keeping them active. This is why Stephen invites people to stay on his land and use it, with the understanding, of course, that they will vacate it when he is ready to use it himself (for example, on Land 2 he allows a man to stay and farm 'for the purpose of securing the land boundaries', in the same way mothers keep the land claims of their sons credible by farming the land).

The crucial element of use in relation to land claims emerges during attempts to resolve disputes. The evidence brought forward at in situ gatherings of local authorities is usually a combination of physical marks in the landscape and oral testimony about their history. For example, in 2014 the chairman of the Awach Sub-county Court Committee told Susan Whyte, Mette Kusk and Alice Adongpiny about a case the committee had recently heard:

> The evidence that made Ojok win were mango and pine trees planted by his father, his [the father's] grave and the brothers' graves, and a drainage, *wang kigingi*. An old foundation of a house, *wi obu*, was also there. The Sub-county Court Committee moved around in the area to see this, and the neighbours confirmed it. If two persons claim the same tree, the neighbours will confirm who is right. People will point fingers if somebody tries to claim land that did not used to be theirs.
>
> ... The *wang kigingi* are made because people throw weeds to one side of their fields. This makes a ridge and a natural drainage along the side of the ridge when rain comes. Neighbours with adjacent fields do not

throw weeds on the same *kigingi*; if one throws to the east, the other does the same. It now helps as proof when people are in conflict over land, but it has not been created purposefully as a boundary.

The *wang kigingi* were not boundary indicators like the mark stones of the surveyor. They were built up organically through use – by people weeding their gardens. Memories of use figured in considerations of land claims in many of the narratives we heard: 'yes, we used to eat mangos from that tree of Okumu's on our way to school'; 'Tito had a sweet potato garden there – I remember that it was a problem for him that men drinking at the nearby market used to urinate in his sweet potatoes.'

Graves are the most common marks of use adduced in land disputes, given that the dead are not buried in churchyards or public cemeteries but rest in family land. Graves are evident as mounds, often with a few stones or bricks to mark them. In the past, people used to plant *kituba* trees at graves, which signalled the burial for many years after the mound of earth had disappeared. Today, those who can afford it make graves permanent as rectangles of cement; the ancestral residents of 'the long home' (Land 6) are identified by names and years of birth and death that were scratched into wet cement. While graves are established naturally as part of life courses and not as mark stones in land claims, there is a growing awareness that they affirm a family's link to the land. Perhaps the marking of graves is taking on greater significance in light of growing worries over land, as Shipton (2009: 96) has argued for the Luo of western Kenya.

Stephen hopes that Land 6, his ancestral land, will be his 'long home' someday, but for now he is thinking of diversity in agricultural and income enterprises on different kinds of land. This logic is evident more widely in people's livelihood strategies. Income diversification is common. Bryceson (2002) writes of 'the scramble in Africa' for non-agricultural sources of livelihood as exports of agricultural commodities decline. At the same time, she notes that agricultural foundations and the production of subsistence crops remain important for household economies. The pattern of diversification in northern Uganda encompasses both agricultural and non-agricultural activities. People like Stephen who have a regular salary invest in livestock and tree plantations and renting out buildings. Atim and Awor (Chapter 5) are trading fish in the market as well as cultivating land where they can. Daniel (Chapter 4) raises pigs and cabbages and worked for an oil company for a period. Brickmaking and charcoal burning are often combined with subsistence agriculture, as is distilling and selling snacks. This kind of multiplicity means that it is useful to have different kinds of land in different locations.

Rural land serves many purposes in addition to agriculture, as Ferguson (2013) has emphasized. A rural homestead is a base for migrants and people who have retired after working elsewhere. It is a platform for trade and small businesses, often with links to urban centres. It is a place where sick and disabled family members can be cared for. Importantly for our arguments in this book, it is an anchor for belonging, as shown in Chapter 6. Ferguson argues that rural land is a basis for distribution as well as production; rural homesteads are where resources are shared and where those who have more will assist those who have less. This is certainly true in Stephen's case.

Multiple Relational Positions

Karl Marx is often credited with the insight that property is not a thing but a social relation between an object and an 'owner' and a group willing to recognize the relation between them. But it was Sir Henry Maine (1861), writing around the same time about property as a 'bundle of rights', who more directly influenced anthropological approaches. The appreciation of multiplicity captured in the 'bundle' metaphor has been evident in anthropological writings on property, law and social relations for many decades (F. von Benda-Beckman, K. von Benda-Beckmann, and Wiber 2006: 32, note 16).

The notion of property as bundles of rights can be a way of analysing social relations. Hann (1998: 7), for example, proposes that we should analyse property as 'the distribution of social entitlements', inviting us to consider who has which kinds of entitlements vis-à-vis whom. For him, the notion of social 'embeddedness' is key. Here he is inspired by Karl Polyani (1944), who first used this concept to underline the ways in which, historically, property and economic processes were deeply entwined with social relations and cultural practices. The idea was elaborated by Granovetter (1985) and adapted by anthropologists studying changes in land tenure in Africa (Colin and Woodhouse 2010; Chauveau and Colin 2010). In relation to land, social embeddedness is the opposite of freehold; land is not free of the claims, entitlements and encumbrances of socially significant others. It cannot be separated from social life and transacted as an independent commodity with absolute property rights (see Chapter 2).

We would like to take these notions of bundles and embeddedness a step further by looking at the practice of negotiating entitlements. Privileges regarding land are not just distributed in some set way according to the elements in an agreed bundle. They are firmly asserted, obliquely denied, grudgingly allowed or generously shared. Access to land, whether by purchase, inheritance or loan, is through social relations, often intimate ones. It is worked out through interaction with multiple others. In this approach, we follow the direction of Cockburn and colleagues to move from thinking about bundles of rights to bundles of relations to performative property practices. They write of '. . . a processual or performative perspective on ownership: property relations are not static but need to be communicated, performed or claimed – actively made and repeated – in order to function' (Cockburn et al. 2018: 8). As their collection demonstrates, these processes are often most visible in contests over property claims.

The conventional image of Acholi society is that patrilineages have land in a given village to which sons, and to some lesser extent daughters, have entitlements. While this picture is generally a fair representation, it does not capture the multiplicity of possibilities that are being worked out by people in different positions and situations. Stephen is a recognized member of a landholding patrilineage, but when he attempted to assert his entitlement, his father's cousin-brother told him that since he was educated and had a good income he could afford to buy land elsewhere. As we will see in Chapter 4, some potential members of a patrilineage are not able to realize their claims because their paternity has not been recognized. Moreover, people can obtain access through links other than membership in a patrilineal descent group. They may mobilize some kind of entitlement through maternal relatives, or because a father or grandfather was given land by a member of another patrilineage, such as an in-law. Stephen mentions that Land 2 was a gift to his father. Among the cases in the chapters to follow, there are similar examples. Atim and Awor (Chapter 5) were living on a plot given to their father's brother by a friend. Daniel and his brothers (Chapter 4) were staying with their mother on her brother's land.

A study on changes in landholding in formerly rural areas around Kampala found an increase in freehold tenure (through conversion from *mailo* land – see the appendix on land legislation), with people with resources buying land for housing developments or large commercial farms. At the same time, those who have continued with smaller scale agriculture have activated multiple forms of access. The researchers identified twenty different types of access mobilized through social connections.

> To negotiate land access, it is essential to have a network of acquaintances, even though mutual aid is today more restricted. An accumulation of forms of land access appears to be the rule more than the exception and it is instructive to relate it to marital or family trajectories (for example, the arrival of a new wife may motivate the acquisition of an extra plot or extra plots might be acquired through wives' acquaintances). (Chalin, Golaz and Médard 2015: 566)

The 'bundle of rights' is large, and the 'distribution of social entitlements' is broad, but they must be negotiated and readjusted as time passes.

People assume a multiplicity of relational positions in pursuing, maintaining, accepting and denying land claims. They engage specific others on grounds that have moral, practical and micro-historical dimensions. Stephen's case illustrates this very well. He interacts as a neighbour with the blind lady, who refused to accept the ruling of the Local Council concerning their boundary on Land 1. His generosity in conceding to her demand might be taken as an example of the moral good of harmonious living (*ber bedo*), which features in several of the other cases we studied (see 'The Land Conflict at Ogul' in Chapter 6 and Obika et al. 2018). Concerning the same land, Stephen interacts as sibling with his brother and sister-in-law who make claims because of the work they have invested in building the house. He positions himself as senior family member towards the cousin's daughter whom he allowed to put up a small building for his sister on the land. On Land 2, Stephen takes the position of employer towards a man he contracted to farm for him, but the man realizes his entitlement to use the land without fulfilling the agreement to grow crops for Stephen. On Land 3, he interacts as business partner with a man who attempts to expand the entitlement beyond their metal fabrication workshop to include use of the land for a kiosk. This development leads to the end of the partnership and the man's entitlement.

Stephen allows people to realize entitlements to use land even as he laments that they are taking advantage of him. Land 4, the grazing land, is a good example. His relatives are keeping as much livestock there as he does but without contributing to the expenses. They have negotiated a social entitlement to use the land (and herdsman) of their kinsman, but Stephen has now grown unhappy about the situation, and his wife, with whom he assumes another relational position, is advising him to end the arrangement.

To say that land claims involve multiple relational positions is to acknowledge that land is embedded in social relations, which in turn involves elements of trust, morality, interest, sentiment and interpersonal history. Relations change over time and thus affect the status of land entitlements. In some cases, it is not that relations become tense because of land conflicts but that relations have already been damaged by tensions that have flared up over other conflicts. Several of the actors in this volume recognize this. In Chapter 3, the land conflict between Sylvia and Lanyuru is linked to Lanyuru's bitterness that Sylvia refused to be inherited by him when her husband died.

> Specific conflicts between men and women over gardens and land rights are often about more than boundaries. They are disputes about status, identity, even legitimacy . . . It was a premise of the Contested Property Claims Project that contesting claims can compel social actors to 'reason about the institution of property.' Our cases suggest that what our interlocutors 'reason about' are the social and historical links that mark their ability to have access to property. (Obika et al. 2018: 209)

The reasoning employed in relation to land access shows that the links are sometimes uncertain and undependable, rendering access insecure.

Sara Berry found a similar multiplicity and uncertainty in relationships among Yorùbá farmers:

> kin-based relations do not provide much security either. People cling to them because trade and politics are risky too . . . Most of my informants said that their primary strategy for surviving or getting ahead has been to keep their options open, which implies both supporting one's kin and exploiting them. . . . The multiplication of options served, in turn, to increase uncertainty and inhibit productive investment. (Berry 1985: 83)

Stephen writes that his experience demonstrates the difficulty in trusting anybody on matters of land. Therefore, he wants multiple pieces of land for insurance; if he loses some to his untrustworthy relatives and neighbours, others will remain. Here he seems to link multiplicity with the risk of duplicity. In a similar vein, the chairman of the Awach Sub-county Court Committee pinpointed mistrust as a constant, when recounting a land dispute where the two parties had seemingly accepted a reconciliation. 'Are they now on good terms?' we asked. Our interlocutor replied: 'They stay well, but you do not know what is inside, deep in the heart. In Acholi: *Gibedo maber, ento pe ingeyo ngo ma i cwinygi* – you never know another person's heart.' The multiple relationships in which land claims are embedded must be activated and considered, not to know their nature for certain but to maintain or revise working assumptions about their viability.

Trust entails a degree of certainty about persons, relationships and situations. Stephen does not feel certain about the present or the future. He cannot count on his family and neighbours; even conditions may change as when neighbouring land is sold or land is subject to compulsory acquisition by the railways. Stephen's strategy is one of insurance rather than assurance; in the face of contingency and uncertainty, he seeks security through multiplicity rather than relying on one trusted and certain relationship (Whyte 2009).

Conclusion

In this chapter, we started with the straightforward point that many people, like Stephen, have claims on more than one piece of land. We used his case to discuss three kinds of multiplicity in landholding. Under multiple forms of tenure and modes of acquisition, we showed that even though the great majority of land in northern Uganda is held under Customary Tenure, multiplicity reigns within that one category. Contrary to the exclusive focus on descent and marriage as the channels through which people access land, we emphasized informal sales on the vernacular land market and the importance of lending, renting and giving as modes of land transaction. A second kind of multiplicity concerns locations and uses. While agriculture in rural areas is the most demanding in terms of extent, land is also important for residence, burial and business. It provides the basis for social life and enterprise in urban centres and country settings. Here multiplicity permits diversity. Finally, we considered the multiplicity of relations around land that follows from its social embeddedness. Even freehold land, which should in principle be less entangled with obligations to intimate others, is not free of social relations, as we saw in 'A Disputed Land Sale', which opened Part I of the book. The land in question was freehold, but the conflict was seen as a betrayal of the trust that should obtain between a mother and daughter.

Stephen Langole, Ph.D., is a Senior Lecturer and former Director of the Institute of Peace and Strategic Studies at Gulu University.

Susan Reynolds Whyte, Ph.D., is Professor at the Department of Anthropology, University of Copenhagen.

Michael Whyte, Ph.D., is Associate Professor Emeritus at the Department of Anthropology, University of Copenhagen.

Note

1. Of course, encroachment and theft are also modes of acquiring land, but here we only consider those recognized as licit.

References

Adoko, Judy. 2017. *Certificates of Customary Ownership (CCOs) are Not What They Seem on the Surface – Risks to CCOs*. Kampala: Land and Equity Movement in Uganda.

Batungi, Nasani. 2008. *Land Reform in Uganda: Towards a Harmonised Tenure System*. Kampala: Fountain Publishers.

Berry, Sara. 1985. *Fathers Work for their Sons: Accumulation, Mobility and Class Formation in an Extended Yorùbá Community*. Berkeley: University of California Press.

Bryceson, Deborah Fahy. 2002. 'The Scramble in Africa: Reorienting Rural Livelihoods', *World Development* 30(5): 725–39.

Chalin, Victoire, Valérie Golaz and Claire Médard. 2015. 'Land Titling in Uganda Crowds out Local Farmers', *Journal of Eastern African Studies* 9(4): 559–73.

Chauveau, Jean-Pierre, and Jean-Philippe Colin. 2010. 'Customary Transfers and Land Sales in Côte d'Ivoire: Revisiting the Embeddedness Issue', *Africa* 80(1): 81–103.

Cockburn, P. J. L. et al. 2018. 'Introduction: Disagreement as a Window onto Property', in M. H. Bruun, P. J. L. Cockburn, B. S. Risager, and M. Thorup (eds), *Contested Property Claims: What Disagreement Tells Us About Ownership*. Abingdon, Oxfordshire: Routledge, pp. 1–20.

Colin, Jean-Philippe, and Philip Woodhouse. 2010. 'Introduction: Interpreting Land Markets in Africa', *Africa* 80(1): 1–13.

De Soto, Hernando. 2000. *The Mystery of Capital: Why Capitalism Triumphs in the West and Fails Everywhere Else*. New York: Basic Books.

Doss, Cheryl, Ruth Meinzen-Dick and Allan Bomuhangi. 2014. 'Who Owns the Land? Perspectives from Rural Ugandans and Implications for Large-scale Land Acquisitions', *Feminist Economics* 20(1): 76–100.

Ferguson, James. 2013. 'How to Do Things with Land: A Distributive Perspective on Rural Livelihoods in Southern Africa', *Journal of Agrarian Change* 13(1): 166–74.
Granovetter, Mark. 1985. 'Economic Action and Social Structure: The Problem of Embeddedness', *American Journal of Sociology* 91(3): 481–510.
Hann, Chris M. 1998. 'Introduction: The Embeddedness of Property', in Chris M. Hann (ed.), *Property Relations: Renewing the Anthropological Tradition*. Cambridge: Cambridge University Press, pp. 1–47.
Joireman, Sandra F. 2007. 'Enforcing New Property Rights in Sub-Saharan Africa: The Ugandan Constitution and the 1998 Land Act', *Comparative Politics* 39(4): 463–80.
Lund, Christian. 2014. 'Of What Is This a Case? Analytical Movements in Qualitative Social Science Research', *Human Organization* 73(3): 224–34.
Maine, Henry James Sumner. 1861. *Ancient Law: Its Connection with the Early History of Society and its Relation to Modern Ideas*. London: John Murray.
Manji, Ambreena. 2006. *The Politics of Land Reform in Africa: From Communal Tenure to Free Markets*. London: Zed Books.
Musembi, Celestine Nyamu. 2007. 'De Soto and Land Relations in Rural Africa: Breathing Life into Dead Theories About Property Rights', *Third World Quarterly* 28(8): 1457–78.
Obika, Julaina A. et al. 2018. 'Contesting Claims to Gardens and Land: Gendered Practice in Post-War Northern Uganda', in Maja Hojer Bruun, Patrick J. L. Cockburn, Bjarke Skaerlund Risager and Mikkel Thorup (eds), *Contested Property Claims: What Disagreement Tells Us About Ownership*. New York: Routledge, pp. 205–20.
Okuku, Juma Anthony. 2006. 'The Land Act (1998) and Land Tenure Reform in Uganda', *Africa Development* 31(1): 1–26.
Peters, Pauline E. 2009. 'Challenges in Land Tenure and Land Reform in Africa: Anthropological Contributions', *World Development* 37(8): 1317–25.
———. 2013. 'Conflicts over Land and Threats to Customary Tenure in Africa', *African Affairs* 112(449): 543–62.
Polyani, Karl. 1944. *The Great Transformation*. New York: Farrar & Rinehart.
Shipton, Parker. 2009. *Mortgaging the Ancestors: Ideologies of Attachment in Africa*. New Haven: Yale University Press.
Shipton, Parker, and Mitzi Goheen. 1992. 'Understanding African Land-Holding: Power, Wealth and Meaning', *Africa* 62(3): 307–25.
Von Benda-Beckmann, Franz, Keebet von Benda-Beckmann and Melanie G. Wiber. 2006. 'The Properties of Property', in Franz von Benda-Beckmann, Keebet von Benda-Beckmann and Melanie G. Wiber (eds), *Changing Properties of Property*. New York: Berghahn, pp. 1–39.
Whyte, Susan Reynolds. 2009. 'Epilogue: Insecurity, Contingency and Uncertainty', in Liv Haram and Bawa Yamba (eds), *Dealing with Uncertainty in Contemporary African Lives*. Uppsala: Nordic Africa Institute, pp. 213–16.

Chapter 2

Transactions

Lotte Meinert and Mette Lind Kusk

Selling Land to Foreigners for a Wind Turbine

It was an afternoon in August 2015, and just outside the village, which overlooks a green valley in the mountains in Ik County, Kaabong district, Komol and two other Ik elders were waiting on their small wooden stools in the shade of a tree. Lemu, his adult daughter Elizabeth and granddaughter Martha arrived on a motorbike. Lemu, a local farmer, wore a large suit jacket over his T-shirt, and the two women were also dressed up for the occasion. Komol got up and introduced Lotte, who was doing fieldwork in the area with Daniel, a local farmer and research assistant. Komol asked if we could all walk to the site in question. As we walked up the hill, Komol told us about the ongoing issue of selling land for building a wind turbine near the village.

In July 2014 representatives from an Asian company had come to survey a piece of land together with a local broker called James from the Ik community. They said they were going to buy a plot of land and build a pilot wind turbine to test if this would be a feasible site for producing electricity. James, a member of the local educated elite, had acted as a middleman (see Chapter 8) between the investors and Komol, who was asked to identify 'the owners of the land'. Komol was approached as an elder and a clan leader and because he was considered a custodian of the land, *Amazeya jumui*, which in the Ik language means 'leader of the soil'. Komol was one of the local traditional authorities who would show people what land they could use if they had moved from another area due to conflict or other issues. Identifying 'the owners of the land' was a tricky task, according to Komol, since many families had been using the land in the past due to the semi-nomadic settlement patterns and recurrent conflict in the area. There were no 'official owners' of the land in terms of land titles or documents but long lines of intimate entanglements of families who had been using the land and who made claims to it. The elders, represented by Komol, had decided that the families of Chilla, Lochol and Lemu were those who were going to be presented to the buyers as the owners. They were from three different clans, and not from the poorest families in those clans.

Lemu explained that a representative from the Asian company had come for a meeting with the sub-county chief, the local broker James, Komol and the three family heads. At the meeting in the sub-county office, Komol and the family heads thought they were going to discuss the terms of the land transaction and negotiate the price, but in Lemu's words they were simply 'presented with money and asked to sign papers'. This was a land sale, not a lease or rental agreement, but none of the local families had been involved in a land sale previously, so they did not know what to expect or what they could possibly ask or demand.

They were told by the company representative that the price, which the company called compensation, had been set at 7.8 million UGX (around 2,200 USD at the time) for the plot of land measuring 150 x 150 meters. In this local context where the cash economy is limited, this appeared to be a significant amount of money. They were told that the division of money was going to be even among the three so-called 'original owners': each family head would get 2 million UGX. A land sale fee to the sub-county was set at 350,000 UGX, and Komol, the elder, was given only 20,000 UGX as a transport refund. On our way up the hill, we did not figure out how the balance of the money, 1,430,000 UGX, was divided or spent. Later Lotte asked others about this again, but they did not know about the balance and did not expect to be able to find out.

When news about the money being paid to the three families reached other members of the community – probably through hearsay and families' suspicious monitoring of others' spending – there was dissatisfaction with the process and the creation of 'original owners'. Other families claimed that they too used to farm in that particular area and lamented: Why were those families given money and not us?

Lemu was upset about the reactions from other community members, and the reason he had travelled with his daughter and granddaughter was to have a discussion with those who were dissatisfied. The families who had claimed they also used to farm on the land were not present, but Lemu spoke as if they were listening. As we reached the sold plot of land on the hilltop, Lemu and his daughter eagerly pointed out trees in the landscape and talked about the crops they had grown over the years. Lemu said: 'My father Aperit was instructed by his grandfather Isiokalem and by his great grandfather Longok to use this land.' Lemu recognized that there had been other users too but claimed 'we were the original owners of this land'. Komol, the elder, backed him up and confirmed his authority by saying: 'I remember who used this land, and I contacted the right people – others should respect that and not claim they were all here.'

After the debate had cooled down, the parties agreed that the process of selling the land had not been good. Komol explained: 'They [the company and the LC3] convinced us to sell the land by saying that the whole place will be bright [i.e. receive electricity]. That is why we accepted to sell.' Elizabeth, Lemu's daughter, was annoyed about the way the sale was done and regretted that they had not proposed the option of rent or lease of the land:

> This was not proper selling. We were just told 'this is your money'. We were not given a chance to negotiate or to understand what was involved ... They [The company] should have called for a community meeting ... They did not explain how they divided the money, and they did not tell about the size of the land or the plan for the wind turbine.

The sub-county chairman, who had hosted the meeting, was less critical of the process and thought that the families should be grateful because they had received compensation. The chairman's perspective was that: 'This area needs development, and electricity will help that.' The chairman had not been informed about the detailed plans to provide power, and it was unclear whether the power would be joining the main grid hundreds of kilometres away or provided locally to villages, and whether families would be expected to pay for it. The chairman was satisfied because at least the company had gone through the official channels to buy the land. They had first contacted the district chairman, then the sub-county chairman and they had the meeting and the land transaction in his office, the sub-county office. The chairman's point of reference was that other outsiders, such as the missionaries who had arrived recently, as well as a foreign couple, had just bought or acquired land locally without involving district or sub-county officials.

The land was located very near the border to Kenya and also near the Timu Forest Reserve. The chairman explained that he had had many questions about the size of the land but there had been no time to answer these questions in the meeting with the company. It turned out that the land that had been sold was actually inside the Timu Forest Reserve, in breach of regulations. It is not unthinkable that Komol and perhaps the families knew this all along. Ik families had been farming, gathering and hunting in the area for generations and had never entirely agreed with the forest authorities about the boundaries of the reserve or which activities were allowed to take place in the forest (see Chapter 9).

The district forest officer, Patrick Nyeko, from the Department of Environment, had not been informed about the wind turbine project and was not aware that the plot that had been sold was located inside the forest reserve. It would obviously not be possible to build a wind turbine inside the forest reserve, since this would be against the law, and it would affect the trees, biodiversity and wildlife. Patrick said that the forest authorities were trying to develop good relations with the local communities and explained how they were trying to bring projects that were compatible with the forest and the people living in the area. The forest officer was obviously less than impressed with how the private company had worked its way through official institutions and procedures because it had not gone through the Department of Environment.

At the beginning of 2016, a new site – also with plenty of wind for building the test turbine – was identified near Lokinene village, close to the main road. The company did not bother to ask the families to pay back the money for the first site in the forest reserve. The company simply wanted to get started on building a fence around the new plot as soon as possible. There were seven other pilot sites for testing the feasibility of producing wind turbine electricity in Kaabong district, and at these sites the test equipment had already been set up. At the new site near Lokinene village, it was agreed between the local broker, the sub-county chief and the local leaders that it would create too many problems if the money was only paid to a select number of families. Thus, the local leaders in the nearby villages, the sub-county chief, the local elders and the same local broker agreed that the compensation money should be paid to the community at large because, as the broker put it, 'land in this area is not really owned by individuals, and the new site is definitely on communal land'. They had to come up with a way of giving the money to the 'community at large'. It was agreed that the money be spent on repairing the community road. Thus 200 inhabitants from the nearby villages who were willing and able to work on the community road were paid 5,000 shillings per day for five days and the road was repaired.

Again, the compensation for the land was set by the company at 7.8 million shillings. This time, the sub-county took a fee of three million. The reason for the change in fee was apparently that a new sub-county chairman had been elected, and furthermore the sub-county was short of funds. Still, the story about the total figure was perplexing. It said that five million was paid to those who worked on the road and three million remained at the sub-county, which makes eight million – so the calculation was 200,000 shillings short. There were disapproving voices saying that this time the money was simply taken by the sub-county, since the sub-county was responsible for repairing the road in the first place, and they were short of funds. Yet the general atmosphere around the second transaction of land was less critical than the first one in which money was given to only three individual families.

In 2017, a team of workers from a Ugandan contractor built cement pillars and put up a barbed wire fence around the new site where the test wind turbine was going to be placed. The team was made up of about fifteen young men, assembled from all over Uganda, who were camping inside the fence during the months when they did the building. The foreman was a young Ankole man, who had been working for the company for eight years. He explained that the wind turbine, together with seven others in Karamoja, was projected to produce around 60 megawatts. After eighteen months of testing the wind turbine, electricity would be available for selling – even to Kenya, the foreman explained. The locals would get free access to power in the beginning and later on they would have to pay for it, but not much, according to the foreman: 'Electricity is now paid like airtime on the phone. You get a card and load your power on it.'

The foreman related how a number of local Ik and Dodoth men had been approaching him to ask for work, but he was not responsible for employing people. This was done centrally by the company. He wished he could hire some of the local people because he could see that they had very few options to earn money. Some of the local older men from Lokinene were complaining too: 'We did not know they were going to put up a big fence like this inside our land – they said they were going to build a wind turbine and provide power to all.' Given their expulsion from the area that was made into Kidepo National Park in 1959 (see

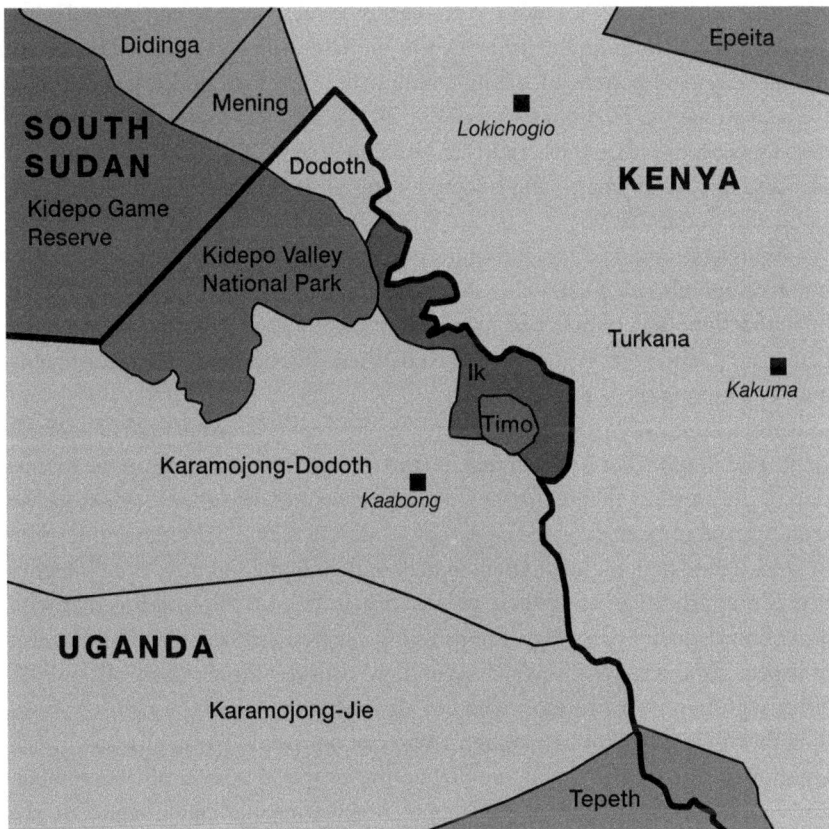

Map 2.1. Ik County, bordering Turkana territory in Kenya, Dodoth Territory, Kidepo National Park and Timu Forest Reserve in Uganda. Map prepared by Nick Leffler.

Chapter 9) and continuous threats of being expelled again from the Timu Forest Reserve, it was no wonder that people became worried when massive cement pillars and a barbed wire fence were put up on their land.

After the fence had been finished and the test mast had been put up to measure the wind, nothing much happened, according to the local broker. A soldier was hired by the company to guard the fence and the test mast. In January 2020, the community had still not heard any news about the prospect of building a wind turbine for producing electricity. But the land had been sold, and the fence and the soldier were clear markers of the land transaction.

Of What Is This a Case?

The sale of land in Ik County was a complicated affair, not least in its consequences. It spurred new creations: of owners, of fences, of arguments for or against land sales, of regulations for transactions, and of ideas about how money gained from a land sale should be spent. It did not end with a signature on a paper and handing over money. Rather, those acts were a starting point for ongoing negotiations and arguments. On the face of it, this is a specific case of the more general pattern of selling communally held land and transforming it from customary to freehold tenure (Wily 2011). It is also a concrete example of dispossession of indigenous land (Laltaika and Askew 2021) and divergent understandings about what a land transaction entails (Colin and Woodhouse 2010; Lund and Boone 2013).

Transactions of land include selling and buying but also lending and borrowing, renting, inheriting and being shown where to use land. These different kinds of transactions and transfers of use rights are not always experienced as clearly demarcated, and what is understood to be their duration and degree of finality may vary among the actors involved.

In the remaining part of this chapter, we first consider some fundamental assumptions about what is transferred in land transactions, building on the discussion in the previous chapter about forms of tenure and modes of acquisition. We then proceed to examine three aspects of transactions as social actions in relation to trust. First, we look at their embedded and embodied nature: the difference between transferring access while physically standing on the land together with other knowledgeable people and transferring a representation of land in the form of papers, data, maps and surveys. Second, we consider the actors involved: individuals, groups or institutions, who can claim that they have the right or power or authority to make the transaction. Who can represent whom, and how much say should others have? Third, we discuss the temporal aspects of land transactions as processes, attending to the ways in which people may disagree on the time perspective of a transaction.

What Is Transferred in a Land Transaction?

As we saw in Chapter 1 on Multiplicity, land tenure may be understood as bundles of entitlements vis-à-vis other persons. Freehold tenure entails the most comprehensive bundle, while customary tenure may involve different kinds and extents of entitlements to use the land. So when land access is transferred, the question is: what entitlements does the recipient gain and what if anything does the giver receive? As Colin and Woodhouse (2010: 8) point out, we must attend to the content of land transactions, especially the rights and obligations exchanged. There is a great variety of arrangements: land transfers entailing particular obligations and rights for the buyer, temporary transfers, and transfers entailing rights to use but not to sell the land in question, and so on (Colin and Woodhouse 2010: 3–4).

In the case of the wind turbine sale, we saw how a large bundle of land access rights were exchanged for money – a common global measure of value. Interestingly, there was no discussion or disagreement about the monetary price of the land – no negotiations, haggling and bargaining about the amount. This is unusual but was probably due to the fact it was the first instance of selling land in the county, and thus there were no points of reference for comparison. Furthermore, the price seemed extraordinarily high to the local sellers, so they had no quarrel to make. The price was presented as 'compensation', a term governments use when expropriating land for a public works project. People being compensated do not have a say about the amount of compensation. It seems that those who transferred the land to the company did not understand the extent of the access entitlements they were providing. Elders complained that they did not know that a big fence would be erected on their land so that they could no longer access it. Moreover, social relations between the parties to the transaction, minimal in any case, ceased once the compensation was paid. There were no jobs for local people at the wind turbine site.

Such a land transaction contrasts with the more common type of transfer, where entitlements are socially embedded and subject to adjustment. These are based in values of cooperation, reciprocity, harmony, sympathy and entrustment for the future. Money can be exchanged for a given entitlement (for example to dig clay for bricks or grow crops for a season), but the presence of money in a transaction does not necessarily excise land access from social relations. Of course, there may be disagreement about the entitlements transferred. As we saw in the case of Stephen's multiple landholdings (Chapter 1), his intimate others did not always accept his definition of the transaction.

Land that is sold in a manner that alienates the entire bundle of rights may later be subject to a reassertion of social embeddedness if family members attempt to reverse the sale. As was the case in Côte d'Ivoire, a sale may be disputed on the grounds that 'my father should not have sold the land' (Chauveau and

Colin 2010: 98). If it is not possible to cancel the sale, the proceeds can at least be shared, thus recognizing the embeddedness that has been denied, as happened in the second sale of land to the wind turbine company.

(Dis)embedded and (Dis)embodied Transactions

Deterritorialization – that is, a process whereby distance and place become irrelevant – is part of global modernity (Eriksen 2007: 16). When it does not matter where something was made or takes place, it has been physically disembedded (ibid.). Disembedding also has a more comprehensive social meaning, according to Giddens, who defines disembedding as the lifting out of social relations from local contexts of interaction and their restructuring across indefinite spans of time-space (1990: 22). This gradual movement from concrete and tangible to the abstract and virtual is also highly relevant in land transactions.

Unlike most other kinds of physical property, land is fixed in space. In a land transaction, land is not moved. Rather, it is people who willingly move or are compelled to move, or their entitlements change. In that sense, land is not property (Lund, this volume). We may refer to land as if it was a 'thing' that is transacted, but in reality it is the bundle of rights to use and settle on the land that is transferred though recognition. The fixity and materiality of land does not mean that its social characteristics are obvious. Its units and borders are often not visible to the unknowing eye because very little land is fenced or demarcated with clearly visible signs. When land is transacted, as we saw in the case from Ik County, the embodied knowledge of people is brought into play. They are aware of the extent of the land being transferred, its history and the kinds of rights to use the land. That is why when a piece of land is entrusted from father to son in the Ik tradition other family members and neighbours ideally have to be present to witness the process, and they often physically walk around the plot and mark or touch trees and stones to show and witness that this is the unit for which rights are being transferred. In this way, a transaction is both physically embedded (happens in situ), socially embedded (takes place with the involved parties present) and it is embodied (with footsteps, touch and sight). Land transactions in northern Uganda almost always involve some action on the ground, some of the involved parties, and some form of embodiment.

Yet in some cases (and for some of the parties) a land transaction is also, or even only, an abstracted process where actors make use of representations of the land: a map representing the landscape, cadastral measurements and numbers, a land title document. When land is represented by papers and measurements, it is not necessary to engage the land physically. The transaction may take place in an office where a limited amount of information is registered and key potential stakeholders are not present. An extreme example is given in Chapter 7 on Aspirations. The sub-county authorities sold plots of land in the Town Board to buyers who had not yet seen the plots they were purchasing. The general location and the measurements of the plots were known, but it was not until later in the process that the buyers were shown the specific plots that they were acquiring.

When the plot of land in Ik County that was sold to the Asian company turned out to be located inside a forest reserve, this made some of these basic issues about land transactions clear. Even though some protocol followed – money was transferred, signatures were put on paper, meetings were held – the transaction was not successful because in the end it turned out that another authority claimed rights to the land – The National Forest Authority; and this trumped other authorities. Because of the fixed nature of land, the company could not simply take what they had paid for and leave but had to give up the first transaction and embark on buying a new plot, because land, even when turned into a commodity, is physically embedded, grounded – it is the ground. Land transactions make power relations and institutions manifest (Lund 2008), and they point to the role of the state and the different actors as citizens (Lund 2016), foreign investors and clan elders and the authority they hold (Lund and Boone 2013).

The knowledge about the land in the Ik case was embedded in memories and relationships between people, as well as in maps and documents. The middleman and the clan elders had given their perspective on the land, which they had used for many generations. They had stories about the land, and they could tell on the ground how the land had been used and say who had used it. This was in line with indigenous Ik ideas about land as an embedded and embodied resource to be used and entrusted to others. The middleman and the elders embodied the history of the land and may not have walked around the plot together with the buyer but were physically present and could point to trees and stones that marked boundaries. This embodied practice of being present on the ground in question was considered appropriate by the local actors, and it was accepted by the foreign buyers, who on these terms could proceed with a meeting in the sub-county office. The meeting in the office, however, was somewhat foreign to the local elders and families. It was characteristic of modern land transactions as disembedded, mediated and disembodied. The transaction took place far away from the land in question, by means of representation: a map represented the land, the three heads of households represented families and clans, a piece of paper represented the agreement between people, signatures represented individuals, and money represented the value of the land. The role of the middleman was largely to assure the parties that they could trust each other's ideas about the transaction and the forms of representation. The foreigners too had to trust the embedded and embodied practices of transaction.

It was only when the abstract, mediated elements of the process proceeded that the company discovered other information about the land. Not until the company wanted to have the purchase registered with the official authorities in the capital did they discover the coordinates were located inside a government-owned forest reserve. When they did the second purchase of a plot of land, they made sure to check the official maps ahead of the transaction.

Embodied knowledge and a physical meeting on the land are considered important for transparency and trust in transactions in northern Uganda. Land transactions should not be hidden. As one man selling portions of family land in Awach remarked: 'Land is not sold at night.' When transactions are questioned in a forum for conflict resolution, a new transaction may be made if the parties accept mediation and the decision of the forum. Here too disputants and witnesses often walk the boundaries of a plot and remark on evidence of use. In the case of 'The Land Conflict at Ogul' reported in Chapter 6 on Belonging, people stood on the boundaries of their farmland while a knowledgeable elder, who was unable to walk, was rolled past them on a bicycle. The chairman of the Sub-county Court Committee in Awach explained that land disputes were always first heard in situ so the Committee members could walk the land and listen to the explanations of immediate actors.

In the entrustment practice (Shipton 2009), land transactions are embodied and ideally witnessed during 'daylight' through the physical presence of all parties involved (social embodiment) at the site in question in question (physical embeddedness). The trust invoked is of a very tangible and personalized kind. Transactions in the cadastral, mediated and disembodied system take place far from the land – they are physically disembedded – through the means of papers, measurements, signatures and stamps. The transaction is based on a more abstract form of trust in institutions and an acceptance that land can be disembedded from immediate social relations to familiar others. When people hold different ideas about a land transaction, as the company and parties in the case from Ik County did, this often creates confusion and potential conflict.

Actors in Land Transactions

Land transactions involve, at a minimum, a giver or seller, a receiver or buyer, and an authority who can approve the transaction. The person transferring rights to access the land must be recognized as having the right to do so. Power and authority are more or less explicitly at play. Doubt about a party's competence to make a transfer throws the transaction into uncertainty. A woman living on the land of her father's clan may allocate the right to build a house to her grown son. But this transaction could be challenged by clan members, who may question her authority. In contrast, successfully conveying or overseeing land transfers enhances authority (Lund 2007).

Establishing the rightful inheritor, owner or representative of a group can make the transfer a conflictual issue and a question of trust. Who has the qualifications to be a buyer, who can veto a sale? Who will be accepted to act as a middleman? Who, or which institution, can approve and confirm a transaction? Who has the position to cancel a transaction retrospectively? These questions all relate to matters of power and trust, in terms of actors' ability to position themselves as authoritative when it comes to land matters among locals as well as in connection to outsiders.

The case of the wind turbine land sale is unusual, but it raises these questions very explicitly. The company buying the land needed owners whom they could buy it from, and they needed a recognized authority in order to make it a formal and rightful sale. The Oxford English Dictionary defines 'owner' as: 'A person who holds something as his or her own; a possessor or proprietor; a person who has the rightful claim or title to a thing.' Following from this definition, to be an 'owner' is tightly connected to an individual's possession of a thing. The term 'rightful' indicates a relationship between an individual and the thing that is formally recognized by law. As such, it indicates a straightforward relationship between an individual person and his or her rights to a thing. In relation to land ownership, it leaves the impression of a person possessing full rights to a clearly defined physical area.

In northern Uganda, indeed in many parts of Africa (Lund 2008: 15), people rarely use a word that would translate as 'owner' when describing their relationship to land they use or have authority over. As further discussed in Chapter 6 on Belonging, words such as 'custodian' or 'caretaker' of land are used (*Amazeya jumui* in Icetot – the Ik language – means 'leader of the soil' and *won ngom* in Acholi could be translated as 'father of the soil'). According to the OED, 'custodian' is defined as follows: 'A person or organization which has custody or guardianship of something or someone; a guardian.' A caretaker is defined as 'one who takes care of a thing, place, or person; one put in charge of anything.' It is obvious that there is a significant difference between being a custodian, caretaker of land or leader and father of the soil and being a landowner. Two different understandings of the relationship between people and land are at play here, which are expressed in the vocabulary used. The wind turbine company holds a conventional, capitalistic approach to land, viewing it as property owned if not by any single individual then by a few individuals; thus the company depended on identifying the owners in order to purchase land.

In Ik County, 'landowners' as such do not exist; rather, long entangled lines of users, custodians and caretakers have engaged actively with the land in the area over time. To be a custodian or caretaker of land does not imply exclusive rights; rather both terms indicate a degree of responsibility for the land. Likewise, in parts of the Acholi sub-region, people say that traditional land (*nyom kwaro*) belongs to the ancestors; it is borrowed by people who use it and keep it in trust for future generations. Being custodians or caretakers of land in northern Uganda does not only entail responsibility for the land per se but also for the complex relations – current, past and future – that are connected to the land.

It is of little surprise that it requires some inventiveness and work when investors request owners in order to buy up land. The complexity of indigenous entrustment systems creates a problem for buyers in a conventional capitalistic transaction system. However, in the Ik case the sub-county chief responded pragmatically to the company's request for owners by asking a respected elder to identify the 'original owners'. He was probably well aware of the illusion it involved but eager enough to witness 'good development' in the area to go through with it. At the same time, the sale also confirmed the authority of the sub-county chief and in this way helped to create the need for this institution. As Christian Lund (2007, 2008) has shown, the competition for authority over land matters is often great between local actors in African and other contexts, where institutional multiplicity is in place, and where jurisdiction over land matters is different depending on the situation. When, for example, a land sale is conducted for the first time, as was the case with the wind turbine in Ik County, it offers an apt opportunity for actors to cement their jurisdiction within the realm of land.

There was something intrinsically curious about the creation of 'original owners' in the case. It worked to the extent that the land was actually sold and money paid to the 'original owners' as well as the local authorities. But as soon as the news seeped out into the community, most people viewed the move to create owners and individualize what is usually considered a common resource potentially available to more people as unjust and short-sighted. It spurred tensions and debates. Thus, in the second land purchase, the creation of original owners followed a different tack and resulted in a collective payment to the community, through the repair of the common road. In this instance, 'the community' was created as the original owners of the land, which is more in line with indigenous Ik ideas about land. But still the conception of 'owners' rather than caretakers is different.

Furthermore, the process of selling the land created a set of relationships and hierarchies that the families involved did not necessarily agree with, such as the higher status of the middleman and the authority of the sub-county chief. They were dissatisfied with the fact that there was no public community meeting where those who felt they should be included could be present to hear with their own ears and ask questions about the sale, if they wished so.

When one person takes on the authority to sell or transact land without consulting others with whom the rights to the land are also embedded, it is taken as a betrayal of trust. This was abundantly clear in 'A Disputed Land Sale', which opened Part I of the book. Elisabeth felt that her daughter Grace had arrogated to herself the position of landowner by selling the land. The Local Councillor apparently believed that Grace was the owner and thus lent the authority of the political structure to the sale. But a higher level of authority, the assistant to the Resident District Commissioner, recognized the rights of Elisabeth, who claimed that she was holding the land in trust for her grandsons. Here, as elsewhere, the failure of communication went hand in hand with a failure of trust. Elisabeth felt that the sale had been done 'by night', as it were, thus keeping her in the dark by excluding her from involvement. The transaction was re-opened with the agreement that a portion of the money realized in the sale should be given to Elisabeth. It was completed when the buyer (not Grace the seller) paid Elisabeth. But trust was never re-established between mother and daughter and communication came to an end. Elisabeth remained bitter even after she received the money because the land was out of her hands for good. There was no possibility of reversing the transaction.

As we saw in the Introduction of this book, the mysterious 'Not for Sale' signs posted on buildings and land indicate this same mistrust. People holding property collectively are suspicious that one among them may claim the right of 'owner' by selling the property behind their backs.

Land Transactions as Temporal Processes

In the case of Stephen's attempt to gain freehold on his land in Gulu (Chapter 1 on Multiplicity), we saw how land transactions that are registered often take a long time due to the process of acquiring cadastral measurements, documents and land titles. Yet, the process is meant to have an end point; a finality is built into the trade relationship. When it is over, the involved parties are supposed to be equal and done with each other; the former landholders are no longer embedded in relations around the land. The importance of time minimization for closing transactions is testified in the World Bank project on land tenure in Uganda, where success is measured in the number of days it takes to access land records and make transactions. The project states that in 2006 it took 435 days to access records, but in 2018 it was instant, due to digitization. Registering a land sale took 52 days in 2013, and in 2018 it took only 30 days (World Bank 2018). The idea that speed and acceleration in transactions are positive features may be characteristic of late modernity; the price for acceleration is alienation (Rosa 2021). Acceleration in land transactions was a common feature in the global land rush that followed the financial and food price crises in 2007 and 2008 (Gabbert 2021: 4). Yet among the agro-pastoral Arbore in Ethiopia it is said that 'land cannot be rushed' – cultivation cycles and movement of cattle have to be timed and tuned, and decisions about land transactions should likewise not be made in a haste (Gabbert 2021: 5).

In the case with the wind turbine, the first transaction was made in haste, from the point of view of the local stakeholders. The transaction was supposed to have ended with the transfer of money, the signatures on the contract and the registration of the sale. But as is often the case, this became the starting point of a conflict and further negotiations that eventually led to a new transaction. In the end, after the second plot was bought, the transaction was concluded, and a fence was put up around the plot to confirm this. Yet the permanence of the land transaction was perceived as a provocation by some of the inhabitants, who did not approve of this way of governing land. Lemu's daughter Elizabeth expressed her disagreement with the tempo and terms of permanence in the sale. She said that 'this was not proper selling' because the landholders did not get a chance in the rushed sale to understand that the land was gone for good. As mentioned, Elizabeth wished they had suggested that the company rent or lease the land, so that eventually it could be returned to the community.

When land is transferred as part of the entrustment system, there are other temporalities at play. If a father shows a son or wife where to plant their gardens, there is an aspect of duration that depends on need and actual use as well as the social relationship between the involved parties; but the transaction is not permanent as it is when the entire bundle of entitlements is transferred upon sale. When a clan leader like Komol shows people from other clans a piece of land 'they can use for now', it is meant to be temporary, and it is meant to create an ongoing relationship of reciprocity and sharing. It is like the temporality of gifts; they are not expected or supposed to be returned immediately, nor with the exact same value (Mauss 1990 [1923]; Bourdieu 1977, 1997).

First and foremost, gifts cement a relationship of reciprocity between giver and receiver that stretches out over time. In this sense, entrustment transactions of land resemble some aspects of the payment of bridewealth, a process that takes place over many years, and rather than ending a relationship is supposed to open and continue it over time through the continued exchange of gifts. Lentz (2010: 63) found an explicit analogy between marriage with bridewealth and transfers of land among Sisala and Dagara people in northern Ghana and Burkina Faso (and notes a similar parallel among Kikuyu in Kenya). Land, like a daughter or sister, is never totally alienated; transferring rights while retaining a connection is the basis for an ongoing relationship with the other party. Yet as Lentz also shows, the temporal aspects of marriage and affinal relations, like those between land givers and receivers, are liable to different interpretations as years pass. When clan leaders or families show a guest or nephew where to farm in the understanding that this is temporary and with a flexible time horizon, the guest and host may in time come to disagree on how temporary and flexible it is. The guest may refuse to leave, and the transaction thus gains a temporal quality of finality, from the guest's perspective, that may not have been the intention of the clan leader. As Woodhouse and Colin emphasize, referring to studies from Côte d'Ivoire (2010: 3), land transactions sometimes go awry partly because people do not agree on the temporal aspect. Is a transaction a permanent deal or a temporary agreement? Is a transaction a loan with some compensation or is it buying?

The wind turbine company probably wanted a transaction that was final because they had no interest in a longer exchange relation with the local population. From their perspective, this could make their investment seem insecure.

Conclusion

The wind turbine case may be seen as marking the beginning of a (partial) transition from entrustment systems of land transactions, where land rights are embedded in social relations, to market-based transactions, where the whole bundle of land rights is alienated for good. The values involved seem to have shifted from ideals based on trust and reinforcement of social relations to the worth of cash and contracts and a move from collective ownership and transactions to the privatization of resources. But as we have shown in this chapter, such contrasts do not exhaust the issues at play. Chauveau and Colin (2010) point out that we often assume a unilineal evolution from embedded to disembedded land transfers, but in reality both kinds of characteristics exist at the same time, as in the Ik case. Here the transaction was partly embedded, as people could stand on the land and talk about its history and marks of use, and partly disembedded, as information was mediated on paper and even sometimes registered in a government office.

The involvement of potentially interested actors is key to studying transactions. The nature of communication and perceptions of exclusion and secrecy generate mistrust in a transaction and can lead to re-negotiations. Here and in the chapters to follow, we see how power, authority and legitimacy are invoked and sometimes changed in the course of a transaction. The temporal aspects of transactions are particularly important because of the socially embedded and bundled nature of land rights. Insofar as land transfers are part of continuing social relations, their temporal horizons are not fixed, and possibilities for continuing negotiations about specific entitlements remain open. However, in the wind turbine case, the local sellers permanently lost access to the second plot that they transacted to the international company. The transaction of the first plot, inside the forest reserve, was undone by the authorities, but the company had the financial power to simply purchase another plot and close the deal. This points to the issue of inequality in transactions. When parties in a deal are more or less equal, they may be more open to bargaining and keeping the transaction open-ended. When a financially powerful company enters the scene, the rules of the game change, and potentially, if resources are found and something turns out to be profitable, companies can in principle buy the land and make locals landless.

In this situation of multiplicity and potential, the general question remains: what kind of values and moral economy will guide land transfers and to the benefits of whom?

Lotte Meinert, Ph.D., is Professor at the Department of Anthropology, Aarhus University.

Mette Lind Kusk, Ph.D., is Assistant Professor at Via University College.

References

Bourdieu, Pierre. 1977. *Outline of a Theory of Practice*. Cambridge: Cambridge University Press.
———. 1997. 'Marginalia – Some Additional Notes on the Gift', in Alan D. Schrift (ed.), *The Logic of the Gift: Toward an Ethic of Generosity*. New York: Routledge, pp. 231–41.
Chauveau, Jean-Pierre, and Jean-Philippe Colin. 2010. 'Customary Transfers and Land Sales in Côte d'Ivoire: Revisiting the Embeddedness Issue', *Africa* 80(1): 81–103.
Colin, Jean-Philippe, and Philip Woodhouse. 2010. 'Interpreting Land Markets in Africa', *Africa* 80(1): 1–13.
Eriksen, Thomas Hylland. 2007. *Globalization: The Key Concepts*. Chicago: Berg Publishers.
Gabbert, Echi Christina. 2021. 'Introduction: Futuremaking with Pastoralists', in Echi Christina Gabbert, Fana Gebresenbet, John G. Galaty and Günther Schlee (eds), *Lands of the Future: Anthropological Perspectives on Pastoralism, Land Deals and Tropes of Modernity in Eastern Africa*. New York: Berghahn Books, pp. 1–38.
Giddens, Anthony. 1990. *The Consequences of Modernity*. Cambridge: Polity Press.
Laltaika, Elifuraha I., and Kelly Askew. 2021. 'Modes of Dispossession of Indigenous Lands and Territories in Africa', in Echi Christina Gabbert, Fana Gebresenbet, John G. Galaty and Günther Schlee (eds), *Lands of the Future: Anthropological Perspectives on Pastoralism, Land Deals and Tropes of Modernity in Eastern Africa*. New York: Berghahn Books, pp. 99–122.
Lentz, Carola. 2010. 'Is Land Inalienable? Historical and Current Debates on Land Transfers in Northern Ghana', *Africa* 80(1): 56–80.
Lund, Christian. 2006. 'Twilight Institutions: Public Authority and Local Politics in Africa', *Development and Change* 37(4): 685–705.
———. 2007. *Twilight Institutions: Public Authority and Local Politics in Africa*. Malden, MA: Blackwell.
———. 2008. *Local Politics and the Dynamics of Property in Africa*. Cambridge: Cambridge University Press.
———. 2016. 'Rule and Rupture: State Formation through the Production of Property and Citizenship', *Development and Change* 47(6): 1199–228.
Lund, Christian, and Catherine Boone. 2013. 'Introduction: Land Politics in Africa – Constituting Authority over Territory, Property and Persons', *Africa* 83(1): 1–13.
Mauss, Marcel. 1990 [1923]. *The Gift: The Form and Reason for Exchange in Archaic Societies*. London: Routledge.
Rosa, Hartmut. 2021. *Alienation and Acceleration: Towards a Critical Theory of Late-Modern Temporality*. Malmö: NSU Press.
Shipton, Parker. 2009. *Mortgaging the Ancestors: Ideologies of Attachment in Africa*. New Haven: Yale University Press.
Wily, Liz Alden. 2011. '"The Law Is to Blame": The Vulnerable Status of Common Property Rights in Sub-Saharan Africa', *Development and Change* 42(3): 733–57.
World Bank. 2018. 'Land Administration Reforms Cut the Red Tape', 20 April. Retrieved 13 March 2021 from https://www.worldbank.org/en/news/feature/2018/04/20/land-administration-reforms-cut-the-red-tape.

Chapter 3
Conflicts

Irene Winnie Anying and Quentin Gausset

Navigating Legal Pluralism

> I know everybody here has mentioned that they prefer to use the *Rwot Kweri* because they know the land boundaries and resolve the cases faster and more cheaply . . . but for me I would prefer to consult the resolution bodies according to the help they can offer. If local leaders are the ones who say that women have no rights, then I would rather go to people who respect and understand me . . .

Sylvia caught Irene's attention when she disagreed with other participants during a focus group discussion on land conflicts organized in Amuru sub-county. By coincidence, on the way to the market the same day, Irene had met Lanyuru, who is Sylvia's brother-in-law and the person with whom Sylvia was having the land conflict. Lanyuru had just been elected as a member of the Area Land Committee for Amuru sub-county and was about to undertake training in the roles of 'Protecting the Rights of the Vulnerable' (including widows, orphans and people with a disability), provided by the NGO that Irene was working for.

A bit careful and reluctant at first, Lanyuru later opened up to Irene and started giving his point of view on the conflict. According to him, Sylvia married Acaye Peter (Lanyuru's brother) in 1979 and had six children with him (two sons and four daughters). Acaye was a police officer; he worked in towns outside of his home area most of the time. In 1990, while they were living in Gulu town, Acaye became sick and violent, and Sylvia's family withdrew her from Acaye. Sylvia was taken to her natal home, which is only about 4 kilometres from her marital home, together with all six children. She continued to receive financial support from Acaye and returned for his burial when he committed suicide in 1992. She also processed Acaye's gratuity as his widow, which she used to look after the children and herself from her natal home. In about 1996, as everyone moved to Internally Displaced Persons (IDP) Camps, Sylvia moved into a camp near her natal home. The impression Irene had was that Lanyuru, Acaye's eldest surviving brother, who used to live with Acaye while studying in Gulu (Acaye was paying for his school fees), resented the fact that Sylvia had taken his late brother's property after abandoning him.

When Irene asked Lanyuru about the dispute with Sylvia, he declared that the issue had already been settled in early 2014 with the help of a Non-Governmental Organization, which had also promised to provide further assistance in planting boundary trees between him and Sylvia. When Irene prompted Lanyuru on whether this was necessary, since they were in-laws, Lanyuru explained that Sylvia is never satisfied. 'It is her who wanted this,' he said. Lanyuru has accepted this idea of planting trees to avoid further problems with Sylvia, whom he described as a very ambitious woman. At this point, Lanyuru informed Irene that Sylvia had wrongly accused him twice before of destroying her huts, but the police had found no merit in the case and simply requested them to settle the matter from home as a family.

Three weeks after talking to Lanyuru, Irene scheduled an interview with Sylvia. Sylvia first told the story of her marriage, which confirmed Lanyuru's account. She then explained that in her land dispute with Lanyuru she had asked the help of almost all the leaders including the *Rwot Kweri*, clan elders, the Local Council chairperson and the Non-Governmental Organisation. Sylvia noted that the dispute with Lanyuru started way back in 2007. She said that when most people in IDP camps started returning to their pre-displacement homes, she informed Lanyuru that she would be returning to her late husband's home and not her own father's home, where she had lived prior to displacement after having left her husband. Sylvia observed that she faced a lot of resistance from both Lanyuru and his mother, who were hesitant to allocate her space for her hut and a garden to dig. Sylvia decided to involve some clan elders and the Local Council 1 in 2008. Both of these advised Lanyuru to provide space to Sylvia.

In 2009, when Sylvia finally returned with the hope of resettling on her late husband's portion of land, Lanyuru was loath to allow her into the family home. Lanyuru had already put up his home on a piece of land where Sylvia and her late husband had had a hut in the late 1980s, which they used whenever they came for holidays in the village. Lanyuru used to live with them in Gulu and would also come back and stay with them during holidays, in the same compound that he was now claiming to be his. Despite Lanyuru's resistance, Sylvia started to put up a hut about 80 meters from Lanyuru's compound without his consent, on a piece of land that she claimed belonged to and was used by her late husband. While she was putting up the hut, Lanyuru verbally insulted her, accusing her of bringing back the same witchcraft that she had used to kill his brother Acaye (Sylvia's husband). A week later, before she thatched the hut, she found her hut broken, an issue she reported to the police, accusing Lanyuru. Sylvia rebuilt the hut and followed up this case with the police until 2010.

At the same time, the Catholic church offered to construct a hut for Sylvia (who was an active member of the church) on part of the church land where they build huts for the vulnerable. Sylvia rejected this offer and preferred to stay amidst Lanyuru's disturbances. Sylvia felt that if she accepted the church's offer, then she would never get back her husband's portion of the land. She felt she needed to stand and defend this land for her children. In Sylvia's words, 'If I don't stand strong, where will my sons find land? I am fighting because of them.' Sylvia also brought up this issue during one of the main clan meetings held in late 2012.

At that clan meeting, Lanyuru asked Sylvia to refund the bridewealth because she had abandoned her husband. The elders resolved that she did not have to refund bridewealth and could stay on her late husband's land. Despite this dispute resolution, Lanyuru continued to disturb Sylvia. Lanyuru would farm up to 10 meters from Sylvia's hut and continued to insult and threaten her, claiming that Sylvia had killed her husband and was bringing witchcraft to the family. Lacking farming land around her, Sylvia used land at her natal home, and she also borrowed land from an elder of her husband's clan. According to Sylvia, both judgements made by the clan elders and by the big clan meeting had advised that she should not be chased away, but she was not satisfied with these rulings, because there was no boundary settlement indicating the limits of the land she would be given.

The clan meeting had advised that Sylvia and Lanyuru should work with the *Rwot Kweri* to finalize the details of the land demarcation, but Sylvia said that she had no trust that the *Rwot Kweri* would be fair to her, as he was closely related to Lanyuru. After some preliminary meetings with the *Rwot Kweri*, and sensing that his decision would not be in her favour, Sylvia decided to report the case to an international NGO (Action Aid) with a field office in Amuru as a case of domestic violence. Action Aid referred her to Ugandan Land Alliance, a national NGO in Amuru, which specializes in land dispute resolution. A meeting was organized in which the NGO, the LC1 and some of the elders were present. At the end of the meeting, the land was divided equally among all the brothers in the family, including those who had passed away but had had children. Notably, land was allocated to two daughters of Acaye's late brother in case they ever returned from their maternal home (Sylvia is currently digging on this land). The two daughters were not present during this division; they were still young at the time, between 15 and 17 years of age.

As Irene was walking back late one evening to find a place to eat at a local restaurant, she met Lanyuru and the *Rwot Kweri*. As they chatted casually and the discussion drifted to Sylvia's case, Lanyuru and the *Rwot Kweri* told Irene that they did respect the rights of women, but that some women, like Sylvia, liked to take advantage of being women and ran everywhere with false accusations to get support. (Having been trained by Irene through the NGO she worked for, Lanyuru may well have wanted to assure her about his commitment to women's rights.)

The following day, Irene visited Lanyuru's compound for the first time. Lanyuru's home is located along the highway about two kilometres from the sub-county headquarters and 10 kilometres from the Town Council. While this place used to be of little significance in the past, the value of land along the highway has skyrocketed since the return phase commenced in 2006 and since Amuru was declared a district in 2007. Lanyuru showed Irene Sylvia's hut and said: 'If I had chased her away, would her hut still be standing there?' Irene's impression was that Lanyuru did not want to disobey the clan elders but also did not want to give Sylvia space beyond the hut. Lanyuru wanted to remain in control of the land. He had planted cassava up to 10 meters from Sylvia's hut and Sylvia only had a hut and no garden. Lanyuru claimed that he had allocated farming land elsewhere to Sylvia but that she had rejected his offer.

Up until this point, both parties had had a very good rapport with Irene. They knew that Irene was talking to both of them. In November of 2015, after almost a year, Irene met with Sylvia again. The demarcation trees had not yet been planted; the NGO was still waiting for funding. Sylvia was still complaining that Lanyuru was insulting and threatening her. However, Sylvia was excited about her daughters' impending marriage. She mentioned that two of her daughters would be married soon, and to Irene's surprise, she said that Lanyuru was helping with the organization and would be standing in as the father to her daughters, since he was her husband's eldest surviving brother. Sylvia's daughters had started to construct a permanent house for her on part of the land that was allocated to her. The house was at the foundation level.

Sylvia was quick to note that she did not in any way hate Lanyuru; it was just Lanyuru who had problems that Sylvia did not understand. She said that Lanyuru did not like her last-born son, a 15-year-old boy called Reagan, and always shouted at him. Noticing Irene's surprise at the age of the boy, she seemed a bit uneasy. She then said that Reagan is the son she had from Ocaya, a clan brother to her late husband, who inherited her after her husband's death.

> Madam, I don't like bringing this up, but I think Lanyuru still holds a grudge against me because I refused to be inherited by him. . . . It would have seemed really wrong to be inherited by him because Lanyuru is like a son to me. He used to live with us when my husband was still alive, we paid his school fees, and when he got his wife he stayed in my house . . . .

Despite the conflict with Lanyuru, Sylvia seemed to recognize his traditional authority as the legal heir to her late husband's family. Yet, she despised Lanyuru as an irresponsible drunkard who had done nothing with his school education except get wasted. She alleged that Lanyuru did not even look after his wife let alone himself.

A follow up visit in early 2016 revealed that Sylvia now had five new huts in her compound: three for herself and two for her last-born son from her marriage with Acaye. The boundary trees had not yet been planted; she complained that Lanyuru and her mother-in-law continued to be indifferent towards her. Sylvia then started talking about her relationship with Ocaya, the clan brother of her late husband, who had inherited her. In Sylvia's opinion, Lanyuru and his mother thought that Sylvia was taking Acaye's wealth further from the family to transfer it to Ocaya, although she only stayed with Ocaya from 1998 to 2004 and the relationship ended there. (Sylvia was not comfortable talking about the reasons why the relationship ended.)

Sylvia continued to complain of the unfairness in the land division and insisted that the land that was divided was the portion she and her late husband utilized. Sylvia was now calling for another clan meeting to plant trees on the boundary between her and Lanyuru, to make sure that no one would be trespassing boundaries in the future. Prior to Irene's visit in early 2016, Sylvia had reported Lanyuru for trying to bewitch her, and her accusation had been taken up in a clan meeting.

Later, in another interview, Lanyuru openly talked to Irene about his feelings on Sylvia's relationship with Ocaya. He had no kind words for Sylvia: 'She should be ashamed of herself to even want to have a voice here . . . She disappeared with all the wealth my brother left, moved out with so many men, and now comes back after 20 years as a wife in this home.' Lanyuru noted that he was merely respecting the clan's decision that Sylvia be allowed to return because of her sons. However, he thought that Reagan, the son Sylvia had with Ocaya, should be looked after by Ocaya and be allocated land at Ocaya's place. 'I want him to take responsibility; he should give the boy space for digging. It feels like he benefited, and he is now bringing back all the burden to us.' On the other hand, he had no problem allocating land to Sylvia's other sons.

Irene then paid a visit to Ocaya (more than 30 km away from Lanyuru's home) to get his point of view. Ocaya was about three years older than Sylvia and looked in a much better financial position than Lanyuru; he was a retired soldier who had returned home from Kampala around 1997. His land was about three hundred hectares, and he lived there with his two wives. In Ocaya's opinion, Sylvia and Lanyuru were not really disputing land ownership; the matter was that Lanyuru still held a grudge against Sylvia for refusing to be inherited by him. Ocaya also offered Sylvia digging space at his home, but she declined the offer.

He offered the same for his son Reagan, as he had no problem taking full custody of him, but Sylvia was unwilling to let Reagan live with him.

When Irene had a chance to speak to the Local Council 1 chairperson later in the evening at the trading centre, she found out that Lanyuru and Sylvia had long had disagreements from the time when Acaye was very ill and immediately following his death. They also had a dispute over Acaye's gratuity payments. Lanyuru felt that Sylvia had no right to take this gratuity, since she had abandoned her husband while he was sick and gone to stay at her natal home. However, the administrative authorities ordered Lanyuru to leave this gratuity for Sylvia as Acaye's widow. Irene also understood from the Local Council 1 chairman that the family land stretched over 3 to 4 kilometers off the roadside but that only the land along the roadside was divided (Lanyuru and his other brothers continue to farm on the undivided land). The LC1, who took part in dividing the land, thought that both Lanyuru and Sylvia were specifically interested in the land near the roadside because of its speculative value.

Of What Is This a Case?

Post-war northern Uganda is characterized by numerous and serious land conflicts. It is also characterized by many competing institutions involved in conflict resolution. In this chapter, we take as a point of departure the case of Sylvia, a woman who has been involved in a long land conflict with her in-laws, and who has succeeded in gaining what she wanted, against all odds (see also Anying and Gausset 2017 for another discussion of this case). Hers is a specific example of the general practice of forum shopping – that is, selecting from among a variety of conflict management institutions, according to an actor's assessment of convenience, fairness or advantage, and trustworthiness. We discuss some of the weaknesses of the current forum shopping practice (located mainly in the strong focus on mediations, an approach that is cynically manipulated by some to gain undue advantages). Sylvia's case illustrates how those involved in disputes put their trust in some institutions above others. Often this has to do with the social conflicts found at the root of land conflicts – a point which is often overlooked by scholars, who tend to focus primarily on the issue of rights and power. The existence of underlying social conflicts gives traditional authorities a prominent role in conflict resolution.

We suggest that the different fora are more collaborative than competitive in resolving land conflicts. And we conclude by acknowledging the positive role that the plurality of fora and the practice of forum shopping have had in successfully resolving land conflicts and securing more peace in northern Uganda.

Among the fora that were in play in Sylvia's case, some are mandated by the Land Act to handle dispute resolution. Others deal with land conflicts even though they are not mandated to do so. This plurality of fora is thus both normative and empirical; normative because it is embodied in legislation that recognizes different fora and stipulates how they are accommodated within the state and interact with each other, and empirical because people experiencing conflict have recourse to a variety of institutions, including some that have no normative or official role to play in conflict resolution; these fora might not exist *de jure*, but they exist *de facto*.

Normative Pluralism

The Land Act cap 227, which regulates land relations in Uganda, recognizes both the Traditional Institutions as well as the land tribunals and mandates the Magistrates' formal courts and the Local Council Courts to manage disputes relating to customary land tenure. (See sections 76 and 88 of the Land Act).

Local Council Courts (LCC) System

The Local Council Courts (LCC) were established under the Local Council Courts Act of 2006, which regulates their jurisdiction and mode of operation. LCCs are the lowest units with administrative, legislative and judicial powers on behalf of the central government. There are three levels of courts: 'sub-county' (LCC3), 'parish' (LCC2) and 'village' (LCC1).[1] Appeals from the LCC3 lie with the Chief Magistrate, and if the appeal involves a substantial question of law or appears to have caused a substantial miscarriage of justice, it goes to the High Court.

In Customary Land Dispute Management, the LCCs are only bound by geographical jurisdiction. They are obliged to handle matters within their geographical limits (village, parish or sub-county). The sitting areas are flexible; the court sessions may be held at any place so long as it is within the designated geographical limit. The procedures are simplified, and hearings are informal, conducted in indigenous languages. The claims are instituted by making an oral complaint to the chairperson of the court, which is committed to writing by the chairperson or any other person appointed to do so. The court is in no way obliged or required to follow any technical rules of evidence or procedure but is guided by principles of natural justice.

At the time of this research, the LCCs had no legal mandate to sit as a court and pass judgment, as per the constitutional court ruling, until fresh elections were held, which occurred in 2019. However, the courts continued to operate at the grassroots, receiving cases, holding hearings and charging fees. They also continued to pass judgments, declaring winners and losers. The LCCs were, however, aware of their legal status, and in most cases if their decisions were not respected they referred cases to NGOs or to the government offices. The LCC of Lamogi specifically claimed they wielded political authority, which is the very reason why the other fora such as the *Rwot Kweri* have to cooperate with the LCC. The individuals interviewed for the study paid no attention to the legal status of the LCCs. In practice, disputants continued to follow the hierarchy of the LCCs; in the first instance they made calls at the LCC1 and followed through the hierarchy up to the LCC3. During the hearings, the respective LCCs invited members of the Traditional Institutions as witnesses.

Formal Court System

Generally, the state system of conflict management is based on English models introduced during the colonial times (1900 to 1962) and comprises Western-style laws and institutions. Uganda's state judicial system is relatively simple: Uganda has a three-tier judicial system with the Supreme Court as the apex court (Art. 129 Constitution). Below it is the Court of Appeal, which hears appeals from the High Court or special tribunals set up by an act of parliament. Below the Court of Appeal is the High Court of Uganda, which has unlimited original jurisdiction, which means that it can try any case of any value or crime of any magnitude. Appeals from Magistrates' Courts go to the High Court. Below the high court are the subordinate Courts, which include the Magistrates' Courts and the Local Council Courts levels 3–1 (sub-county, parish, and village). The Magistrates' Courts handle the bulk of civil and criminal cases in Uganda. They were legally the first point of contact for customary tenure land cases, since, as mentioned above, the LCCs had been declared illegal until fresh elections. The procedures before the Magistrates' Court takes a minimum of 60 days before a hearing can officially begin. An analysis of Amuru Court Registry made for the purposes of this research in 2015 indicates that cases take on average over 5 years to be resolved (see also Burke and Egaru 2011).

The grade 1 Magistrates' Courts are situated at almost all district headquarters. In northern Uganda-Acholi sub-region, there are two chief magisterial areas with five grade one Magistrates' Courts. One of the greatest challenges that is today facing the Magistrates' Courts is the backlog of cases. The cases take from a minimum of one year up to 5 years or even more. Statistical data obtained from the land registry (2012 to 2014) of Amuru District court in 2015 indicates that out of the 191 land cases filed between 2012 and 2014, only 33 had been finalized. And even then, many of these were dismissed because neither the plaintiff nor the defendant appeared before the court when the suit was called for hearing.

The trial before the Magistrates' Court is characterized by many adjournments and transfers of magistrates. Most of the disputants interviewed for the purpose of this study expressed weariness with following up their cases before the Magistrates' Courts. As a result of this, many litigants lose interest and try other fora that are faster and less expensive. This resonates with the view expressed by most individuals interviewed but also stakeholders, who noted that filing cases before the formal courts is used to compel the other party to cooperate. As one litigant expressed during a focus group discussion: if you are tired and have no money to spend, then you just have to abandon your case or seek help from somewhere else.

Enforcement of land judgments are particularly challenging. Land issues, especially when it comes to evictions, are very sensitive in post-war northern Uganda. For an eviction to take place, more than one stakeholder must get involved in the execution of the judgment. This includes both those who are legally mandated and those who are not.

Traditional Authorities

The role of traditional institutions is officially recognized under the Land Act. Although there is no uniform composition of the traditional power structure in Acholi sub-region, it can be broadly sketched as hierarchical, ranging from household level to the level of the chiefdom. The region is composed of chiefdoms, which are made up of various clans. The clans are subdivided into hamlets and further into households. The chiefdoms are headed by the *Rwot* (clan chief), and clans are headed by *Ladit Kaka* (clan heads). At the hamlet level, one finds heads of households (*Won Ot*), followed by heads of families (*Won Paco*). The land dispute resolution structure within the traditional institutions emanates within its socio-political structure. At the hamlet level, we have the head of household followed by the head of family and then the 'Chief of the Hoe' (*Rwot Kweri*, formally elected), a position created during the colonial administration. At the clan level, one finds the representative of the chief (*Lawang Rwot*) and the clan head (*Ladit Kaka*), and finally the clan chief (*Rwot Moo*), who is a member of the 'royal clan' dominating the region. Despite the hierarchy of traditional leaders/authority, there is no appeal structure within the traditional institutions. Cases are transferred back and forth among the leaders. Disputants therefore have the possibility to begin at the lowest level and gradually go higher up in the hierarchy if they are not satisfied with the outcome, or they can begin directly at the top of the hierarchy, or even go to more than one of the leaders simultaneously.

Choosing which traditional leader to approach is determined by several factors, including physical accessibility of leaders in terms of distance as well as fairness and comfort (Anying 2012). The other factors also include the nature of the conflict and the parties involved. The Chief of the Hoe (*Rwot Kweri*) is the most consulted traditional leader in land dispute resolution, but as emerged in Sylvia's case, he may not be trusted if he is on close terms with the opposing party.

The procedure before the traditional institutions is very informal, like that before the LCC. It is initiated through a verbal complaint to any of the traditional leaders within the hierarchy. In most cases, when a complaint is lodged, a letter is written to the person against whom the complaint is made, with a scheduled date for the mediation meeting. The 'respondent' in this case does not have to reply to the letter; he or she only has to make a physical appearance if he or she wishes.

Generally, the procedure before the Chief of the Hoe is very similar to that of the LCC. This is attributed to training that has been provided to them mainly by the NGOs on concepts such as natural justice and the rights of women and persons with disability. Traditional leaders try to work in close coordination with the other fora, namely the NGOs, the formal court system, and the LCCs. They must adapt to the procedures of other fora and to borrow from their concepts to remain relevant in the game of conflict resolution.

Instead of judging who is right and who is wrong, traditional leaders rely mainly on mediation and persuasion to try to find a peaceful solution. A mediation is a negotiation in which the third party (the mediator) facilitates the finding of a consensus among conflicting parties but has no right to decide or settle the issue (Nicolas 2020). In mediations that Irene attended while collecting data for this book chapter, the opening statements made by the traditional leaders reveal their approach. In the words of one of them: 'we want *ber bedo* [loosely translated as harmonious living]. We are not a court and are not looking for a winner, in the past we lived in harmony, blood is thicker than water, and this is what we should look forward to.' Consequently, the parties are often asked to compromise by letting go of some portions of the land for the sake of harmonious living. In instances where one of the parties is adamant, the practice varies from one Chief of the Hoe to another. Whereas some of them nonetheless go ahead and make a decision based on the majority views, others prefer to make no decision. It is important to point out that they do not just look at the question of ownership or land boundaries. Their decisions go well beyond legal questions, and they dig deep into local history and social relationships, including witchcraft allegations. This gives the traditional institutions an edge over the other fora such as the LCC or even the formal court system, which are more restricted. One officer of an NGO explained to Irene that the advantage with the traditional leaders is their ability to look at land rights from a social perspective. In his opinion, it is one of the reasons why some disputants insist on dealing with the traditional leaders as opposed to the courts or the LCC.

There is no provision in the law that stipulates how the decisions of the traditional institution are to be enforced. Accordingly, the outcome is not in any way legally binding on any of the parties. The parties are merely under a moral obligation to respect the decisions (Anying 2012). In Chapter 1 on Multiplicity, we saw how the clan meeting in 2015 attempted to deal with the conflicts on Stephen's ancestral land (Land 6). But the decisions were not implemented, and the disputes on the southern and northern boundaries remained unresolved.

Generally, however, whenever the decisions of the traditional leaders do not build on consensus and are not respected, the party who does not accept the decision files a case with either the Local Council Court, an NGO or even with the Magistrates' Court (Anying 2012). In such a scenario, the case is taken as a fresh suit, and the mediation results may be used as evidence in proceedings before the court, but it is not in any way mandatory, and the court can come out with a completely different judgment.

Empirical/De facto Pluralism

In addition to the fora expressly mandated under the Land Act, there are a number of institutions that play a de facto (non-official) role in conflict resolutions, including elected and appointed government officials and NGOs.

Elected and Appointed Government Officials
The appointed government officials that are most consulted for help in solving land conflicts are the Parish Chief at the Parish level, the Sub-county Chief and Community Development Officer at the Sub-county Level, and the office of the Resident District Commissioner at the District level.

Among the elected leaders, one also finds the head of the Local Council 5, who is the political head of the district. Save for the Resident District Commissioner, the other offices are legally mandated to play a role in land administration management, but none of them have any judicial function as far as the resolution of land disputes is concerned. The disputants, however, perceive them as having power, since they are government agencies. Consequently, when a letter is issued by these offices to either the LCC or even the traditional institution leaders such as the Chief of the Hoe (*Rwot Kweri*) they always act upon it.[2] The consultation and or consideration of the non-judicial government offices in the resolution of land matters is attributed to a reduction in power and penetration of the formal state courts, which continued immediately after the conflict.[3] Consequently, disputants view government officials as an alternative to traditional institutions.

The Resident District Commissioner (RDC) often plays a key role in land dispute management, as we saw in Case I, 'A Disputed Land Sale'. Although not mandated per se by the laws regulating land dispute management, the role of the RDC has become more prominent. This is because of their position within the districts but also because of the sensitivity of land disputes in post-war northern Uganda. The RDCs are mandated as substantive chairs to the district security committee. Since land disputes have become rampant following the declaration of return from the IDP camps, and since this is being viewed as a source of potential insecurity in the recovery of the region, the RDCs of northern Uganda have focused a lot of their attention on land issues and have intervened in land dispute management through organizing mediation meetings between and among the disputing parties. In this way, mediations have provided access to justice while at the same time relieving ordinary courts of law from heavy caseloads and backlogs (see also Bognitz 2020). These are either conducted at the invitation of one of the parties or at the initiative of the RDC when he or she feels that a particular dispute may lead to insecurity or turn into a violent situation. Although it is not within the law, it has become a common practice that the Resident District Commissioner sanctions a legal judgment before it is enforced.

Non-Governmental Organizations

In addition to the existing avenues for land conflict management, Non-Governmental Organizations (NGOs), community-based organizations (CBOs) and faith-based organizations (FBOs) also play a role in land dispute management. In post-war northern Uganda, the increase in number of land disputes set the stage for pronounced emphasis on land issues by civil society organizations and NGOs as they transitioned from war-related interventions to post-conflict and development activities (Hopwood and Atkinson 2013).

The NGOs provide legal aid including court representation for those who cannot afford legal fees, as well as legal advice and mediation between and among parties in a dispute. In addition, a number of NGOs also conduct community awareness sessions, targeting not only the community but also the local council leaders and the traditional institutions. The sensitizations focus on several issues including rights of women to property, general land rights as embodied in the Land Act, and general human rights issues as embodied in national and international instruments. They also offer training targeting specific groups such as LCC members, traditional leaders, Area Land Committees and women's groups, among others. They seek to empower the vulnerable groups but also the traditional institutions with knowledge on national and international human rights law through sensitization (Hopwood and Atkinson 2013). Specific procedures vary from NGO to NGO, but generally they require that any litigant asking for their help must have had the dispute attended to by a local leader, which includes either a traditional leader at any level within the locality or the LCC (preferably LCC1 or 2).

The Possibilities in Pluralism

As can be seen, the plural terrain presents possibilities for disputants to approach any of the institutions. The choice that people must make is not just between formality or informality but between five different types of institutions (Magistrates' Courts, Local Council Courts, traditional leaders, government officials and civil society organizations) and between different embedded or independent actors within each of the five types described. Forum shopping can be successive (when litigants try one institution after another) but is most commonly simultaneous (several institutions are involved at the same time). Forum shopping can also be horizontal (involving different kinds of institutions), or they can be vertical (involving hierarchical actors within one kind of institution). Disputants can thus file a case before many different institutions – before the case is resolved and even after the case has been resolved, a situation that would otherwise be considered res judicata (Helfer 1999; Unruh 2003). These possibilities are not restricted to the plaintiff; they also extend to the defendant. Since forum shopping is unregulated and the different institutions do not complement each other, all institutions may indeed make decisions over the same case. The only thing that extinguishes the thirst for new fora is the satisfaction of both parties in a conflict – that is, the consensual resolution of the conflict.

A few general observations can be made at this level. First, even though it is not the case in Sylvia's dispute, there is room for resolutions and mediations to go in opposing directions and contradict each other. In local communities, many people have links to local leaders, and this can affect the independence and objectivity of the solutions proposed. As we saw in Sylvia's case, she did not trust the *Rwot Kweri* because of his friendship with her opponent Lanyuru. Forum shopping can here appear as a kind of security against arbitrary judgements. But it can also be a source of insecurity when two resolutions provided by two different fora are in opposition. For example, some disputants can prevent the resolution of a conflict by refusing any settlement and by constantly involving new institutions until they are granted what they want. This renegotiation of authority and legitimacy in situations of institutional multiplicity is explored in several works (Francis and James 2003; Vandekerckhove 2011; Kobusingye, Van Leeuwen and Van Dijk 2016; Van Leeuwen 2017).

The general focus on finding a consensus rather than judging who is right and who is wrong or who is telling the truth (see Schlee 2020) can also be cynically exploited by an actor in bad faith, in that they can grab the land of someone else until mediation persuades that person to give up part of his land, as a conciliatory gesture and for the sake of social peace. In these cases, forum shopping and legal pluralism appear to be sources of insecurity.

Second, another key element is that many conflicts about land appear to be by-products of social conflicts. Personal relations and history play a big role in such conflicts: love, betrayal, jealousy, births, deaths, inheritance, and witchcraft accusations are often found under the surface of land conflicts. The authority of a family head in allocating land, or the land rights of a family member, can become challenged at the same time as the inheritance of power, the legitimacy of marriage or children, or the morality of a person is questioned. Land conflicts are at the centre of complex strategies to weave or sever social ties.

While Sylvia does recognize Lanyuru's authority as head of the family whenever it suits her needs (she asks his help to organize the marriage of her daughters and to solve the problems of her sons), she refuses Lanyuru's authority when it goes against her own interest, because she wants to establish her own independence. The fact that Sylvia succeeded in her endeavour, despite all odds, shows that women are not always powerless and marginalized, and that they can use forum shopping strategically to further their advantages (Anying and Gausset

2017). But the main point here is that this gives customary authorities a prominent role to play, since they remain the forum that deals primarily with social and family conflicts.

The entanglement of land conflicts with other social conflicts follows from the embeddedness of land entitlements, as we saw in Chapter 1 on Multiplicity. Land is not 'free' of social relations, and therefore conflicts such as that between Sylvia and Lanyuru are expressed as land conflicts. Attempting to deal with such land conflicts may exacerbate or defuse other conflicts.

Third, while most of the classical literature supports the popular thesis that legal pluralism is characterized by competition between and among the multiple fora for power and authority (Berry 2002; Unruh 2003; Tamanaha 2008; Sikor and Lund 2009; Mwangi 2010; Van Leeuwen 2014, 2017; Kobusingye, Van Leeuwen and Van Dijk 2016), our case and our understanding of the situation in northern Uganda points towards cooperation rather than competition. The competition described by scholars ranges from what norms, rules and procedures should apply in conflict resolution, to which organizations/institutions should be authorized to take charge under what particular circumstances (Van Leeuwen 2014). The competition is also presented as a venue for establishing and consolidating authority for the actors and institutions involved (Berry 2002; Boege 2006; Lund 2006; Sikor and Lund 2009; Huber 2010; Lund and Boone 2013). According to our cases and research, however, it appears that no forum in northern Uganda can succeed in resolving land conflicts alone. The weakness and slowness of the Magistrates' Court necessitates other fora. The local courts rely on the help and advice of customary chiefs. NGOs had recourse to the Magistrates' Court as a threat to push for mediation agreements. And customary authorities need the back-up of official institutions to have legitimacy. The different fora are interdependent, and even though their collaboration may at times be seen as a necessary evil, our research documents a genuine collaboration and a remarkable convergence and homogeneity in the advocated resolutions of a variety of cases. The widespread collaboration that is witnessed in practice between all fora can be interpreted both as a sign of weakness of each institution taken separately, and as a sign that each of them gains strength when joining forces with others. The multiplicity of fora can also be interpreted as the result of a grassroots demand for justice rather than as the result of resource capture by the different institutions involved.

Conclusion

Post-conflict northern Uganda is characterized by extreme confusion in land matters (Branch 2007, 2008; Rugadya, Nsamba-Gayiiya and Kamusiime 2008; Dolan 2009; Vaughan and Stewart 2011; Whyte et al. 2013). After 10 to 20 years being interned in camps, people were asked to 'go back to where the war found them'. For people who were displaced several times during the conflict, determining where the war had found them was anything but an easy matter. The conflict has also created a lot of family problems, such as children born out of wedlock, sometimes as the result of rape by belligerents, often because of a lack of cattle to pay bridewealth. As a result, many children do not have a proper or clear clan membership and thereby lack the right to access customary land. Some families have been split by brothers fighting in opposite camps, which makes it difficult for them to cohabit on the same land. Adding to this the fact that the new Land Act was passed during war time when people lived in camps, that huge land speculation and commodification developed during the 20 years of conflicts, and that field boundaries (and many elders who knew about them) had disappeared during all the years in the camps, one can understand easily how land conflicts have become one of the most serious and most pressing problems in the region.

Despite this explosive situation, the level of violence in land conflicts has generally remained relatively low, and the institutions involved in conflict resolution have played an important role in creating order within an initially chaotic situation – even though there is still room for instrumentalizing legal pluralism to gain illegitimate advantages, as described above. All in all, we must recognize that the plurality of fora, despite some inconveniences and weaknesses, has been successful in resolving complex land disputes, and thus in furthering peace in an extremely difficult and pressing context, while at the same time securing the rights of vulnerable citizens.

The marginal role (not to say the failure) of Magistrates' Courts in solving land disputes at a reasonable speed and cost has been compensated by a diversity of institutions that although competing in theory have been mainly collaborating to find reasonable settlements to the many conflicts that erupted after the return from the camps. More remarkably, this diversity of fora has also made it possible to address the social conflicts that are often found at the root of many land conflicts. Whereas modern institutions such as Magistrates' Courts, government officials or NGOs tend to focus almost exclusively on rights and tenure when it comes to land conflict, traditional institutions have had much less difficulty in seeing land conflicts as symptoms or proxies of social conflicts and have been much better at addressing witchcraft accusations, problems of marriage and of clan membership (and thereby issues of land inheritance), and other social conflicts that are fuelling land conflicts. In other words, they address intimate governance, the theme of this book's next section.

Irene Winnie Anying, Ph.D., is a Ugandan Human Rights Lawyer and Advocate of the High Court of Uganda. She lectures at the Faculty of Law, of Gulu

University. She is specialized in access to justice and has over ten years' experience working and researching on both formal and informal justice systems.

Quentin Gausset received his Ph.D. in anthropology from the Free University of Brussels and is currently Associate Professor at the Department of Anthropology at University of Copenhagen. He is specialized in environmental anthropology and has over twenty years' research experience in the management of conflicts over natural resources.

Notes

1. The LCC1 and LCC2 are composed of members of the executive committee, implying that the local councilors, who hold an elective position, play two roles: as executive officers of the local council and at the same time as (quasi) judicial officers of the LCC. LCC3, situated at the sub-county level, consists of five members appointed by the Town Council, division council or sub-county council on the recommendation of the respective executive committee. Hence unlike LCC1 and LCC2 members, LCC3 members only execute judicial functions.
2. In one of our focus group discussions, the Parish Chief of Amuru pointed to instances where people have been denied a letter of referral from a lower LCC to a higher LCC or even the Magistrates' Courts. When they do write referrals or even letters to such adamant leaders, they act upon instruction and refer the parties as required. This view was confirmed by a former sub-county chief of Amuru, who has himself participated in a number of mediations in his capacity as a sub-county chief.
3. In Amuru, for example, where most of this field data was collected, there was no district court until 2012. Even when the court was formally instituted in 2009, it was about 120 kilometers away from the district headquarters.

References

Anying, Irene Winnie. 2012. *Re-envisioning Gender Justice in Access and Use of Land Through Traditional Institutions: A Case for Customary Tenure of Land Ownership in Acholi Sub-region, Northern Uganda.* The Danish Institute for Human Rights (DIHR).
Anying, Irene Winnie, and Quentin Gausset. 2017. 'Gender and Forum Shopping in Land Conflict Resolution in Northern Uganda', *The Journal of Legal Pluralism and Unofficial Law* 49(3): 353–72.
Berry, Sara. 2002. 'Debating the Land Question in Africa', *Comparative Studies in Society and History* 44: 638–68.
Boege, Volker. 2006. *Traditional Approaches to Conflict Transformation-Potential and Limits.* Berlin: Berghof Research Center for Constructive Conflict Management.
Bognitz, Stefanie. 2020. 'Mediation in Circumstances of the Existential: Dispute and Justice in Rwanda', in Karl Härter, Carolin Hillemanns and Günther Schlee (eds), *On Mediation: Historical, Legal, Anthropological and International Perspectives.* New York: Berghahn Books, pp. 95–115.
Branch, Adam. 2007. *Fostering the Transition in Acholiland: From War to Peace, from Camps to Home.* Gulu: Human Rights Focus.

———. 2008. *Gulu Town in War . . . and Peace? Displacement, Humanitarianism and Post-War Crisis*, Crisis States Working Paper Series No 2, Working Paper 36. London: London School of Economics.
Burke, Christopher, and Emiat Emmanuel Egaru. 2011. *Identification of Good Practices in Land Conflict Resolution in Acholi*. Kampala: United Nations Peace Building Program.
Dolan, Chris. 2009. *Social Torture: The Case of Northern Uganda, 1986–2006*. New York: Berghahn Books.
Francis, Paul, and Robert James. 2003. 'Balancing Rural Poverty Reduction and Citizen Participation: The Contradictions of Uganda's Decentralization Program', *World Development* 31(2): 325–37.
Helfer, Laurence R. 1999. 'Forum Shopping for Human Rights', *University of Pennsylvania Law Review* 148(2): 285–400.
Hopwood, Julian, and Ronald R. Atkinson. 2013. *Land Conflict Monitoring and Mapping Tool for the Acholi Sub-region*. Human Rights Focus and United Nations Peace Building Program, Final Report.
Huber, Jessica. 2010. *Model for Land Tenure Security*. Kampala: USAID/SPRING.
Kobusingye, Doreen Nancy, Mathijs van Leeuwen and Han van Dijk. 2016. 'Where Do I Report My Land Dispute? The Impact of Institutional Proliferation on Land Governance in Post-Conflict Northern Uganda', *The Journal of Legal Pluralism and Unofficial Law* 48(2): 238–55.
Lund, Christian. 2006. 'Twilight Institutions: Public Authority and Local Politics in Africa', *Development and Change* 37(4): 685–705.
Lund, Christian, and Catherine Boone. 2013. 'Land Politics in Africa: Constituting Authority over Territory, Property and Persons', *Africa* 83(1): 1–13.
Mwangi, Esther. 2010. 'Bumbling Bureaucrats, Sluggish Courts and Forum-Shopping Elites: Unending Conflict and Competition in the Transition to Private Property', *The European Journal of Development Research* 22(5): 715–32.
Nicolas, Andrea. 2020. 'What is Mediation? Definitions and Anthropological Discomforts', in Karl Härter, Carolin Hillemanns and Günther Schlee (eds), *On Mediation: Historical, Legal, Anthropological and International Perspectives*. New York: Berghahn Books, pp. 69–94.
Rugadya, Margaret, Eddie Nsamba-Gayiiya and Herbert Kamusiime. 2008. *Northern Uganda Land Study, Analysis of Post Conflict Land Policy and Land Administration: A Survey of IDP Return and Resettlement Issues and Lessons, Acholi and Lango Regions*. Retrieved 3 March 2020 from https://mokoro.co.uk/wp-content/uploads/northern_uganda_land_study_acholi_and_lango.pdf.
Schlee, Günther. 2020. 'Mediation and Truth', in Karl Härter, Carolin Hillemanns and Günther Schlee (eds), *On Mediation: Historical, Legal, Anthropological and International Perspectives*. New York: Berghahn Books, pp. 116–31.
Sikor, Thomas, and Christian Lund. 2009. 'Access and Property: A Question of Power and Authority', *Development and Change* 40(1): 1–22.
Tamanaha, Brian Z. 2008. 'Understanding Legal Pluralism: Past to Present, Local to Global', *Sydney Law Review* 30: 375–411.
Unruh, Jon D. 2003. 'Land Tenure and Legal Pluralism in the Peace Process', *Peace & Change* 28(3): 352–77.
Vandekerckhove, Nel. 2011. 'The State, The Rebel and The Chief: Public Authority and Land Disputes in Assam, India', *Development and Change* 42(3): 759–79.
Van Leeuwen, Mathijs. 2014. 'Renegotiating Customary Tenure Reform – Land Governance Reform and Tenure Security in Uganda', *Land Use Policy* 39: 292–300.

———. 2017. 'Localizing Land Governance, Strengthening the State: Decentralization and Land Tenure Security in Uganda', *Journal of Agrarian Change* 17(1): 208–27.

Vaughan, Jenny, and Tim Stewart. 2011. *Land Disputes in Acholiland: A Conflict and Market Assessment*. Edinburgh: Mercy Corps.

Whyte, S. R. et al. 2013. 'Remaining Internally Displaced: Missing Links to Security in Northern Uganda', *Journal of Refugee Studies* 26(2): 283–301.

Part II
Intimate Governance of Land

Case II

Disputed Land and Broken Graves

Sophie Seebach

Edward lived on the land of his ancestors. Many of his relatives lived in the surrounding clearings, their homesteads connected by well-worn footpaths created through years of daily visits. And as Edward and his relations lived their lives on this land, their ancestors were buried beneath it. Their graves were dotted around the compounds, many of them marked permanently by cement rectangles, their names and dates of birth and death etched into the wet cement to remind their

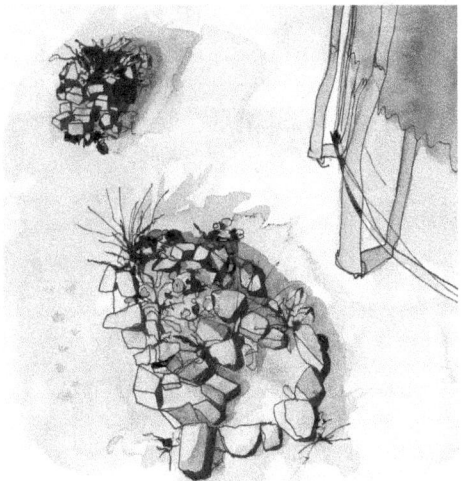

Figure CII.1. Traditional grave © Mette Lind Kusk.

Figure CII.2. Cemented grave © Mette Lind Kusk.

descendants of their continued presence in death. One day, Edward met a young man named Oyo. Oyo had been cast out of his own clan, and taking pity on him, Edward invited him to come and live with him and his family. Edward treated Oyo like a son, and for a while they lived amicably together, sharing everyday life on Edward's land. When Oyo found a woman he wanted to marry, Edward helped him with the arrangements and contributed to the bridewealth.

Then, the war came. The rebels of The Lord's Resistance Army snuck out of the bush to strike civilians and military alike, abducting children, killing and spreading terror. And in their efforts to strike down the LRA, the government forces were no less merciless in their treatment of the civilian population. The time came when Edward and his extended family were no longer able to live on their ancestral land. They were forced to relocate to a camp for the internally

Figure CII.3. Community meeting © Mette Lind Kusk.

displaced, and though life was hard, the family stuck together, and Oyo remained like a son to Edward.

When finally the war ended, Edward and his family were able to move back home to their ancestral land, to commence repairing what was damaged and overgrown, plant new crops and rebuild life after the years of insecurity. For two years, the family lived like this, happy to be home. But then one day, as Edward was planting his garden, Oyo stopped him and said, 'This area is mine!' They argued, and after Oyo accused Edward of trying to encroach on his land,

Figure CII.4. In the office of the LC1 © Mette Lind Kusk.

Edward called the elders of the clan, pointing out that it was actually Oyo who was encroaching.

The elders tried to reason with Oyo. They told him that he should remember that Edward had taken care of him, that he had been good to him. They urged Oyo not to go against Edward in this matter. To try to reach a compromise, the elders suggested that Edward perhaps give Oyo a piece of land, and Edward accepted this. But when they tried to divide the land, Oyo was not happy with the size of the land he was allocated; he wanted the biggest piece. To settle it, they then went to the LC1.

The LC1 did not accept Oyo's demands: 'This land is not yours!', he said. 'You should only use the land that has been given to you.' Furious, Oyo went first to the LC2 and then the LC3, both of whom refused his claim. The LC3 told him: 'Don't turn against those who have brought you up! You should respect them. They did not chase you away.' The LC3 advised him to use the land given to him and be satisfied. Still Oyo would not give up, and he took the matter to the Magistrates' Court. But here he realized that he could not win. One night, Oyo went to Edward's home with some friends, and under the cover of darkness they destroyed six cement graves. When Edward and his family rose the following morning and saw the broken graves, they were horrified. They called the local leaders and asked them for help in finding the suspects; they knew it must be

Figure CII.5. Destroying graves at night © Mette Lind Kusk.

Figure CII.6. Shocked family members © Mette Lind Kusk.

Oyo. It was not long before Oyo was captured, and he readily admitted that he had destroyed the graves, but he argued that he had the right to do so, because they were on *his* land.

The family were afraid that the spirits of the people buried in the destroyed cement graves would turn vengeful and perhaps decide to harm Oyo, so they had to conduct some rituals in order to calm them down. They also forced Oyo to pay for the reconstruction of the graves. In the Magistrates' Court, Edward brought photographs of the destroyed graves to show what Oyo had done. The Magistrate

Figure CII.7. Community meeting © Mette Lind Kusk.

judged that Oyo had a bad heart because he had turned against someone who had taken him in and treated him like a son. He judged that Oyo had to leave the land, and that he was not even to have the little piece of land that was first allotted to him. 'But where should I go?' Oyo cried. This, the Magistrate could not answer.

Later, Oyo went to Edward to plead his case. He told Edward that someone had given him bad advice, that someone had told him that Edward had taken the land from Oyo's father. Yet Edward did not relent. Breaking the graves, he said, was beyond what was acceptable, and Oyo should follow the court's ruling and leave him in peace. Defeated, Oyo went back to his own clan, which had cast him out, but they also did not want to take him in, because he had behaved so atrociously. In the end, he bought a small plot of land for himself and settled there, away from his own clan, and away from Edward.

Figure CII.8. Oyo leaves the community © Mette Lind Kusk.

Sophie Seebach, Ph.D., is Head of LEO Historical Archives and Museum.

Chapter 4

Generations

Esther Acio, Lioba Lenhart
and Susan Reynolds Whyte

The Insecure Nephew

Daniel's grass-thatched hut was clean and tidy. It was evidently the house of someone with resources. The floor was cemented, and curtains separated the sleeping area from the space for receiving visitors. A crucifix and a rosary hung from the centre pole along with a wire basket containing a blister pack of pills, tubes and other small things. The first time we visited Daniel at home, it looked as if he had prepared for our coming. As we took the seats he offered, we saw on a table in front of us items that showed different aspects of his life and work. It seemed he had been a bit more exposed to the outside world than other youth in his community. A copy of the Book of Mormon contrasted with the rosary. There were boxes of male and female condoms, which he distributed as a youth leader tasked with, among other things, instructing his peers on how to use them to prevent HIV/AIDS and STDs. Some papers next to the boxes indicated past engagements. There was material from Green Watch, an environmental advocacy organization, which had employed him in 2012–13. He showed us documents about a National Agricultural Advisory Services (NAADS)-supported piggery project run by disabled people, who had invited him to become a member of their group and facilitate the work, although he was not disabled himself. There was a certificate from an oil company for which he had worked, and a photo of him and four other young men together with a Dutch engineer. Other material revealed hopes for the future: brochures promoting seeds and agrochemicals, which he spoke of passionately as the sort of thing he would buy when he was able to engage in serious farming someday. Daniel was already doing some small-scale agriculture but, as we learned, accessing land for farming was a challenge.

We had met Daniel the day before in Purongo, at the sub-county offices, where the Chairman of LC3 had called him in response to our request to talk to some youth. The Chairman introduced him as a youth leader, since Daniel had served as a youth representative on the local council. He was 24 years old, at that time, in early 2014. Later, Esther and Lioba met him frequently during their field stays in Purongo, where both had rented a place. Esther developed a close relationship with Daniel, who became not only one of her most important respondents but also her research assistant. He shared many insights about his life and experiences as a youth in the community, identified and connected her to interlocutors, and helped her with translations. She regularly visited him at home and was introduced to his family members, with whom she interacted whenever she went to Purongo. During our first visit and meetings later on, Daniel shared his life story with us. We also talked to his brothers, his mother and his maternal uncle.

Daniel was the third child in a family of five sons. He lived with his mother Aber and three of his brothers on the same compound. An elder married brother lived in Gulu town with a wife and children. Of the five huts in the compound in Purongo, one was for his mother with whom his youngest brother stayed when he was home from school. Another was for an older married brother and his wife and children. They used one of the two kitchen huts, while his mother cooked in the other. Daniel shared his own well-built hut with a younger brother, until that brother married in 2016 and constructed one of his own.

Daniel's parents had separated during the insurgency. His father went with other women, and there was some insinuation about witchcraft in the home that we never fully understood. When people in the area were forced into IDP camps, Aber did not go with her husband but instead took refuge in a camp near her natal home in Purongo. Her elder brother Okot had received her and the children well and taken care of them ever since. Okot had used the bridewealth from Aber's marriage to bring his own first wife to the home, so he had a special obligation to her. But because Okot had also to look after his seven biological children, he could not afford to pay school fees for Daniel and his brothers, as they had hoped, so they had to struggle on their own. His elder brothers proved to be rather successful. One became a primary school teacher in Purongo, whereas the other got a job as a petrol station manager in Gulu. Daniel, however, eventually dropped out of O-level secondary school. He joined a technical school, where he took a course in carpentry and joinery, which he did not complete due to lack of school fees. However, he and his elder brothers made sure that the younger brothers could complete their O-level education. The two oldest brothers contributed from their salaries, and Daniel helped whenever he managed to earn some cash.

Daniel's uncle Okot was born into a family of six children, three boys and three girls. Two of his brothers died, so that he, as the only male child alive, had become head of the family and natal home of Daniel's mother. Two other sisters lived in their marital homes. Okot had married four wives. He was separated from one, and two of them had passed on, but he was still living with his first wife. The first wife had delivered two girls, who were already married, as well as two boys, who were still in school. Okot had three children with his second wife, one boy and two girls, who were married and lived in Purongo. The boy had two wives but had not yet paid bridewealth for either of them, something that Okot wanted to help him achieve. The third wife had delivered two children who died, and he separated with the fourth wife before they had a child. In addition to his own biological children and his sister Aber's children, Daniel's uncle was also looking after other relatives' children; five of them were still in school.

Over time, we learned more about Daniel's endeavours to access land. He told us that his uncle Okot had inherited over thirty acres of land from his father. In 2007, when they left the camps, Okot had given Daniel's mother two acres of land. It was not much for both residence and farming, but as she stated, 'In Acholi, when a girl returns home, she has no power to say anything regarding land matters; therefore, whatever she is given is what she takes, whether it's enough or not.' Okot explained: 'It is our father's land, and Aber has the right to be allocated land to use with her children. But there is no ownership given to the children; they just use it. I am now the owner of the land; they have to ask me for land when they want to use it.' Daniel and his brothers could have claimed their father's land. However, Aber explained that after she had returned to her natal home in Purongo with her sons, her husband had not supported them at all but married another wife, with whom he had four children, two boys and two girls. She stressed that Daniel and his brothers should indeed claim land from their

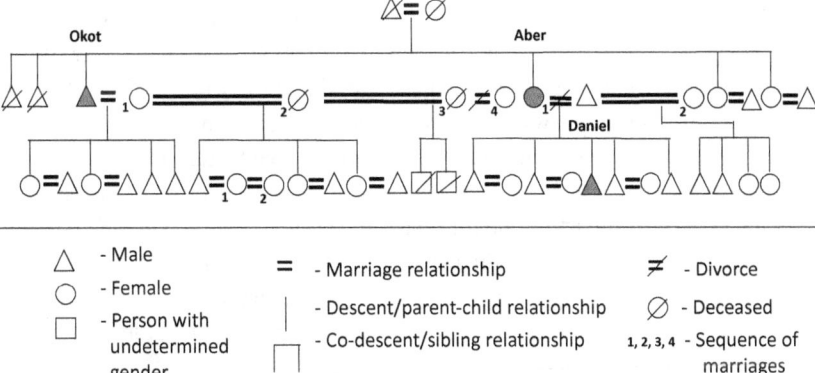

Figure 4.1. Daniel's family ties showing the marriages and children of his mother Aber and her brother Okot. Numbers indicate the seniority of wives © Lioba Lenhart.

father, but they would not do so, because they now identified more with their mother's side. Moreover, their father's land was contested, and neither her sons nor she as good Christians would want to be involved in any land conflict. She said she hoped to get money one day to buy land for her sons so that they can have a say on that land.

Of the two acres Okot had allocated to them, Daniel, his mother and his brothers used one and a half acres for residence. The remaining half acre was for planting food crops such as beans, cassava and sweet potatoes, which were mainly for home consumption. Daniel also showed us another five acres of land in a valley close to their homestead, which his uncle had given him for cultivation. The uncle had also entrusted him to manage the land in case other relatives wanted to use parts of it. Okot felt that he was no longer strong enough to use this land, which was quite wet. There, Daniel had planted sugarcane, which he regarded as a good source of income. He proudly told us that he had earned about one million Uganda shillings from his sugarcane harvest in 2013. He had also planted green vegetables and prepared a nursery bed with small cabbage plants. The valley was crossed by a small stream. Daniel had made drainage channels to irrigate the crops. He was also thinking of growing watermelons and other fruits, which he hoped to sell to one of the companies he once had worked for. 'This land has helped me a lot,' Daniel said.

However, when Daniel was given the land, his uncle Okot had told him: 'Know for sure that this is not your land, and when I ask for it, you have to give it back.' The uncle had stressed that a man in Acholi society can only own land when he has achieved a certain social status as a married man with children. But he also had another point to make. In Acholi society, land is usually transmitted from fathers to sons. However, Daniel and his brothers did not live on their father's land but with their mother on her brother's land. In Purongo, they were nephews and therefore – unlike Okot's own male children – had no customary rights to the land.

Daniel stressed: 'Youth have no voice in land matters. It is the elders. When you are grown up and you are married with children, you may have a say. When you are a youth, you may dig anywhere but the land is not yours.' This was particularly true for nephews. Daniel was given part of his maternal uncle's land to provide for his mother and siblings, but not to own or sell it. The uncle had taken good care of them since they were young; they appreciated and respected their uncle for what he had done for them, and they listened to what he said. He had treated them like his own sons and given them access to land, which some other young people were not lucky enough to have because they could not be trusted, since they were not humble and respectful towards the older generation like Daniel and his brothers.

Nevertheless, Daniel and his brothers could not be sure for how long they could stay on the uncle's land and engage in cultivation. Possibly, the uncle's sons would claim this land in future, using patrilineal inheritance as an argument to exclude them. Okot had other pieces of customary land that he inherited from his own father and grandfather, but they were located in other areas. As the only surviving son, Okot had authority over all this customary land. Recently, he had started to sell parts of the family land to outsiders – the local church, an LC3 councillor, and others whom Daniel and his mother and brothers did not know. They had only heard about it by chance. The fact that Okot had sold land without even informing his own sister made them worry.

When the uncle returned from a drinking place where he had consumed a lot of local brew, he sometimes spoke roughly about them; one time he had even told them that they would have to go back to 'where they belong', namely to their father's place. All this was triggering worries that the uncle might also sell the land on which they lived. Daniel's brother Robert lamented this state of uncertainty: 'We live here like visitors, and one day we will be required to leave.'

Daniel and his brothers took the selling of parts of the family land by their uncle as an eye-opener 'to do something before it is too late'. For them, it was not an option to return to their father's place and fight over land with their father's other children. They were also not willing to quarrel with their uncle's children over the land where they were staying. While they continued cultivating the uncle's land, they were thinking about saving money to buy land elsewhere. They had started to hire land from other people to plant crops such as rice, sesame and groundnuts, which they sometimes sold.

Daniel was the first among them to buy his own land. In March 2016, he acquired two acres near Hoima, a town far away from home. He had earlier worked for an oil company there that had just paid him his salary arrears, which had accumulated to a total of five million Uganda shillings. A former colleague and friend from that area told him about the two acres of land that were for sale by an old man who wanted to move to Kampala to live with his daughter. Daniel bought the land at 4.8 million Uganda shillings. He still had 200,000 Uganda shillings left, which he spent for his transport fares and other requirements. Interestingly, Daniel has only told one of his younger brothers, whom he says he trusts, about the land he purchased.

Daniel had no land he could unambiguously call 'ours'. The closest was the two acres allocated to his mother and the valley land over which his uncle had given him authority. The 'ours' in this case refers to his mother and brothers. In his account, the land and the livelihood it provides are part of his belonging and obligations to this family. The purchased land he can now call 'mine' is also somewhat ambiguous in that he says it will be for his future children. In other words, it will become 'ours' for the next generation. The fact that he has only told one brother about this land suggests that he is uneasy that his brothers will treat it as 'ours' or that he will be forced to sell it to meet family obligations. This had already happened in relation to other property he had acquired.

In 2012, Daniel had started a livestock project with eight goats and two pigs. However, in late 2013 he had to sell his animals because he had to contribute money for a relative's funeral, pay school fees for his youngest brother, and cover the medical bills for his sick mother. Not long afterwards, he ventured into a poultry project for some time, but it also did not last long as he did not have enough money for treatment when the birds fell sick, and so they died. In 2015, Daniel started another piggery project together with his younger brother Robert. The number of piglets had multiplied when Robert came up with plans to marry. So, they sold all the pigs in order to finance the marriage that took place in mid-2016. 'We were all so happy for Robert and his achievement,' Daniel said, expressing firm solidarity with his brother and the 'achievement' of a church wedding.

Daniel, however, was not yet ready to marry his girlfriend from West Nile, although she and his mother had pressured him 'to settle down'. Instead, he separated from her. 'I do not have money to marry now,' he said. 'I first have to secure land for my future children's future.' He explained that he had plans to acquire land nearby and start a business in livestock production and agriculture: to raise pigs, goats and poultry – do 'some serious farming'. Daniel did not just sit back and wait for things to happen or land to appear. He had always struggled in one way or another to secure his birth family's livelihoods, and he aspired to become an equally responsible husband and father, which in his view implied having secured land as a foundation for family life.

Of What Is This a Case?

Daniel was in many ways an exemplary young man: a good son and brother, a respectful nephew, a hard-working farmer, and a socially conscious 'exposed' youth representative on the Local Council. He could be taken primarily as representative of 'the nephew problem' (*nero ki okeya*) in that he was living on his mother's brother's land to which he had no claim according to Acholi patrilineal conventions. But we will take this as a specific case of an even more general phenomenon: the interplay between generations around access to land. It is also a concrete case of more abstract principles of genealogy, historical disruption and the generation of alternatives.

In this chapter, we consider three meanings of generation – genealogical, historical and productive – which structure our consideration of the wider implications of Daniel's story. Together with gender, generation is the axis of kinship, so anthropological studies of kin-based African societies have long focused on the links between genealogical generations. Careful attention has been accorded to the relations between parents and children, grandparents and grandchildren, parents-in-law and children-in-law, aunts and uncles and their nieces and nephews, and, of course, descent groups. In the last decade or so, scholars and policymakers have approached generation in another way. They are concerned with youth as a historical generation – a cohort born around the same time with similar experiences of war, HIV and lack of economic possibilities, but also education, communication technologies and exposure to new discourses and aspirations for a life different from that of their parents. Although the emphasis is on young people in these studies, the contrast to their seniors is always implicit. As a verb, to generate means to produce or create. The efforts of parents and children, of older and younger people, to deal with land issues in contemporary northern Uganda have generated new ideas and practices with important consequences for their interrelations.

Gerontocracy and Genealogical Generations: The Patrilineal Ideal

Acholi society is patrilineal in principle. Descent and therefore generational relations are fundamental for identity and access to resources. Children are considered to belong to the clan (*kaka*) of their fathers. Customary land is held by smaller descent groups traced through the male line; these patrilineages are also called *kaka*. Sons have a claim to their fathers' land so that a neighbourhood consists of the homes (*dogola*) of men related agnatically and descended from a common ancestor. The term for the land that they share, *ngom kwaro*, usually translates to 'ancestral land', implying a relation to previous generations.

The androcentric perspective in patriliny is tempered by the key position of women and gender relations (Shipton 2009: 105–8). Since descent groups are exogamous, wives from outside are necessary for the creation of further generations of lineage members. Traditionally, sisters married out, bringing in bridewealth to ensure that their brothers had the wherewithal to bring wives to cultivate their ancestral land. Daughters are expected to move to the home of their husbands' families, residing virilocally and cultivating gardens there, which their sons will inherit someday. They have residual rights to use the land of their fathers and brothers should they fail to marry durably. Their children often stay with them, thus living on the land of their maternal uncles, as did Daniel and his brothers. If neither bridewealth nor the payment to recognize children (*luk latini*) is given to the family of a mother, her children should be considered members of her clan and allowed to claim land from their mother's brothers, according to one source (Ker Kwaro Acholi 2008). Yet this is often problematic, and in practice the status of such children is often ambiguous.

Patriliny and virilocality are normal and normative, in the sense of being common and considered right. Still, they are neither inevitable nor absolute. Girling (1960: 37–38) reported families living on the land of mother's brothers and wives' fathers during the late colonial era. Gauvin did a full village genealogy in 2012 and found people who had been living on land from the maternal side for generations (Baines and Gauvin 2014: 299–300). Likewise, Hopwood and Atkinson (2013: 6) state that many of the 'guest' families in core clan villages 'were the households of women returning to the clans into which they were born, usually with their husbands, but sometimes as women-headed households after leaving their husbands' clan, and clan land, because of divorce or other serious difference or difficulty'.

In his classic work on kinship among the patrilineal Tallensi in West Africa, Meyer Fortes (1949) distinguished between the significance of paternal and maternal kinship links. Filiation is the recognized status of being the child of a parent, a mother or a father. Descent refers to the link by a parent to ancestors. In patrilineal societies like the Tallensi and Acholi, it is paternal filiation that links sons, and to some extent daughters, to the descent groups through which they access land. Links to mothers, and through them to her consanguineal relatives, were dubbed 'complementary filiation' by Fortes (1969: 254). (In a matrilineal society, the 'complementary filiation' is on the paternal side.) He suggested that maternal links had a different quality; Girling (1960: 39) made a similar observation in his Acholi study. Fortes asserted that these matrilateral ties deserved equal attention despite the ideological weight given to paternal descent. For our purposes here, what is important is the acknowledgement of the most fundamental relationship of generation – that between a mother and child. Daniel lived on his uncle's land because of his mother.

Sons have a claim to land through their fathers. Through links to an agnatic descent group, they are entitled to use ancestral land: son to father and on to father's brothers, and father's father, all sharing the land of their paternal forefather. Conventionally, fathers show their sons the portion of land they may use at the time they marry. Again, however, women's position is key. The portion sons are most likely to be given is where their mothers had gardens (Obika et al. 2018: 208). Thus, a mother's labour helps to secure land for her sons. Land disputes are often based on the entitlements mothers establish through use; evidence of such use – ditches or lines where weeds were thrown – may figure in dispute negotiation. If a man has several wives, there may well be tension between them and their children over portions and boundaries.

Children have land entitlements through their parents, especially their fathers, but also in some ways through the efforts of their mothers. Women who leave their husbands often go to some length to secure their sons' claims in patrilineal land. As we will see in Chapter 5, Awor explained that she farms on the land of her ex-husband in order to secure the land for her sons. It is not always realized that the reverse also holds: parents have claims through their children. Having children, especially sons, supports the entitlement of a wife to use her husband's land. In the case of Sylvia (Chapter 3), the clan elders decided that she should be allowed to return to her late husband's land because of her sons. Obika and colleagues (2018: 216) write that: 'Being the mother of recognised clan children cements a woman's claim to garden land.' Especially if she has sons, a woman may be entitled to use land even if she is estranged from their father; her sons will one day bring wives to cultivate where their mother had gardens. Likewise, if her husband dies, her security on his family land is firmer if she has children. Having children is also important for men's claims to land. The clansman without children is in a weaker position regarding land. One of Langole's informants, Watmon, struggled to get a share of family land. He was told to leave their father's land for siblings who had children.

As Shipton (2009: 111) points out, land use entitlements are passed from one generation to another through inheritance at death, and through devolution during a senior man's life, typically when a young man marries and a father allocates a portion of land to him. But as we have seen in the case of Daniel, devolution may take different forms. His mother's brother assigned land for his use but underlined that the land was on loan. The difference between devolution and lending may not always be clear.

Nearly all land in the Acholi sub-region is held under customary tenure; it is not registered with state authorities. Through inheritance or devolution, it passes from one generation to another. Authority over the disposition of land rests with the senior generation. As an older man summed it up: 'customary tenure means that the elders are in control' (Whyte and Acio 2017: 24). Governance of land by gerontocracy, in Acholi as elsewhere in Africa, is often attended by tensions and open conflicts between sons and fathers. In Bugisu, eastern Uganda, where land is in short supply, such conflicts have, in the past, been linked to high rates of patricide and filicide (LaFontaine 1967; Heald 1989). In Acholiland, open clashes are rare; instead, there is a marked pattern of filial humility and respect. As we have suggested elsewhere, patient, respectful waiting is a strategy for youth hoping to acquire a share of ancestral land; as one young man put it: '. . . the elders are the ones who are involved in giving or allocating land to us young people, which means that as you grow up, you have to wait until the elders give you land because they are the ones who know which land to give you' (Whyte and Acio 2017: 26). Those who are impatient and demand a share may be condemned as 'big-headed'. Deference towards 'the one who cares for the land' is also wise on the part of those staying with maternal relatives, as Daniel's example shows.

An essential element of gerontocracy is the assumption that older men have a monopoly on legitimate knowledge. The elders are 'the ones who know'. And legitimate knowledge is knowledge about the past. Which grandmother had gardens where? Who planted those mango trees? Who lived where the faint ruins of a house foundation can be traced? Who lies buried under the stones on that mound of earth? Material marks in the landscape are evidence only if they are interpreted by a person in authority. No matter what forum is used for dispute management, the voice of the senior generation is given greater weight.

Historical Generations: Challenges to Patriliny

Deference to authority is precisely what is lacking among the youth of today, according to many older people in Acholiland. They claim that the youth who came of age during the war and in the IDP camps were morally spoiled – they respected neither their elders nor the virtues of Acholi life. They had not learned how to farm. They were lazy and avoided the hoe. They wanted the amusements of town life: videos, gambling and drinking. They did not form responsible partnerships; girls fell pregnant at a tender age and young men did not support the children they begot. A repeated assertion was that male youth just wanted to sell land to buy motorcycles to use as taxis in town.

Young people in turn criticized their male elders for secretiveness, greediness and selfishness. They did not share knowledge about the land. They sold land for their own individual benefit without consulting their children and grandchildren, they drank too much, they favoured the children of one wife over others and they did not care for orphans left by deceased lineage members. They used witchcraft and connived unfairly to exclude some young paternal relatives. Often these criticisms were aimed at specific older men; sometimes they were generalized to senior males across the board.

Karl Mannheim (1952 [1927]) drew attention to the way that young people who came of age under momentous historical conditions had to reconcile the cultural heritage they had from older generations with the new experiences they had undergone. He suggested that such a cohort might develop a distinctive generational consciousness. Several scholars have found the concept of historical generations useful in the study of youth and generations in Africa (Cole and Durham 2006; Alber, Van der Geest and Whyte 2008). Vorhölter's (2014) study of Acholi youth discourses in Gulu town analyses the generational consciousness of the 'war generation' so often criticized by their seniors. She argues that they see themselves at a crossroads, between tradition and modernity, the past and the future, Acholi and Western culture. This in-between, both/and, neither/nor situation is ambiguous as Verma (2013) shows. That is why, she explains, they are seen as *lakite* – 'somehow' tricky, changeable and unreliable. Young musicians in Gulu are explicit about the ambiguity of their generational position (Meinert and Schneidermann 2014).

It seems that the war contributed to generational consciousness: 'we are youth at the crossroads' and 'the testimony of older people is more reliable'. In the negotiations over land at Ogul described in Chapter 6, it was explicitly stated that the 'children of the camps', those who came of age as Internally Displaced, should not be part of the meetings. Partly it was assumed that such young men can turn violent and partly that they did not know how land had been used in the past. As is often the case, the consciousness of generational belonging was oppositional: 'the older people do not share knowledge with us' and 'youth today do not respect us'. In this historical conjuncture, mistrust between generations is common, both in general terms and in specific instances. Daniel and his brothers did not trust their mother's brother in matters relating to land. He sold land without telling his nephews; they heard about it from someone else. Lack of communication fuelled their uncertainty – maybe he would even sell the land where they were staying.

Intergenerational tensions around land often revolve around the morally reprehensible sale of ancestral land. Joireman, doing research in Acholiland in 2015, examines children as victims and agents in land matters following the disruptions of AIDS, war and displacement. She found as we did that elders accused youth of selling clan land. Although she describes this as a statement made by her older informants, she accepts that it is indeed the case and argues that children in this way are vectors of institutional change. 'Resource conflict there – and specifically access to land – has taken on an intergenerational quality as young adults take advantage of the growing market in land and eroded social institutions to sell clan land' (Joireman 2018: 94). There are surely some such cases, but they cannot be very common given that authority over land is seldom in the hands of young adults. (In another sense, it is always children who sell ancestral land; if it is understood as passing down generations, then it is sold by children of previous generations – although those 'children' might be middle-aged men.) Like Daniel, most young men are more in the market for buying than for selling land. We agree with Joireman's point that members of the 'war generation' were both disenfranchised and motivated to find new alternative ways forward, thus acting as vectors of change. However, we emphasize other tactics.

There can be no doubt that the war and displacement to camps disrupted the patrilineal ideal in fundamental ways. The authority of senior men and the reproduction of agnatic descent groups rested on marriage. Older men controlled not only the disposition of land but also the circulation of bridewealth. When the Acholi people lost their livestock to the depredations of the Karamojong, the LRA and the UPDF, and then were confined to camps, the giving of bridewealth was impossible. The formalization of partnerships through open courtship (*cuna*), including visits and exchanges between families of the couple, declined drastically (Baines and Gauvin 2014). Together with the fact that links were lost through death or disregard, this meant that women had children without recognized fathers. The most common recourse for them was to stay in the homes of their parents and brothers. While such arrangements had long existed, they became far more common after the war and internment. When sisters' sons grew up in their mothers' homes, where should they get land? This was the quandary facing Daniel and his brothers, even though their situation was different in that their mother had been properly married with bridewealth and their father was still alive.

Children without a relationship to their fathers and who are not absorbed in their mothers' lineages are precariously positioned in patrilineal societies. Perhaps the most extreme examples are the 'children born of war', whose mothers were abducted and whose fathers were LRA fighters. When those women return, they are not always welcomed by their families and neighbours because of their association with violence. Their children are derided as 'children of the bush' whose unidentified fathers were brutal rebels. The children themselves want to know their fathers' families, where they should properly belong. The Justice and Reconciliation Project sees the establishment of paternal descent as a source of healing for these children and has been undertaking an effort to help mothers and 'children born of war' to trace paternal families. 'Many children continue to ask their mothers the whereabouts of their paternal homes and find that not knowing their home can be a painful void in their sense of identity. Additionally, knowing one's "home" (paternal village) is an integral component of *social belonging* in Acholi culture' (Justice and Reconciliation Project 2018).

More numerous even than the fatherless children of the LRA are the children who have no relationship with their (non-combatant) fathers. In some cases, this is because their mothers were mistreated and broke ties with them, as did Daniel's mother. In other cases, the mother never told them who their father was; in still others the father died and his agnates did not recognize them. Perhaps most commonly, the father never acknowledged his child, either by paying *luk* or by giving support. Poverty was often invoked as the reason why men did not undertake responsibility.

Baines and Gauvin address this widespread problem of 'illegitimate children' and note that there is a resurgence of lineal authority reflected in efforts to recognize paternal filiation and descent. Such efforts include attempts by maternal families to make paternal ones take responsibility, and the willingness of some fathers or paternal relatives to acknowledge and support children whose mothers were never wives. The backside of this resurgence of lineal authority is what can be called 'patrilineal fundamentalism', the contention that only agnatic descent gives entitlement to land (Whyte et al. 2013: 294), thus excluding sisters' sons and descendants of friends who were given land in earlier times.

Langole's (2014) study of male and female youth in Gulu town traces generational relations in detail. 'Slippery paternity' was a problem for several of the young mothers, who had no further interaction with the fathers of their children (Langole 2014: 73). Like other researchers, he found that children, especially sons, had an existential need to know their paternity, a need that could have serious mental health implications (Whyte and Oboke 2022). This did not necessarily mean having a personal relation with their genitor. Paternal grandparents, aunts or uncles might also give them recognition and support (Langole 2014: 77). Sons might even hope to be given access to land. Yet their entitlements were far from secure.

Fortes' old notion of complementary filiation seems oddly out of place in such situations. When generational links are mainly maternal in a patrilineal society, it is more a matter of 'noncomplementary filiation'. Without social recognition of agnatic descent, maternal filiation is primary not complementary. While single motherhood and the 'nephew problem' are associated with the war in northern Uganda, the decline of formal marriage and the failure of fathers to support their children is not limited to that part of the country.

Generating Alternatives: Our Land and My Land

'This land is from our grandfathers; we are caring for it so that our children will use it in future.' These words capture the notion of entrustment that is so pronounced when Acholi people speak of ancestral land held under customary tenure. Despite the consequences of war, most of the male youth in northern Uganda access land through their parents and guardians. Some are even entrusted with large shares. For instance, at an early age, a young man we interviewed acquired about 300 acres of land from the Panakorach clan to which he belongs. After the death of his father, the clan decided to give him his father's share. In other words, he inherited the authority over the communally owned family land. His new responsibility denotes a change in his social position within the family and community. He has become a part of a new generational category and is no longer merely a son but one who has replaced his late father. His social position as a first-born male entitles him to the family authority, including the authority over the communal family land.

However, authority over land should not be confused with ownership, as this concept does not exist within customary tenure. Adoko and Levine (2005) propose the concept of stewardship to describe how land is held in trust for the next generation. Thus, the family land does not belong to the young man who has now gained the authority but belongs to his family and his clan. Land is in this way deeply embedded in social relations and hierarchical organization. Vice versa, access to and authority over land also shapes social identities, evident in how the young man's stewardship of the land provides him with a new social position in his family and local community.

Land is about livelihood, social belonging, trust and obligation. Parker Shipton (2007: xi), writing of the Luo of Kenya, whose social and cultural fabric resembles that of the Acholi, uses the term 'fiduciary culture', which he characterizes as 'shared, learned ways of thinking and acting that involve some sense of obligation'. In this regard, he highlights reciprocal forms of entrustment as well as serial transfers passed between the generations that are part of reproductive, ritual and symbolic life and are consciously expressed and emotionally felt by the people. Thus, it is 'hard to distinguish activities that are economic from the ones that are not' (Shipton 2007: xi). The attachment of the Acholi to their land, which they regard as a source of belonging and livelihood security, demonstrates this pattern. Entrustment goes together with obligation both laterally to the living and lineally to preceding and succeeding generations. The interdiction on selling ancestral land reflects the positive value of stewardship across generations. The principle that land belongs to a descent group, not to an individual, obligates sharing while bounding the sharing unit to those filiated to fathers and through them to ancestors.

Generational attachment to land is manifested in graves. The burial of a parent or grandparent is often considered evidence of a person's attachment and entitlement to land. This is illustrated in the case which opened Part II of our book, about Oyo, who destroyed the cement graves of Stephen's ancestors, claiming they were on his land. Graves are not only deployed as evidence in disputes but they also have a spiritual purpose in that the spirits of the dead are thought to demand recognition and respect. The efforts families made to exhume the bodies of those buried in the IDP camps and rebury them properly in their rural homes testify to this (Meinert and Whyte 2013).

However cosmopolitan, however removed from the agricultural life of ancestral land, burial should be on 'our land' near the graves of agnates. In his study of intergenerational relations of youth in Gulu town, Langole distinguishes between kinds of homes, arguing that the true home is where the grave, the 'long home', will be located. He gives two examples of men with prestigious positions and luxurious houses in Gulu Town. When their fathers died, the burials had to take place on their ancestral land. Neither man had invested in houses and roads there, so their 'working-class' friends and colleagues found only dilapidated huts when they arrived for the funeral. 'After the burial, it became the talk of the town. "Ezekial does not have a home – death can really expose the real person"' (Langole 2014: 89). The burial of a parent is a 'reality check', Langole suggests; generational relationships are enacted on ancestral land, which is the socially significant home.

As young people grow older and have children of their own, it becomes more important for them to have an attachment to ancestral land if possible. Two of Langole's interlocutors were boda-boda riders, the very epitome of 'the youth of today', who want town life rather than the life of the hoe, according to the stereotype. Still, both have houses near their parents on their lineage land, which they visit regularly. They have agricultural projects there and plan to shift there as they get too old for boda work, an occupation primarily for younger men. Their trajectory was similar to that of Tito, a 30-year-old from Purongo, who explained to Esther Acio:

If you want to have money, you should have land. As well . . . if you want to marry, you should have land where to stay with your family. I left town because life was so difficult for me with no job, so I came to the village, where I was given land by my father's brother.

The attachment to ancestral land remains, as does the patrilineal ideal associated with it. Yet the history of war, displacement, AIDS and poverty has made the inclusion in ancestral land problematic for many who are not so fortunate as Tito. For some, like Daniel and his brothers, there were complications in the parental generation that pre-dated the war.

> You see, access to the customary land is a challenge. My mother and siblings live in the village, but the elder sons of the other two co-wives grab land from children of the deceased relatives and claim that it is for them and their own children. That is why I left the village and stay here in the centre. I don't want to go to the ancestral land, and I will only go back home when the two co-wives are no more, including their elder sons, who grab land from other vulnerable relatives. At least I will struggle to buy my own land, rather than go back there. (Dominic, youth from Purongo)

The events and conditions of the past decades have been generative in that they have problematized the entrustment of ancestral land. It can no longer be taken for granted that all male members of succeeding generations will accept to wait patiently for their share, nor is it certain that shares will be provided. Many young men, like Dominic, wanted to buy their own land, not necessarily instead of but in addition to their share in customary land.

> We live on customary land and my father has never allocated land to us, so I have no authority to say this land is mine or even to sell it. I want to shift from my father's land, but first I have to struggle and buy even one plot of land for me to move to first. If my father decides to distribute the land one day, he has to give me my share too even if I will have my own land. (George, youth from Purongo)

George would like to have a share of 'our land' as a member of his father's descent group, and he would also like to own 'my land' as an individual.

In the uncertainty about traditional, collective and customary tenure, some youth expressed that they wanted to own land with titles bearing their own names, which would be under their authority. 'If you want land in your own name, you must buy it because the customary land is not yours . . . I own a plot of land (30m x 15m), which I want to keep and register in my names since it is mine . . .' (Peter, Purongo). Yet even these dreams of individual land title were not divorced from considerations about generation. Like ancestral land, individual land often held assumptions about entrustment. In the case of 'A Disputed Land Sale', Mama Elisabeth had inherited a plot of freehold land, which she hoped would benefit her grandsons one day. Men were often concerned about their children: 'I want to buy my own land in the future, when I get money, and build a permanent house. I feel that I should farm more to raise money to pay school fees for my children . . . that is why I need to buy land' (Albert, Purongo youth). Daniel said he was delaying marriage because 'I first have to secure land for my future children's future'. Another young man declared: 'I hope that I will be able to buy my own land one day and my children can say, "this is my father's land". I would also love to say, "this is my land and not our land"' (Whyte and Acio 2017: 33). The irony is that for his children the land he bought will be 'ours' after he dies.

The alternative to ancestral land that young men aspired to was individual land – and not only young men had such aspirations, as the case of Stephen Langole (Chapter 1) showed. But this was out of reach for the majority and certainly for most women. A more feasible alternative that diminished dependence on older males was to borrow or hire land. This tactic had the advantage of flexibility from season to season for both parties and obviated the sale of ancestral land. Lending and renting land were extremely common, both for growing subsistence crops and for cultivating cash crops such as rice, sunflower and sugarcane. It is striking that borrowing and hiring land are seldom noticed in the discussions of customary and freehold tenure. Yet they provide ready alternatives for people affected by tensions and generational conflicts.

Betty, whom we met in Purongo, had left her marriage and returned to her paternal home with her three children from two different fathers. (Later the father of her sons came and took them with him to his village.) Her father was dead, and her paternal uncles and brothers were in charge of the customary land. One elder brother, Akena, who stayed on the land and assumed the authority of their father, gave her a house and a piece of land for digging. Her crops did not do well, and she went away to Kamdini, where she worked in a hotel for six months. When she returned home to Purongo, she found that another brother was using the acre of land that she had been given to use previously, so she did not bother her brother Akena for land again. Luckily, in 2014 she got a job with the water office on an eight-month contract. The following year, she joined the sub-county as a cleaner for seven months. Thereafter, she did not have a job for some time but kept looking for petty work such as digging for people in their gardens, sorting rice at the milling grounds and washing clothes for the traffic policemen (whose uniforms must look smart). By this time, Betty had moved from their home and was renting in the trading centre. She said that she did not have much interest in the land at home because her brother Akena was hiring it out to other people and had told her frankly that there was no land for her to dig. Instead, she combined efforts and money with a friend of hers and they hired an acre of land on which they agreed to plant ginger and popcorn. This was in addition to the petty jobs that she continued to look for.

Betty's story reveals the variety of livelihood strategies that many women employ. Even though she was able to earn a salary for periods of time, she did not give up farming. In her account, we also see the tenuousness of claims by daughters and sisters to use the land of their fathers and brothers. Although the

Acholi cultural organization Ker Kwaro Acholi (2008) specifically confirms the rights of daughters and sisters in ancestral land, their claims are less firm than those of sons and in practice may be ignored. Notably, it was Betty's brother, not her paternal uncles, who first welcomed and then excluded her in order to hire out their ancestral land to others. We have seen other examples in which brothers are reluctant to provide land for unmarried sisters while fathers are more accommodating. Juliet and her sisters provide a case in point: their brothers complained that they should stay with their husbands and use land there, while their fathers declared that all children, male and female, could use family land (Whyte and Acio 2017). Brothers with their own wives, often with growing families, are more concerned about keeping land use within the patrilineal line.

Just as Betty navigated among a variety of livelihood possibilities because she could not rely on access to land through her generational links, so did many men. We have considered these alternatives particularly in relation to the 'war generation' – those who came of age in the IDP camps (Whyte and Acio 2017). But as we saw in Chapter 1 on Multiplicity, even older men try to secure land through means other than generational claims. They may sell it again, or they may lose it in a land wrangle. But much of the land that is acquired through connections other than kinship will pass to the next genealogical generation, confirming the fundamental significance of consanguineal kinship for access to land.

Conclusion

In Acholi society, intimate governance of land is obviously a matter of relations between generations. Access to land passes from parents to children. This genealogical understanding of generation is prominent in everyday considerations and practices of allocating land for use. Filiation, being recognized as a child, is a precondition for most land access. In a patrilineal society, sons, and to some extent daughters, expect to get land through their fathers and his agnatic group. Yet this is by no means a hard and fast rule, as we have seen. Some children, like Daniel, gain land access through their mothers, even if their fathers are living. In the case that opened Part II of our book, Oyo was treated as a son and given land to use by a man from another clan. Such variation in genealogical patterns has long existed but has become far more pronounced in the wake of war, displacement and the decline of marriage.

The concept of historical generation reminds us that broader changes in political economy transform conditions for generational consciousness and interactions, thus affecting access to land. In the Acholi sub-region, such far-reaching shifts are attributed to the LRA war and camp internment. However, other factors may be in play as well – factors widespread throughout the country, including commercialization of land and impoverishment. Mistrust between generations is expressed generally in stereotypes about violent and disaffected youth and images of self-regarding, secretive elders. In specific cases, it often colours relations between sons and their fathers or fathers' brothers, between nephews and mothers' brothers, and between women and their partners' parents.

People have responded to these difficulties through another kind of generation: the creation of alternative modes of accessing land and livelihood. Mistrust arises in situations of dependence where reliability should prevail. By seeking to obtain 'my land' instead of depending on the elders for 'our land', and by borrowing or renting land, young people attempt to secure themselves in difficult situations. Yet most parents and children hope and reckon that their links will be confirmed through land.

Esther Acio is Lecturer at the Institute of Peace and Strategic Studies, Gulu University.

Lioba Lenhart was Associate Professor at the Institute of Peace and Strategy Studies, Gulu University (2009–2021), and is now Programme Advisor for Participatory Transformation of Land Conflicts in Northern Uganda, Civil Peace Service Programme, German Federal Ministry for Economic Cooperation and Development (BMZ) and GIZ.

Susan Reynolds Whyte is Professor at the Institute of Anthropology, University of Copenhagen.

References

Adoko, Judy, and Simon Levine. 2005. 'Land rights: Where We Are and Where We Need to Go'. Kampala: Land and Equity Movement in Uganda.
Alber, Erdmute, Sjaak van der Geest and Susan Reynolds Whyte (eds). 2008. *Generations in Africa: Connections and Conflicts*. Münster: LIT Verlag.
Atkinson, Ronald, and Julian Hopwood. 2013. *Land Conflict Monitoring and Mapping Tool for the Acholi Sub-region*. Kampala: United Nations Peacebuilding Programme in Uganda by Human Rights Focus.
Baines, Erin, and Lara Rosenoff Gauvin. 2014. 'Motherhood and Social Repair after War and Displacement in Northern Uganda', *Journal of Refugee Studies* 27(2): 282–300.
Cole, Jennifer, and Deborah Durham. 2006. 'Introduction: Age, Regeneration and the Intimate Politics of Globalization', in Jennifer Cole and Deborah Durham (eds), *Generations and Globalization: Youth, Age and Family in the New World Economy*. Bloomington: Indiana University Press, pp. 1–28.
Fortes, Meyer. 1949. *The Web of Kinship among the Tallensi*. Oxford: Oxford University Press.
———. 1969. *Kinship and the Social Order*. London: Routledge.
Girling, Frank Knowles. 1960. *The Acholi of Uganda*. London: Her Majesty's Stationery Office.
Heald, Suzette. 1989. *Controlling Anger: The Sociology of Gisu Violence*. Manchester: Manchester University Press.

Joireman, Sandra. 2018. 'Intergenerational Land Conflict in Northern Uganda: Children, Customary Law and Return Migration', *Africa* 88(1): 81–98.
Justice and Reconciliation Project. 2018. 'Reintegration of Children Born of War through Family Reunions'. Justice and Reconciliation Project website. Retrieved 10 April 2020 from: https://www.justiceandreconciliation.org/initiatives/child-reintegration/.
Ker Kwaro Acholi. 2008. *Principles and Practices of Customary Tenure in Acholiland.* Gulu.
LaFontaine, Jean. 1967. 'Homicide and Suicide among the Gisu', in Paul Bohannon (ed.), *African Homicide and Suicide.* New York: Atheneum, pp. 94–129.
Langole, Stephen. 2014. 'Urban Youth in Post-conflict Northern Uganda: Networking Livelihood Resources'. Ph.D. dissertation. Gulu: Gulu University.
Mannheim, Karl. 1952 [1927]. 'Essay on the Problem of Generations', in Pál Kecskeméti (ed.), *Essays on the Sociology of Knowledge.* New York: Routledge & Kegan Paul.
Meinert, Lotte, and Nanna Schneidermann. 2014. 'Making a Name: Young Musicians in Uganda Working on The Future', in Anne Line Dalsgaard, Martin Demant Frederiksen, Susanne Højlund and Lotte Meinert (eds), *Ethnographies of Youth and Temporality: Time Objectified.* Philadelphia: Temple University Press, pp. 153–74.
Meinert, Lotte, and Susan Reynolds Whyte. 2013. 'Creating the New Times: Reburials after War in Northern Uganda', in Dorthe Refslund Christensen and Rane Willerslev (eds), *Taming Time, Timing Death: Social Technologies and Ritual.* Farnham: Ashgate, pp. 175–93.
Obika, Julaina A., Ben Adol Otto, Sulayman Mpisi Babiiha and Michael Whyte. 2018. 'Contesting Claims to Gardens and Land: Gendered Practice in Post-war Northern Uganda', in Patrick Cockburn, Maja Hojer Bruun, Bjarke S. Risager and Mikkel Thorup (eds), *Contested Property Claims: What Disagreement Tells Us about Ownership.* London: Routledge, pp. 205–20.
Shipton, Parker. 2007. *The Nature of Entrustment: Intimacy, Exchange, and the Sacred in Africa.* New Haven: Yale University Press.
———. 2009. *Mortgaging the Ancestors: Ideologies of Attachment in Africa.* New Haven: Yale University Press.
Verma, Cecilie Lanken. 2013. 'Guns and Tricks: State Becoming and Political Subjectivity in War-torn Northern Uganda', Ph.D. dissertation. Copenhagen: University of Copenhagen.
Vorhölter, Julia. 2014. *Youth at the Crossroads: Discourses on Socio-Cultural Change in Post-War Northern Uganda.* Göttingen: Göttingen University Press.
Whyte, Susan Reynolds, and Esther Acio. 2017. 'Generations and Access to Land in Post-Conflict Northern Uganda: "Youth Have No Voice in Land Matters"', *African Studies Review* 60(3): 17–36.
Whyte, Susan Reynolds, and Henry Oboke. 2022. 'Gender Configurations and Suicide in Northern Uganda', in Lotte Meinert and Jens Seeberg (eds), *Configuring Contagion: Ethnographies of Biosocial Epidemics.* London: Berghahn, pp. 56–92.
Whyte et al. 2013. 'Remaining Internally Displaced: Missing Links to Human Security in Northern Uganda', *Journal of Refugee Studies* 26(2): 283–301.

Chapter 5

Gender

Julaina A. Obika and Hanne O. Mogensen

Atim and Awor: Sisters in Love and War

On a hot afternoon in February 2014, Atim sat quietly sipping a mug of water in the shade of her hut in Pader Town, a small urban centre that had been turned into an IDP camp during the war. Wandering around, Julaina, her research assistant Alice and her co-supervisor Hanne were looking for the fastest opportunity to get some shelter from the scorching sun; they were also looking for a woman to talk to about women's livelihood strategies in post-conflict northern Uganda, the topic of Julaina's Ph.D. project. Atim welcomed the researchers and asked them to join her in the shade. She also willingly started telling them about her life. She explained that she lived with her two sons (13 and 12 years old), who were still in school, and that her sister, Awor, and her five sons lived next to her. Atim also told them that she had two adult daughters (20 and 17 years old) and a son living elsewhere. The land where she was currently living was her late father's land, where she had grown up before she married and moved to her husband's home in Olam. Just before the war began, however, she divorced her husband and returned to her father's home. Her clan brothers had helped to bring her back home because her husband was violent and also, they argued, he had not completed paying bridewealth to the family.

During the interview, orange-red dust along with a few blue, black and white plastic bags strewn along the dirt roads were suddenly lifted into a whirlwind around the homestead. Atim and Alice continued talking while they both instinctively started shooing the whirlwind away with their hands. Julaina and

Hanne looked at each other puzzled and then started laughing: 'What are you doing?' Julaina asked 'Chasing away the *lapiru*', they said. In Acholi, the word *lapiru* refers to a whirlwind that is believed to have an evil spirit in it. While continuing their talk about the hardships of life, the two women discretely warded off 'the evil' whenever it started circling around the homestead.

Atim, 48, told the researchers that she had six sisters and no brothers. Her parents had both died during the war and left the land to them. Three of her sisters were still alive, two of them married and living elsewhere. She lived with Awor, her youngest sister, who separated from her husband during the war. The two sisters had been living well together, but a neighbour was trying to chase them off their land with the help of their clan brothers. These clan brothers and the neighbour claimed that women do not own land according to Acholi custom. The men argued that the two women should return to their husbands' homes, reconcile with them, and thereby gain access to their land. The case had been taken to the LC1 court but at that time was still unsettled.

Atim gave the impression of a woman living in dire conditions, relying on several small-scale businesses such as selling water. She paid 1,000 shillings per month (approx. USD 0.3) for access to a borehole, which was about 300 meters from her home. She would collect about five jerrycans a day and sell them for 300 shillings in the town during the dry season, and 200 shillings in the rainy season. She had also borrowed some land at a distance from her home where she planted potatoes and cassava, crops that can stay for long in the garden without her going to tend them regularly. Sometimes she tried to make bricks and had her children help her. She and Awor helped each other in times of sickness, but they did not trust each other with money. 'In money issues, there are no relatives [to help],' she said, but in any case, she also usually spent the money right away when she had any.

Julaina and Alice went to Atim's home several times after that first meeting, but for some time they were not successful in finding her. They only managed to find her at home again in March 2015. She said: 'I know that you have been checking on me and not finding me at home, but it is because I am doing this business that takes me up to Lira.' In Lira, a neighbouring district, she bought smoked fish that she sold at the main market in Pader. She was happy to see Alice and Julaina again. She called Alice 'my daughter' and told her that she felt relieved when the researchers came and talked to her about her land issues.

The conflict with the neighbour and clan brothers had been resolved. Clan elders who were the allies of the neighbour had told the clan brothers: 'Leave these women alone', which they did. Instead Atim was now fighting with her sister, Awor. Awor had tried to stop Atim's son from constructing his hut on the land. This prompted Atim to think that Awor was telling her that her son's future was not on that land. 'So, my problem now is that I do not know where I am going to put my boys. If they were girls, they would get married and go away,'

Atim said. 'I am not feeling so secure because I am staying with someone who is just pretending to love me, but I do not know what she is thinking in her heart.' The clan elders had been called once more to settle the issue between the sisters. They told them to stay peacefully together, and one elder cautioned them using a well-known Acholi proverb about a mother who had two children. She served them food on one plate, hoping that they would share it equally. The problem was that one of the children was greedy and ate very fast, and the other child suffered for it. The only choice that mother had was to divide the food equally on two separate plates. Likewise, the elders warned that if the two sisters did not live together peacefully on the land, then the next time they were called to settle a problem, they would divide the land equally between the two of them, not forgetting the share of the other two sisters who did not live there.

The sisters promised to try to live well together, and then the clan members warned them about another impending threat to their land. The Town Council was coming up with new plans for developing the town, which all the residents and landowners had to comply with in the very near future or else risk losing their land. The new plans included plotting and registering land as well as tearing down temporary structures, including grass-thatched houses, and putting up permanent structures. Atim pointed to the grass-thatched houses in her compound, including a new temporary structure that she had just constructed. She did not have money to put up the so-called permanent structures that the Town Council was demanding.

After the clan meeting, Atim together with her sister Awor and their elder sister who lived in Soroti had a discussion about how to safeguard their land. The sisters came up with a plan. They decided to cement their mother's grave that had previously been a mound of dirt behind one of Atim's huts. The elder sister, who was somewhat well off, provided all the materials and paid labourers to cement their mother's grave in an attempt to identify the land as theirs. In January 2016, during the TrustLand Project annual workshop, Julaina presented Atim's case and was told by one of the members of local government in Gulu (who was invited to the workshop) that graves within the town may not be accepted by the Town Council, and that the sisters would face problems in the future if they relied on this grave as evidence of their land ownership. They may even be asked to remove it at some point.

During their visit in March 2015, the researchers also learnt new information about Atim's family. Her three children from her first marriage were living with their father. Her two teenage sons staying with her were from a second 'marriage' (to a man with whom she had cohabited during the war).

In February 2016, exactly two years after their first meeting, Atim informed Julaina and Alice that the problem between herself and her sister Awor had escalated. Awor's son attacked Atim (he claimed he was sent by his mother), and Awor had referred to Atim as being a witch. Atim contacted the police and the

LC1 chairman, but they never came to her rescue. She then decided to contact the clan members again. With the aid of his mobile phone, the clan leader quickly gathered a number of young clan brothers. At the clan meeting, Awor's son asked to be forgiven for what he had done to Atim and told the clan that he had attempted to kill her because he just wanted his mother Awor to have some peace.

After listening to both sides, the clan elders had advised both sisters to move away from the land because it was clear that they could not live together peacefully. Awor moved away almost immediately. Before Pader became a district, when land there was still cheap, she had bought a small piece of land. Atim, however, did not move. She was not against moving but needed support and had appealed to her clan brothers to find her some land somewhere and build her a house. 'I would open my teeth to smile, but I really had problems. I would go to bed at night, but I would not sleep,' she said.

During the interview, Julaina and Alice both had the impression that Atim was doing much better than when they had first met her. She looked stronger and less tired than before. She was very open, would crack jokes and talked about her *awaro*, a small retail business between Lira and Pader districts. At the end of their visit, she gave Julaina and Alice quite a lot of groundnuts and lapena (pigeon peas) to share between them. Even when they tried to object to the large quantities, she told them sternly that children do not refuse what their mother gives them when they come to visit her.

The researcher's frequent visits, even when they did not find her at home, meant a great deal to Atim and made her open up more. She started giving information that she had previously been withholding from them. She told them that her second husband – the father of the two youngest boys – was a soldier who went to Somalia to fight and did not come back. Atim had no idea where he was; his phone had been switched off, but she did not think that he was dead. He had probably just abandoned them. She told the researchers that the land on which she lived – and which she had always referred to as her father's land – was actually land that belonged to her father's clan brother. More precisely: her father's brother was a government worker and was 'given' this land by a friend. When Atim's father died, his clan brother inherited her mother, so Atim and her sisters grew up on this land.

When her father's brother died, the son of the man who had 'given' the land to her father's brother tried to reclaim it. The LC was involved. They concluded that the trees and the graves on the land were evidence that Atim's family had stayed on the land for a long time and therefore owned the land. A compromise was made. The original owner's son took back part of the land that didn't include Atim's homestead, the graves and the trees. But for this reason, Atim cannot sell the land. This land is still governed under customary rules of tenure, hence Atim's involvement of clan members whenever there is a problem with the land. But at the same time, being situated in the heart of Pader Town, it has a different set of formal rules of land tenure under the Town Council.

The researchers also learnt that the older sister who lived in Soroti (who organized for their mother's grave to be cemented) now seemed to be conniving with clan brothers in trying to claim ownership of the land. This sister felt that she had invested a lot in the land, not only cementing their mother's grave but also giving financial support whenever meetings were called to resolve conflicts over the land. She thought that she should be given rights over the land because Atim and Awor were fighting constantly and she was herself in a better financial position to develop the land (for example by building permanent structures).

In March 2016, Alice made a return visit to see Atim and talked to her briefly. She was told that the clan members had not yet come to evict her from the land, but her elder sister who lived in Soroti had asked why she had not yet left. When she got the call from her elder sister, Atim had gone to seek advice from their clan leader who had told her to first stay on the land as they sorted things out but reminded her that she could not stay indefinitely. To Atim, this meant that the clan leader was siding with her elder sister. Atim told Alice about the time she argued with her elder sister about the ownership of the land. Her sister had said: 'This land was going to be taken from us by the son of the man who gave it to our father's clan brother. I am the one who went to court and recovered it.' Atim had then replied: 'When you went to court, did you then tell the court that you owned this land?' Her sister had gone silent, so Atim continued: 'Do not think that this land belongs to you only. Our father's property belongs to all of us, but it is only that we could not all go to stand in court, which is why we asked you to stand on our behalf. We did not say that you should own the land.' Atim believed that her sister hated her for saying this so boldly and that she had therefore become the ally of Awor, who had for a long time been trying to chase Atim off the land.

Atim told Alice that she and Awor were now completely estranged. They were doing the same small business in Pader market but would 'sit with their backs to each other' as if they were not sisters. Julaina had been keeping in touch with Alice by phone and asked her to do her best to track down Awor, especially if she was at the market. Alice did manage to find Awor, who agreed to take Alice to her home.

According to Awor, the conflict between the sisters was not so much about land but about their lack of respect for each other as sisters. As the youngest sister, she said, she should have been the one to look after their late father's homestead. In Acholi culture, she said, it is the youngest child who inherits the homestead. This was the first time that the researchers had heard that it was not the youngest son but the youngest child who should inherit the homestead.

Awor now stayed on the small plot that she had purchased during the war, but she still had access to gardens at her former husband's home because she was taking care of their children. She said:

Even if I have separated with my husband, I still go to his land to dig because I need to secure land for my children since they are all boys. That was the land I was using before going to the camp. The moment you leave it redundant, other relatives will occupy it, and it will be very hard to recover it.

She added that: 'For me I am happy here, so I leave all those matters with the other land in the hands of the elders.' She did not know what Atim was planning to do:

Personally I cannot go to ask her, but I think she does not have a place to go, because her husband took all the children. If she had come back to her father's place with the children, then she could now have gone to claim land at her husband's home in the name of her children.

Of What Is This a Case?

In this chapter, we focus on the changing relationships between men, women and land. We show that gender, as a lens for studying land, can help us challenge notions of 'rights' and 'ownership' and hence get a better grasp of the complex land tenure systems in Acholi today (see Nakayi 2013; Kobusingye, Van Leeuwen and Van Dijk 2016 for discussions on complex land tenure systems in Acholi society). Scrutinizing land conflicts from the point of view of gender relations furthermore helps us catch sight of some of the important changes that took place in Acholi society during and after the war.

Many debates on customary land and women's land rights in Sub-Saharan Africa focus on gender-differentiated access to land. It has been noted that women undertake more than 75 per cent of agricultural work and yet own less than 10 per cent of the land (Behrman, Meinzen-Dick and Quisumbing 2012). Women's embeddedness in the household without autonomous access to property is often highlighted (Nussbaum 1999). In patrilineal societies, women's relationship to land is shaped by kinship structures and virilocal marriage practices. Women derive their rights to land through male relations, first their father or brothers and later (ideally) the husband, therefore making the social costs of challenging male authority over property high (Khadiagala 2002; Awumbila and Tsikata 2010). Men have the primary rights (to transfer, bequeath or dispose), and women only have secondary rights of use of land (Rose 2002; Whitehead and Tsikata 2003; Paradza 2011). Women are often portrayed as victims of uncertainty and instability in their difficulty securing access to land in the case of polygyny, divorce or death of a husband (Joireman 2008).

All in all, women are usually represented as vulnerable in terms of rights to land, in Sub-Saharan Africa generally, and in post-conflict northern Uganda in particular. The case of Atim and Awor shows us that women who lack links to male relatives, in particular husbands and fathers, are indeed faced with challenges. But their case also shows us that they work hard to secure land for themselves and their children using a broad range of strategies. In the process of doing so, conflicts arise not only between men and women but amongst women themselves. We will argue that the case of Atim and Awor is a concrete instance of a more abstract principle: that the cultivation of relationships is a means to access land. Here and in other cases, there are various 'unconventional' ways in which women create links to others to obtain resources and to access land. These kinds of strategies are part of the complex land tenure systems in Acholi society today (Göttsches 2013).

Changing Gender Relations

The displacement period marked a dramatic change in the social landscape in northern Uganda. Relations between men and women, youth and elders became fraught with new kinds of tensions and contradictions (Mergelsberg 2012). The process of return and reintegration has furthermore been challenged by population growth, weak governance systems, commoditization of land and an increasing failure of the customary tenure system to accommodate landless people. Northern Uganda has witnessed an increase in the number of widows, orphans and single mothers and created new types of partnership or 'male-female alliances', many female-headed households and ultimately an increasing number of people, in particular women, no longer embedded in the patrilineal kinship structure who are ultimately 'landless'.

Patrilineal kinship and land tenure systems are known from all over Sub-Saharan Africa and have frequently been described by anthropologists, Girling (1960) being the most commonly referred to in relation to the Acholi. In societies based on patrilineal kinship systems, a daughter is expected to leave her natal home and join her husband's family. She and her children will access land through her husband. Before marrying, she cultivates gardens with the household at her natal home. A young man is given his own piece of land after he marries and establishes his own household. Women obtain full access to their husbands' land as their position shifts from clan wives to mothers of clan children. A widow will look after her husband's estate, holding it in trust for her children until they are grown. It is culturally accepted and even expected that a woman who divorces or separates from her husband will find refuge at her natal home, where her brothers will give her land on which to farm and nurture her children, until they, ideally, return to their father's home. In the past, wives of a household possessed ownership rights in food crops under the general authority of the household head, who in turn possessed ownership rights to cattle and cash crops – for example, cotton (Girling 1960).

The patrilineal kinship ideology is accompanied by a particular view on male and female roles, as described by both Girling and later Dolan, who interviewed people (both men and women) in the camps on their notions of male and female roles. According to Dolan's informants, the woman is subordinate to the man, and a wife is the property of the husband. She loses her own clan identity on marriage but does not fully assume the clan identity of her husband and is viewed as an outsider not to be trusted, at least not until much later when she has grown children (Girling 1960: 193; Finnström 2008).

As Dolan (2009: 196) points out, socialization into masculinity begins at a very early age, but its full achievement is impossible without making the transition to adulthood by way of marriage. It is not sufficient to be an economic provider. A man must be a married provider, and marriage cannot take place without payment of bridewealth. Men are taught that they should aspire to and judge themselves by this transition to adulthood through marriage, and both state and society judge and assess them against it (Dolan 2009: 196). Marriage through the payment of bridewealth was, however, practically impossible during the years of encampment, and as a result many people were 'ambiguously' married or simply co-habiting. According to Girling (1960: 167), there have always been men who were too poor to pay bridewealth, but during and after the war it was the case for the vast majority of men (Finnström 2008; Dolan 2009: 199). During the war, most men were prevented from fulfilling expectations of them, both as married men and as providers. Many men simply disappeared and left women to manage on their own. Whyte and colleagues (2013) discuss the missing links of inhabitants in former camps turned into trading centres after the conflict had ended. Many of those who had remained in the former camps had no relatives with land to return to, and many of them were women with children, who had lost husbands or partners, who were 'ambiguously married' and had not become incorporated into their husband's lineage, or who were now rejected by them and had no brothers or fathers with land to which they could return. They remained 'internally displaced', stuck in a no-man's land between fathers and husbands. The same may be said of Awor and Atim, who remained in Pader even after the war. The land on which they lived had belonged to a clan brother of their father, but they had both settled on their husbands' land before the war. Their husbands were still alive but had become irresponsible and badly behaved during the war, and they had no desire (or possibility) to return to them.

Social ties suffered in various ways during the war and the years of encampment, but of particular importance for this chapter is the fact that those years also changed the relationship and power balance between men and women considerably. Dolan shows how the dynamics of violation and debilitation caused a sense of humiliation and a collapse of masculinity. Unable to live up to the model of an adult man being a married provider, which involved relationships of power over women and youth, and neither offered nor allowed to develop any recognized alternative, they experienced a social and often physical impotence. In the face of this collapse of their own masculinity, some resorted to acts of violence – against themselves, through alcohol abuse and suicide, but also against others, through domestic violence, mob justice or by joining armed forces, whether government or rebel (2009: 191). Awor bought a small plot of land during the war, when her husband started mistreating her, and Atim also left her first husband during the war due to his mistreatment. Her second 'husband' abandoned her and their two sons. She did not know why, nor where he was, but she heard that he may have joined armed forces.

Women were often victims of the violence of men, but they were also, even more than was the case for men, subject to an array of supportive interventions in northern Uganda during and after the conflict (see Branch 2011). While men saw their authority and status within Acholi society wane, women saw theirs rise in the camps. Because many men had died, joined armed organizations, abandoned their wives, or turned to alcohol abuse, women were left with the primary responsibility of providing for their families. Food rations and non-food item distributions were inadequate, so women were faced with the need to earn money to feed their families and to buy basics such as soap and clothes.

Displacement caused significant physical hardship and suffering for women, but it also brought women together in new ways. Before displacement, women lived in relatively isolated family homesteads. As a middle-aged woman in Gulu Town reported to Branch: 'we [women] were very far apart in the village. We did not have groups or come together like we do now' (Branch 2011: 138). Combined with resources provided by government and international agencies, the camps created the context in which women could forge new forms of association, mostly for economic empowerment, such as loan schemes, but also for cultural activities. These groups became spaces for women to come together and discuss problems (ibid.). Women gained access to loans both individually and collectively. They could run small businesses and retain possession over produce and save the money. They achieved new education through training by NGOs and government on health and other issues. Much of it was part of the struggle to feed the family in the camps, but many women saw these developments as positive. Alongside all this, discourses on women's rights became increasingly strong (ibid.: 139). Women's organizations started presenting a vision of peace, built not on normalization but on the demand for increasing political and social inclusion of women (ibid.). Branch also reports widespread accusations by men that women's rights are to blame for increased domestic violence (ibid.: 141), and he notes that women whom he interviewed during encampment and in the early phases of resettlement declared their hope that their husbands would accept their new economic and political roles back in the village but recognized that this might not be the case (ibid.: 174).

Dolan reminds us to be wary of the stereotypes of men as idle heavy drinkers with no economic initiative. Some men have moved into what were previously regarded as women's areas of activity. Male groups have sought to create some economic enterprise against all odds, and other men in humble ways take on menial tasks for the sake of their family's survival (Dolan 2009: 204). But in other ways, gender relations *have* changed. Obika's work (2021), which will be discussed below, shows that women have indeed brought their experience from the years of encampment with them and continue to make use of their new networks and of a broad range of livelihood strategies whether they resettled in the village or remained in trading centres. The 'missing links' did not turn out to be as disastrous for women as anticipated. One of the things they had learned in camps was indeed how to make other kinds of links.

Who Owns Land? Claims and Counterclaims

Since Ester Boserup's publication of *Women's Role in Economic Development* (1970), women have often been at the centre of analysis, but they have usually been portrayed as holding powerless positions in terms of land (see Nussbaum 1999). Uganda has been praised for having taken critical steps towards improving women's property rights, including the 1995 Constitution, which is said to be one of the most gender-neutral both in content and language with regard to property rights in Sub-Saharan Africa, including land rights (Joireman 2007; Rugadya in Doss et al. 2012). However, even if women's land rights are protected under statutory law, they may not be guaranteed under customary law and cultural practices. Customary systems often allow for certain flexibility, for various forms of access, and for movement of land between different users (Ossome 2014). However, Peters (2004, 2009) warns us to be wary of discourses on this 'flexibility', which often hide realities of unequal power relations. In the case of Atim and Awor, they both claimed land that they referred to as their father's land but which it was later revealed was given (or even lent) to their father (actually their father's clan brother, who inherited their mother) by his friend. The clan elders did not contest their claim to the land until the two sisters started fighting each other, both trying to secure land for their sons whose fathers were absent. Only then, according to Atim, did the clan elders team up with the oldest sister of Atim and Awor to support her in trying to claim ownership.

In another case from Obika's fieldwork, two widowed women, Akech and Apiyo, who were neighbours but not related, had ended up in a conflict over land that they both claimed a right over through the notion of 'first-comer' (see Lentz 2005 and Chapter 6, this volume, for a discussion of first-comers). Their husbands, who had both died during the war, had been friends. One of them had been a first-comer to the land but had at some stage invited his friend to stay on the land, and then the war came. Both women argued for their husband's status as first-comer, their stories contradicting each other. Both had sons, but Apiyo's was present on the land and supported her to build a case against Akech, whereas

Akech's son was not. Unfortunately for his mother, once he returned, Akech's son's express interest was in selling off the land for a project of his elsewhere. If he had succeeded in doing so, this might have brought an end to the conflict but also jeopardized his mother's attempt to secure land for him and his children. Obika (2021) found that young men often expressed very little interest in staying on family land that was under contestation. Instead, they tried to reason with or convince their elders (particularly mothers) to buy land (where possible) or just move elsewhere.

To understand the impact of both statutory and customary law and gendered power relations, we need to look at these micro-level negotiations over access and use of land. Being married does not necessarily guarantee access to land or security of tenure, and being a single mother does not necessarily translate into tenure insecurity. A common way of phrasing women's relationship to land in Acholi is: 'Women do not own land.' Even though this is true, in reality (as we have seen in previous chapters) neither do men when it comes to customary ancestral land. Land is held in trust by clans on behalf of multiple users, claimants and rights' holders (Adoko and Levine 2005; Hopwood 2015). The concept of 'ownership' does not translate neatly into Acholi, as we saw in Chapter 2, and we lose sight of gendered power relations and what is happening on the ground if we translate various forms of land tenure and negotiations over these into 'one-dimensional' ownership debates (Shipton and Goheen 1992).

A lot of work has already been done on gender and land in Africa, including: land tenure reforms (Yngstrom 2002; Manji 2003; Jirira and Halimana 2008) and the role of law (Manji 2001); large-scale land grabs (Chu 2011; Behrman, Meinzen-Dick and Quisumbing 2012); land rights (Yngstrom 2002; Whitehead and Tsikata 2003); inequalities in customary land tenure systems (Peters 2004; Ossome 2014); and labour and capital accumulation (Berry 1989; Tsikata 2010). Very little research has, however, been done on small-scale land grabs and conflicts between kith and kin and neighbours. Women's lesser access to certain spaces has been studied extensively, but less attention has been given to how they navigate those limited spaces to their own benefit. Hopwood (2015: 389–90) suggests that instead of looking at *rights*, we should pay closer attention to the dynamic flow of *claims* and counterclaims that are being made in the name of custom. Claims are, for example, made in the name of custom for returning to one's father's land, for securing land for one's children, through the cementing of a grave, or through claims of being a first-comer. In other words, we need to pay attention not only to customary law and ownership, but also to how men and women manage, use and access land and how also women may place their mark on land for several years and generations.

Ribot and Peluso (2003: 153) define access as 'the ability to benefit from things – including material objects, persons, institutions and symbols', which in this context suggests that women's access to land is different to, but not necessarily less than, that of men. Neither men nor women constitute homogenous categories. There is a big difference between 'the ability to benefit from things' as a young newly married woman, a widow with grown children, a divorced woman who has returned to her brother's home, or a single woman who is a head of household and managing on her own. Obika (2021) found that few young, newly married women claimed to be involved in any kind of decisions concerning land or land conflict, whereas most middle-aged and older women were often directly involved in land governance and conflicts over land, as victims or (in the view of others) as perpetrators, or as witnesses due to their long experience cultivating land in the area, with different and sometimes similar experiences to their male counterparts. As mentioned above, young men also tend to shy away from land conflicts. Where ownership of the land is in doubt and young men's (e.g. uterine nephews) possibilities for continuity on the land is uncertain, they tend to look for projects of their own, as we see in the case of Akech's son.

Ossome suggests that women's claims to land are stronger and more diverse than usually presented, their strength lying precisely in the social embeddedness that has otherwise often been seen as the reason for women's lack of rights (Ossome 2014). Based on her fieldwork in Acholi, Obika (2021) likewise demonstrates the diversity of women's land claims (and counterclaims) within a socially embedded customary tenure system and how women are able to negotiate, manoeuvre and find pathways to land access in various ways, exactly because they are good at 'cultivating' not only land but also relationships, benefiting as well from the plurality of institutions involved in conflict resolution (see Chapter 3 on Conflicts). We will now move on to discuss this.

How to Cultivate Relationships around Land

A woman once told Holly Porter, who did research on rape in northern Uganda, that the image of a man being powerful is a 'myth'. The power of a man, this woman insisted, is embedded in his relatives, particularly his mother. Despite the narrative of the powerful and proud African man who suppresses his wife, beats his children and determines his destiny, individual men, like women, Porter reminds us, have very little freedom to make independent decisions. They must submit to the wishes of their relatives (Porter 2017: 42). Obika (2021) argues that 'cultivating' relationships in order to 'hold' land takes as much work and effort, if not more, than cultivating the land – preparing, ploughing and planting, weeding and harvesting. And women often put more effort into it than do men.

Akech, for example, whose conflict with her neighbour Apiyo was referred to above, had several fields that she had cultivated when she was younger but not anymore due to old age and physical weakness. Instead, she had given it to her daughters, who used part of it to plant their crops to supplement what they produced from the land they had at their marital homes. She also gave some fields to a friend who had requested her to let him grow his *simsim* on the land that she was not currently using. She agreed to help him because he too may have had his own challenges of accessing land at his ancestral home, but also, this was a way of preventing others from grabbing it and a way of garnering support from others when contesting her claim over the land before various legal and social fora (Obika et al. 2018). She was cultivating relationships using her land and maintaining access through other people's support. She may not officially have been the 'owner' of the land, but she was the one who proved able to control it. In the case of Atim and Awor, we may say that it was their lack of ability to 'cultivate' their own relationship that ultimately had them ordered off their father's land. If they had managed to stay on good terms the clan elders would have left the land for them, even though they were constantly reminded that they were 'daughters who had returned home'. Again, it was a question, not of 'customary law' but of the women's ability to 'cultivate' relationships. Women with many sons, powerful friends, a savings scheme and a well-functioning women's group and other social networks stand a good chance of putting up a fight for their land.

Just as there is seasonality to the cultivation of land, so is there to the cultivation of relationships. During the planting season, fields became defined plots of bounded land and hence of conflicts with relatives and neighbours. During the dry season, fields ceased to exist, in a way, and the land became an unbounded mass. The dry season was a time for carrying out repairs of huts and granaries – and also of relationships. An exception was that domestic violence seemed to increase after harvest, since some men would attempt to sell off the harvest for their personal use. During the dry season, more women went back to their natal homes (or were sent back due to conflicts with husbands), but it did not stop them from working. Many were engaged in small businesses and saving schemes at their natal home, cultivating their relationships there but returning to their husband and his land once the planting season returned. The process of accessing land was for many of them not linear but cyclical, and displacement, we may say, is not always about discontinuity and separation but also about continuity and seasonality, both in rural areas and in town, where some activities also decline during heavy agricultural seasons.

Megan Göttsches (2013), who carried out a study of widows and livelihood in northern Uganda, also found that access to land through friends, neighbours and women's groups was common. She refers to these non-traditional forms of land tenure as 'complex tenure', a term that we adopt to capture the multi-pronged informal pathways taken by women to gain and safeguard access to land and pursue various livelihood strategies in addition to the cultivation of crops on the customary land of husbands, fathers and brothers. In this, women and youth resemble one another, as shown in Chapter 4 on Generations.

Complex Tenure: Livelihood and Land

Most women in rural districts in northern Uganda still depend on land, but their effort to safeguard their land, or at least their access to land, is inextricably tied to their other livelihood strategies. What we begin to see is a pattern of women who move within and between residences (natal, marital and others) to safeguard not only their own but also their children's access to land. Awor moved between her former husband's land, the plot she had purchased herself during the war and (at least in the beginning of Obika's fieldwork) her father's land. She also did small-scale business in the market of Pader Town. Atim had fewer plots of land to move between, though she did at some stage borrow land to cultivate. She had a broad range of livelihood strategies in addition to cultivating her friend's land. She had a small-scale business selling water and later, also, dried fish.

Women's livelihood strategies changed during and after the war and encampment, with many women now doing what used to be considered men's work. As Angee, a woman in her forties told Obika,

> a woman has many things she should do in the home: cooking, farming, smearing the floor of her hut [with cow dung or mud], taking care of visitors, and welcoming people. But these days women do many other things in addition to this. They burn bricks, make granaries and make charcoal, all of which used to be the work of men.

Angee told Obika, as did many other women, that when the war started men became drunkards. If women had remained in the home as they usually did before the war, children would have been neglected and would have slept hungry. Today, she added, some men continue to misbehave, and even the payment of school fees has become women's responsibility. Other women mentioned their participation in stone quarrying, in small non-agricultural businesses, and even about their participation in setting traps and hunting wild animals, which they would then sell on markets. They also talked of renting and borrowing land instead of, or in addition to, cultivating the land of husbands or kin, something that is often overlooked in the literature. It is important to note that even though women clearly experience carrying the largest responsibilities for the well-being of the family, many men are faced with the same challenges of accessing land in various places and having to combine farming with other kinds of livelihood strategies.

Navigating Trust and Access: The Fabric of Intimate Governance

We have suggested that cultivating relationships is an important part of gaining and maintaining access to customary land in post-war Acholi. Manoeuvring and weaving pathways is part of everyday life for men and women alike, in a context where access to land is not a given and belonging to a certain piece of land is, for many, uncertain. Cultivating relationships necessarily raises a question about land access: whom do I trust? As we saw in the case of Atim, Awor and their elder sister, trust and mistrust flowed back and forth between them. Sometimes they were forming alliances and at other times they were living as intimate enemies (Theidon 2006), eventually accusing each other of witchcraft. As Geschiere (2013) suggests, intimacy and trust are relational and often go together with witchcraft or accusations thereof. Obika (2021) found that witchcraft accusations are often intertwined with land conflicts being fought among people closely related (Heald 1989; Ciekawy and Geschiere 1998) and are referred to as the 'dark side of kinship' (Leistner 2014).

We suggest that the constant tensions, pushing and pulling, claims and counterclaims between sisters, brothers, elders and youth, neighbours and kith and kin – these intimate allies/enemies – are the very fabric on which the negotiation and contestation of customary land is built. We have found that whom one trusts today is not necessarily an ally tomorrow, a situation that has come to resemble what Meinert (2015) refers to as 'tricky trust'. Neither security of access nor trust is absolute. It is not a matter of either/or but of more or less, and security requires a continuing effort through the cultivation of relationships. Cultivating relationships is a process of building and increasing trust, which in turn increases one's guarantee of holding on to one's land or at the very least having access to it.

Conclusion

A substantial part of the academic literature on Africa has focused on the vulnerability and victimhood of women after prolonged violent conflict. Without dismissing the mounting evidence of suffering and hardship of women during the conflict in northern Uganda, it also seems to be the case, as Göttsches (2013) has argued, that violent reshuffling of society during and after armed conflict may create novel opportunities, where the current and former gender balance can be re-addressed and renegotiated (see also Denov and Gervais 2007; Utas 2005). It also seems that the cultivation of relationships is crucial to the continued process of safeguarding land – and that women often put more effort into the cultivation of relationships than men do. Our cases have focused on women, not to dismiss men's experiences of land tenure insecurity but to highlight how different categories of women are able to navigate small spaces of land access, precisely because they are relegated to access land through men under customary rules and norms.

Julaina A. Obika, Ph.D., is Senior Lecturer at the Institute of Peace and Strategic Studies of Gulu University in northern Uganda.

Hanne O. Mogensen, Ph.D., is Associate Professor at the Institute of Anthropology, University of Copenhagen.

References

Adoko, Judy, and Simon Levine. 2005. *Land Rights: Where We Are and Where We Need to Go*. Kampala: Land and Equity Movement in Uganda (LEMU).

Awumbila, Mariama, and Dzodzi A. Tsikata. 2010. 'Economic Liberalisation, Changing Resource Tenures and Gendered Livelihoods: A Study of Small-Scale Gold Mining and Mangrove Exploitation in Rural Ghana', in Dzodzi A. Tsikata and Pamela Golah (eds), *Land Tenure, Gender and Globalisation Research and Analysis from Africa, Asia and Latin America*. Ottawa: IDRC, pp. 99–142.

Behrman, Julia A., Ruth Meinzen-Dick and Agnes R. Quisumbing. 2012. 'The Gender Implications of Large-Scale Land Deals', *The Journal of Peasant Studies* 39(1): 49–79.

Berry, Sara. 1989. 'Social Institutions and Access to Resources', *Africa* 59(1): 41–55.

Boserup, Ester. 1970. *Women's Role in Economic Development*. London and New York: Earthscan.

Branch, Adam. 2011. *Displacing Human Rights: War and Intervention in Northern Uganda*. Oxford: Oxford University Press.

Chu, Jessica. 2011. 'Gender and "Land Grabbing" in Sub-Saharan Africa: Women's Land Rights and Customary Land Tenure', *Development* 54(1): 35–39.

Ciekawy, Diane, and Peter Geschiere. 1998. 'Containing Witchcraft: Conflicting Scenarios in Postcolonial Africa', *African Studies Review* 41(3): 1–14.

Denov, Myriam, and Christine Gervais. 2007. 'Negotiating (In)security: Agency, Resistance, and Resourcefulness Among Girls Formerly Associated with Sierra Leone's Revolutionary United Front', *Signs* 32(4): 885–910.

Dolan, Chris. 2009. *Social Torture: The Case of Northern Uganda, 1986–2006*. New York: Berghahn Books.

Doss, C., et al. 2012. 'Women, Marriage and Asset Inheritance in Uganda', *Development Policy Review* 30(5): 597–616.

Finnström, Sverker. 2008. *Living with Bad Surroundings: War, History and Everyday Moments in Northern Uganda*. Durham: Duke University Press.

Geschiere, Peter. 2013. *Witchcraft, Intimacy and Trust: Africa in Comparison*. Chicago: University of Chicago Press.

Girling, Frank Knowles. 1960. *The Acholi of Uganda*. London: Her Majesty's Stationary Office.

Göttsches, Megan S. 2013. 'Access to Land, Securing a Livelihood and Gender Role Renegotiation: A Case Study of Widows in Northern Uganda', *Journal of Peace and Security Studies* 1: 28–48.

Heald, Suzette. 1989. *Controlling Anger: The Sociology of Gisu Violence*. Manchester: Manchester University Press.

Hopwood, Julian. 2015. 'Women's Land Claims in the Acholi Region of Northern Uganda: What Can Be Learned from What is Contested', *International Journal on Minority and Group Rights* 22: 387–409.

Jirira, Kwanele O., and Charles M. Halimana. 2008. *A Gender Audit of Women and Land Rights in Zimbabwe*. Harare: Zimbabwe Women's Resource Centre and Network.

Joireman, Sandra Fullerton. 2007. 'Enforcing New Property Rights in Sub-Saharan Africa: The Ugandan Constitution and the 1998 Land Act', *Comparative Politics* 39(4): 463–80.

———. 2008. 'The Mystery of Capital Formation in Sub-Saharan Africa: Women, Property Rights and Customary Law', *World Development* 36(7): 1233–46.

Khadiagala, Lynn S. 2002. 'Justice and Power in the Adjudication of Women's Property Rights in Uganda', *Africa Today* 49(2): 101–21.
Kobusingye, Doreen Nancy, Mathijs van Leeuwen and Han van Dijk. 2016. 'Where Do I Report My Land Dispute? The Impact of Institutional Proliferation on Land Governance in Post-Conflict Northern Uganda', *The Journal of Legal Pluralism and Unofficial Law* 48(2): 238–55.
Leistner, Erich. 2014. 'Witchcraft and African Development', *African Security Review* 23(1): 53–77.
Lentz, Carole. 2005. 'First Comers and Late-Comers: The Role of Narratives in Land Claims', in Sandra Evers, Marja Spierenburg and Harry Wells (eds), *Competing Jurisdictions: Settling Land Claims in Africa*. Leiden: Brill, pp. 157–80.
Manji, Ambereena. 2001. 'Land Reform in the Shadow of the State: The Implementation of New Land Laws in Sub-Saharan Africa', *Third World Quarterly* 22(3): 327–42.
———. 2003. 'Capital, Labour and Land Relations in Africa: A Gender Analysis of the World Bank's Policy Research Report on Land Institutions and Land Policy', *Third World Quarterly* 24(1): 97–114.
Meinert, Lotte. 2015. 'Tricky Trust: Distrust as a Point of Departure and Trust as a Social Achievement in Uganda', in Sune Liisberg, Esther Oluffa Pedersen and Anne Line Dalsgaard (eds), *Anthropology and Philosophy: Dialogues on Trust and Hope*. London: Berghahn Books, pp. 118–33.
Mergelsberg, Ben. 2012. 'The Displaced Family: Moral Imaginations and Social Control in Pabbo, Northern Uganda', *Journal of Eastern African Studies* 6(1): 64–80.
Nakayi, Rose. 2013. 'The Role of Local Council Courts and Traditional Institutions in Resolving Land Disputes in Post-Conflict Northern Uganda', *Malawi Law Journal* 7: 119–38.
Nussbaum, Martha. 1999. 'Women and Equality: The Capabilities Approach', *International Labour Review* 138(3): 227–45.
Obika, Julaina A. 2021. 'Women Navigating Access: Governing Land (Conflicts) in the Acholi Sub-region', Ph.D. dissertation. Gulu: Gulu University.
Obika, J. A., et al. 2018. 'Contesting Claims to Gardens and Land: Gendered Practice in Post-War Northern Uganda', in Maja Hojer Bruun, Patrick J. L. Cockburn, Bjarke Skaerlund Risager and Mikkel Thorup (eds), *Contested Property Claims: What Disagreement Tells Us About Ownership*. New York: Routledge, pp. 205–20.
Ossome, Lyn. 2014. 'Can the Law Secure Women's Rights to Land in Africa? Revisiting Tensions Between Culture and Land Commercialization', *Feminist Economics* 20(1): 155–77.
Paradza, Gaynor G. 2011. *Innovations for Securing Women's Access to Land in East Africa*. Rome: International Land Coalition.
Peters, Pauline E. 2004. 'Inequality and Social Conflict over Land in Africa', *Journal of Agrarian Change* 4(3): 269–314.
———. 2009. 'Challenges in Land Tenure and Land Reform in Africa: Anthropological Contributions', *World Development* 37(8): 1317–25.
Porter, Holly. 2017. *After Rape: Violence, Justice and Social Harmony in Uganda*. Cambridge: Cambridge University Press.
Ribot, Jesse C., and Nancy L. Peluso. 2003. 'A Theory of Access', *Rural Sociology* 68(2): 153–81.
Rose, Laurel L. 2002. 'Women's Strategies for Customary Land Access in Swaziland and Malawi: A Comparative Study', *Africa Today* 49(2): 123–49.
Shipton, Parker, and Mitzi Goheen. 1992. 'Introduction: Understanding African Land-holding: Power, Wealth, and Meaning', *Africa: Journal of the International African Institute* 62(3): 307–25.

Theidon, Kimberly S. 2006. 'Justice in Transition: The Micropolitics of Reconciliation in Post-War Peru', *The Journal of Conflict Resolution* 50(3): 433–57.

Tsikata, Dzodzi. 2010. 'Gender, Land and Labour Relations and Livelihoods in Sub-Saharan Africa in the Era of Economic Liberalisation: Towards a Research Agenda', *Feminist Africa* 12: 11–30.

Utas, Mats. 2005. 'West-African Warscapes: Victimcy, Girlfriending, Soldiering: Tactic Agency in a Young Woman's Social Navigation of the Liberian War Zone', *Anthropological Quarterly* 78(2): 403–30.

Whitehead, Ann, and Dzodzi A. Tsikata. 2003. 'Policy Discourses on Women's Land Rights in Sub-Saharan Africa: The Implications of the Re-turn to the Customary', *Journal of Agrarian Change* 3(1): 67–112.

Whyte, S. R. et al. 2013. 'Remaining Internally Displaced: Missing Links to Human Security in Northern Uganda', *Journal of Refugee Studies* 26(2): 283–301.

Yngstrom, Ingrid. 2002. 'Women, Wives, and Land Rights in Africa: Situating Gender Beyond the Household in the Debate over Land Policy and Changing Tenure Systems', *Oxford Development Studies* 30(1): 21–40.

Chapter 6

Belonging

Ben Adol Otto, Michael Whyte
and Susan Reynolds Whyte

The Land Conflict at Ogul: Ethnicity and Neighbourliness

'Fighting has broken out between Langi and Acholi people in Lela Ogul – people are slashing each other with machetes!' It was November 2013 when Ben heard from a friend about a dialogue meeting gone badly wrong in Kotomor sub-county of Agago District. In an attempt to deal with land conflicts and increasing tensions between the two ethnic groups, the Resident District Commissioner and the District Police Commander had called for both sides to meet at Lela Ogul, an area where Langi and Acholi farmers had cultivated fields side by side for generations. Instead of dialogue, the meeting culminated in bloodshed. The recent history of the area suggests some background for the violent confrontation at Ogul.

The district as a whole is considered part of the Acholi sub-region, but the part bordering on Otuke District (Lango sub-region) has many Langi residents. During the war, they were in the same Internally Displaced Persons (IDP) camps as their Acholi neighbours. When the camps were closed and people returned to their rural homes, cultivation in Ogul resumed without incident for the first two years. Then in 2009 the Agago district sub-counties were divided, and Kotomor was created as a new sub-county. Its population was mainly Langi-speaking, so the new administrative boundary was seen as an ethnic boundary and disputed as such.

Not long after the establishment of Kotomor as a new sub-county, there was disagreement between two men: Kitenya from the Acholi side and Agong from the new Langi-dominated Kotomor sub-county. Agong alleged that Kitenya maliciously ploughed up his groundnut garden and reported Kitenya to police. It was found that Kitenya was doing the first ploughing of his sesame garden, which bordered Agong's groundnut garden. As the oxen turned at the edge of Kitenya's sesame field, they would uproot some groundnut plants from Agong's adjoining garden. Police confirmed that Kitenya's action was not intentional and recommended that the matter be settled by the leaders of the relevant sub-counties. The two were reconciled in a unique way. The leaders recommended that each accept food and drink and spend a night in the home of the other. Kitenya enjoyed the hospitality in Agong's place, but when time came for Agong to reciprocate by visiting Kitenya, he was advised against it. Agong was a 'born again' Christian, and his fellow church members warned him that Kitenya would drink waragi (hard liquor), which is against Agong's Christian faith, so it was better to avoid the home altogether. Despite that difference, the two made peace and continued to cultivate their sesame and groundnut fields side by side.

Yet in the process of settling this dispute, another issue cropped up – the sub-county border. The Langi alleged that their border ends at Agago River, not the current location next to Kitenya's home. This implied that Kitenya was actually in Kotomor sub-county. The people of the nearby Acholi-dominated village claimed that this was one more example of Langi attempts to encroach on their land, which lies well inside the new Kotomor sub-county around Ogul. A seemingly banal quarrel between two neighbouring farmers kicked off years of land wrangles. It took on political and ethnic undertones that grew to consume two sub-counties and threatened peaceful coexistence between the Langi and Acholi communities. Agago district local government, NGOs and traditional leaders undertook many initiatives aiming to resolve the conflicts, but none of these interventions yielded durable solutions; instead more violent conflicts erupted.

Appeal was made to the President of Uganda himself. In 2010, when he was on his country visit to Lira District in Lango sub-region, the interim chairman of Kotomor wrote a letter to the President. He asked him urgently to intervene on the boundary dispute between Kotomor and adjoining sub-counties, which was causing violent conflicts between Acholi and Langi. The letter, copied to the Agago district authorities, asserted that the boundary of Kotomor was at Agago River. It alleged that Acholi had chased away Langi people from their land and that 120 households had been displaced to Kotomor sub-county headquarters. In response, the President sent the Minister for Local Government to Kotomor to deal with the situation. The Minister found that things were tense, but there was no displacement as alleged in the Chairperson's letter. Nevertheless, the letter caused panic, suspicion and anxiety among both Acholi and Langi. Mistrust was rife.

In this atmosphere, things came to a head in Ogul. The place is also known as Lela Ogul, (Ogul meaning 'flat stone') because of its rock platform with a hole where water collects. People and animals use it in the dry season, and when it dries up a rain ritual is performed by an Acholi elder from a nearby village in Lukwangole Parish. There is no source of drinking water in the area, so no one lives there permanently, but people from the nearby villages grow food crops on adjacent fields. On one side, the population is predominantly Acholi; on the other, it is mainly Langi. The farmers of Ogul were from both communities, mainly from Acwiko village on the Langi side in Kotomor sub-county and Lukwangole Parish on the Acholi side in Patongo sub-county. Conflicts broke out as they began to re-assert claims on their fields. When the LC3 chairperson of Acholi-dominated Patongo sub-county went to Ogul to assess the situation, the chairperson of Langi-dominated Kotomor reportedly called the Agago District Police Commander and accused his Acholi counterpart of moving with a gun to intimidate the Langi. The Gombolola Internal Security Officer (GISO) investigated the allegation and found no gun.

Reports about the land conflicts between Acholi and Langi went to the Agago District leadership, who convened a first dialogue meeting. On that occasion, Ogul farmers from the Acholi side claimed that they belonged to (meaning they were descended from) twelve great grandparents who farmed in Ogul many years ago. Langi claimed that their ancestors, who had worked on land in Ogul since the 1930s, were also about twelve in number. It was agreed that only twelve representatives from each side should turn up for the next meeting, not the entire sub-county population. Meanwhile, farmers from both sides continued to use the disputed land, and more conflicts ensued. In November 2013, the Resident District Commissioner announced over the radio the next dialogue meeting, to be held in Lela Ogul itself.

On the day of the meeting, the Acholi participants claimed that their Langi counterparts had brought in reinforcements from neighbouring Lango districts. This angered the Acholi, who reasoned that Langi seemed to have a hidden agenda. They accused the Langi of encroaching on land that had long been used by Acholi. Both sides gave presentations on the history of the area, but before a round of reactions, fighting broke out, and several people on both sides were hacked with machetes. It was clear the meeting was a total fiasco.

It was at this point that Ben heard about the troubles and decided to follow developments at Ogul. It was a tricky situation for a researcher. Mistrust was so intense that Ben could not openly move from one side to the other. It would have been most direct for him to travel from the Acholi side, where he lives, to Kotomor. Instead, he took a roundabout route by way of Lira, the capital of the Langi sub-region. Ben is a native Acholi speaker, but his grandmother was from Lango, and he could also speak Langi. Moreover, he had a friend whose family lives in Acwiko village near Ogul on the Langi side. That family was deeply involved in the conflict; the father was an elder of the area and was injured in the fighting at the failed second dialogue meeting. Ben had good contacts as well in Lukwangole, the parish near Ogul on the Acholi side. He visited both, but at first did not reveal that he was talking to both sides. Only after he had built trust did he explain that his research required him to understand both points of view.

Ogul itself was hardly accessible for either Langi or Acholi unless they moved as a group. Langi alleged that Acholi youth were hiding in the bush to attack them. Reportedly, in December 2013, Acholi from Lukwangole had built thirty-eight huts north-east of Lela Ogul with the purpose of monitoring encroachment on their land by the Langi. Meanwhile, the district increased surveillance of the area by deploying the police in Acwiko village on the Langi side, about 3 kilometres from Ogul.

On 7 February 2014, the Langi people (mainly from Acwiko village) allegedly mobilized, burnt those thirty-eight huts and also destroyed some cassava. Although this act of aggression was reported to police, no arrests took place. Both communities expressed their lack of trust in the ability and will of their leaders to resolve the stalemate. Lukwangole people recalled that Agago district authorities stopped the use of Ogul land in 2012 until the disputes were resolved, only to learn in the fall of the dry season that Langi actually cultivated sesame and cassava and nobody stopped them.

On Easter Monday 6 April 2015, an unspecified number of community members from Lukwangole Parish, Patongo sub-county, violently attacked people of Acwiko village in Kotomor sub-county. The attack was a response to the suspected abduction of an older man from Lukwangole by a group of Langi who found him digging with two young men in the disputed land. The two young men managed to escape, leaving behind the elder whom the Langi took to an unknown destination. Worried about his fate, the people from Lukwangole side mobilized in large numbers, armed with spears, bows and arrows, and machetes, to 'rescue' him. Upon reaching Acwiko village, the group started burning huts and granaries and beating up people. After a while, the police and the army jointly rushed to Acwiko to resolve the situation. A total of twenty-four suspects from both sides (fifteen from Lukwangole) were arrested and detained at Patongo central police station.

The raid in Acwiko village led to the death of a 3-year-old boy, who was stabbed in the neck and died shortly after admission to Kalongo Hospital; fifteen others (mainly women and children) were injured, and a lot of property was destroyed. In this stand-off, communication between Acholi and Langi from the two areas ceased, and fear of revenge attacks was high in Lukwangole. There was blame on the district leadership for persistent failure and on Acholi former politicians from the area, who were suspected of fuelling violence in order to take over land from Langi. Local NGOs went to Acwiko village to document the magnitude of the damage, and more army and police were deployed in both Acwiko and Lukwangole. No solution to the land conflict was in sight.

In this situation of leadership void, Hon. Justice Owiny Dollo, the High Court Judge in Uganda who hails from Patongo sub-county, returned home and mobilized both Acholi and Langi for talks with the aim of peacefully resolving the conflict. Dollo expressed disappointment at such violent conflict between the two communities that had lived together for generations. He also refuted the allegations that land conflicts reflected hostility between Acholi and Langi, as there were more conflicts among the Acholi themselves in many other places.

Justice Dollo denied the accusation that he was behind the conflict and wanted to take over the land to mine minerals or to open a ranch in Ogul. Some leaders in Agago district had reportedly circulated the allegations to get political mileage. It was also alleged that Dollo bought local waragi and gumboots and promised people of Lukwangole a hefty amount of money if anyone managed to hack the Langi of Acwiko village when they went to dig in Ogul. The Hon. Justice ignored the falsehoods and went ahead to mediate the conflicts.

The two communities expressed support for the plea made by Dollo, who proposed to work with elders of high integrity to mediate the conflict. Names of elders from both sides were put forward and approved or disapproved by both. Twelve people from each side were nominated to form the mediation team, and Dollo contacted them individually. He also proposed that a lawyer from the side of Lango be brought on board to help in building trust in the mediation team. A priest from Patongo Catholic parish provided spiritual guidance.

Another task was the selection of representatives of disputants from both sides. Again, twelve people were proposed, but this was not to include the so-called *lutino camp*, 'children of the camps', who grew up not knowing the situation before the war and the history of land use around Lela Ogul. Each side had a leader to present its issues. Three follow-up meetings to plan mediation were held at Owiny Dollo's place in Patongo, attended by all the twenty-four representatives of the conflicting parties. The district leadership, the army and the District Police Commander attended the meetings. A local NGO called Passion for Community Transformation provided drinks, meals and secretarial services to the mediation team.

The meetings, including site visits to the disputed land, were largely informed and guided by stories and recollections from Mzee Kamilo Okot Imato ingolo Biteng. Then in his 90s, Kamilo was the only surviving person in the area who had worked with parish chiefs and *rwodi kweri* (Chiefs of the Hoe at village level) in guiding farmers and demarcating boundaries between Acholi and Langi for cotton growing during colonial administration. He narrated the history of the area, confirming that the Langi and Acholi communities had lived harmoniously together in former times. Despite the administrative division of land between Acholi and Langi, people continued to acquire land from both sides by buying, renting and borrowing. In all these arrangements, conflicts never erupted. Kamilo took the mediation team and the representatives of Lukwangole and Acwiko villages to the land he had been using since colonial times. He showed them evidence of activities that had taken place in the area, such as sites for heaping potatoes by the people of Lukwangole. The mango trees were planted by Acholi of long ago, showing that the land belonged to them as they belonged to the land. The Langi could point to the tamarind trees planted by their ancestors. People had intermarried across ethnic lines. As some noted, this continued to the present day. One man from Acwiko on the Langi side said that he would not be harmed in the conflict because he had an Acholi wife.

Mzee Kamilo also told of the rain ceremonies at Ogul rock (Lela Ogul). Both sides agreed they were carried out by the family of Mzee Raphael Owor, already in his 90s. 'They belong to this land because they did the ritual.' Ben had earlier interviewed this old man, so he knew that Mzee Raphael was the only surviving son of the late Ngaa Koko Rom. Mzee Raphael claimed that his father was the one who gave land in Ogul to his Lango friend around 1939. The first-comer's mystical entitlement to control rain was implied in a story Ben heard from Mzee Raphael, which the Langi from Acwiko also confirmed. Wanting to enact control over Ogul, a Langi elder carried out the rain ritual; thereafter, lightning struck dead four of his bulls, demonstrating that he had no right to do the ritual.

The mediation team later met in Lela Ogul to hear specific disputes between land claimants. The land conflict between one Layika from Lukwangole and Owor from Kotomor side was singled out and discussed in-depth. Both claimed that their fathers owned the same piece of land. After a lengthy discussion, the two agreed to divide the land equally. Layika and Owor hugged each other and promised to finish up the process of dividing the land without having to involve everybody. The meeting was adjourned to the next day.

All the boundaries of farms in Ogul area were to be inspected. Rwot Okori Layika (88 years), who was county chief under the colonial government and chairperson of the mediation team, led the walk along the boundaries. Being of advanced age, Rwot was rolled on a bicycle along the land boundaries. Dollo called the land claimants and told each of them to stand on their gardens. Two disputants, Yacinto and Odongo, were given special attention; people were asked to walk along their contested boundaries to ascertain the truth. After nearly a half-day of walking, the mediation team managed to resolve the boundary issue between Yacinto and Odongo. It was resolved that all conflicts should be solved in the same way by negotiation between the individuals involved. Anybody making new claims to land in Ogul was to be looked at as a problem causer and should be stopped by both communities.

In his concluding remarks, Mzee Okori Layika emphasized that 'everyone gathered here should prioritize peace and reconciliation above all else. The people of Agago have historically lived without discrimination. As a song goes . . . *Wan jo agago wacamo kalara warubu kinyige* . . . meaning there is no discrimination in Agago. Hence everybody is welcomed to coexist harmoniously.' The RDC of Agago district was tasked with monitoring the security situation as the two communities implemented the mediation agreement.

When Ben visited the area six months later, he found that the resolutions of the mediation team were still holding. Although there were instances of alleged encroachment, hostilities had ceased, and Langi and Acholi had resumed relationships. People from Acholi-dominated Lukwangole village were attending the market in Langi-dominated Kotomor. There was a plan to engage lawyers from both sides to compute the costs of damaged properties before *mato oput*, the ceremony of reconciliation after a killing, could be arranged.

Of What Is This a Case?

On the face of it, the conflicts in Ogul were based on ethnic oppositions. The division between Acholi and Langi was administratively set in 1959 when the colonial authorities drew a boundary between them. Tensions have flared up and waned over the years, partly due to land issues and partly due to national political conjunctures, including the fact that Milton Obote, from Lango, was twice president of Uganda. Seemingly, the Ogul story is a specific case of a general pattern of ethnic conflicts over land reported from many African countries (Boone 2017). However, it is also a concrete example of more abstract issues concerning the concept of belonging. It suggests that belonging is multiple and that dimensions of belonging are situational. And it shows that multiple attachments are played out in practice, even performed, illustrating the different forms that belonging can take. In Ogul, ethnic belonging was mobilized to the point of violence. But other forms of belonging were also brought into play: political belonging to the nation and to its administrative categories, neighbourhood attachments and belonging through descent and marriage. Even religious attachments had a brief role to play when they prevented Agong from visiting the home of his erstwhile opponent Kitenya.

In this chapter, we review some concepts of belonging in relation to land. Then we move to a discussion of the inclusive and exclusive dimensions of belonging as they are brought to bear on land access. Finally, we take up the practices of attachment to people and land as they emerged in our research and as they have been considered in studies from elsewhere.

The Meaning of Belonging

Belonging has at least two common meanings in English. One denotes membership, being a part of, having affinity with, as when people belong to families, workplaces and nations. The other meaning is often written in the plural, belongings, and it denotes property, objects that are owned; it implies a subject-object relationship (Cockburn et al. 2018: 6). Agong belonged to the Langi ethnic group and his groundnut field belonged to him. That said, much analysis of property unpicks ownership relations in ways that blur the distinction. If property rights are bundles of entitlements embedded in a multiplicity of social relations (see Chapter 1 on Multiplicity), then belongings are closely linked to belonging or attachment to groups or persons.

If we think in terms of bundles, then 'ownership' and 'belonging' must be disaggregated and specified. What kinds of entitlement are involved? The problem is revealed in attempts at translation: in Acholi, the word *won* is rendered 'owner' in English, just as with similar words in Ugandan Bantu languages. One can speak of the owner of the ceremony (the sponsor), the owner of the girl (her father or husband), the owner of the pregnancy (the genitor) and of course the owner of the land. Often 'owner' might better be termed 'the one responsible for' or 'the keeper', as the relevant word in Teso and Akarimojong denotes (see Chapter 2). In the same way, belonging in the sense of being a part of some group, category or place is often more or less, rather than either/or. Geschiere (2009: 86) wrote of the 'half-hearted belonging of the external elites'; in Chapter 8 we discuss such external elites as 'inside/outsiders'. As has already been seen, belonging is situational; the farmers of Ogul belonged to a common neighbourhood on some occasions and to opposing ethnic groups on others.

Belonging can be understood as attachment, the term Shipton (2009) used in his book subtitled *Ideologies of Attachment in Africa*. This helps to remind us that belonging is not only about membership in a group or category but also about links to another individual; for example, to a friend who offers the use of a piece of land. As we suggested in our discussion of embeddedness (Chapter 1 on Multiplicity), attachments are asserted and can be questioned. They must be practised in order to gain strength. Because belonging is multiple, performing one dimension of belonging may diminish the significance of another potential kind of belonging. This was the strategy of the Honourable Justice Dollo. By dealing with conflicts as disputes between individual farmers, he emphasized neighbourly belonging over ethnic affinity and avoided a large-scale clash with heavy political and economic costs.

The distinction between belonging as 'attachment to' and belonging as 'being owned by' tends to break down in interesting ways. Cockburn and colleagues (2018: 6) write: 'In many cases, people and things mediate belonging. This is the case when people belong to one another through what belongs to them, as when they live together in a house or village, or work together in the same workplace (e.g., Edwards and Strathern 2000).' The farmers of Ogul belonged to a community of neighbours by virtue of the fields that belonged to them as individuals or families. In a similar vein, Lentz confirms the common rural African principle that belonging gives access to land but recognizes also that owning land is a symbol of belonging (Lentz 2013: 4–5). As Lund (2011: 74) puts it: 'Citizenship and belonging can be avenues to secure property, and property may bolster claims of belonging and citizenship.' Here again, the double meaning of belonging merges in the one point that land, people and belonging must be considered together.

Or, as Shipton (2009: 110–11) writes: 'People do not just own or inherit land, in an East African way of seeing things; they also belong to it. Belonging to land is part and parcel of belonging to other people – in groups, networks, or open categories.' Our TrustLand colleague Quentin Gausset raised the question: 'Does land belong to people or do people belong to land?' The answer must be both, potentially; we will suggest that both are achievements that must be worked at. This kind of work is most relevant in rural contexts, where people are concerned to confirm continuing claims on ancestral land even if they are not continuously residing on it.

Inclusion and Exclusion

The creation of Kotomor as a new sub-county seems to have enhanced consciousness of ethnic belonging. While the old sub-county comprised both Acholi and Langi, the new one was bounded so as to be almost exclusively Langi. The dynamics are similar to those that have emerged around the creation of new districts: 'far from alleviating ethnic tension and spurring development, it is clear that the creation of new districts has led, in many cases, to increased levels of ethnic conflict' (Green 2010). Researchers have pointed to the connection between decentralization, the creation of new administrative boundaries, opportunities for local elites, ethnic belonging and land conflicts (Green 2008; Geschiere 2009; Sjögren 2015). In the case of Ogul, the conflicts between individual farmers escalated into ethnic conflicts that were related to the boundaries of the new sub-county. Belonging as Acholi or Langi took on a local territorial dimension within Agago District.

The increased emphasis on ethnicity is a prime example of what Peters (2009: 1321) calls 'narrowing definitions of belonging'. In Ogul, new administrative boundaries were related to a greater exclusiveness based on ethnicity. Other factors too are commonly at work in narrowing definitions of belonging. The growing value of land, shortage of land and increased concerns about the security of land can all mean that belonging and thus entitlements are more exclusively defined. In the West African forest belt, conflicts between landowners and immigrants have taken on ethnic tones, with land for perennial crops like coffee and cocoa becoming increasingly monetized as land laws were changed and as national governments became increasingly involved. Yet the dimensions of belonging at play are never only ethnic. Kinship has always been important as is adherence to one or another earth shrine (Lund 2008; Chauveau and Colin 2010; Lentz 2013). Perhaps it is not so much that definitions of belonging are narrowing as that one kind of belonging is given more weight than others in certain situations. It is important to consider what kinds of authority and legitimacy are deployed to underwrite a claim to belonging.

Autochthony is one such argument for legitimacy and authority over land. Indeed, to be autochthonous is to be 'a self of the soil', according to the Greek roots of the word. Throughout the world, autochthony is deployed as the most authentic and legitimate form of belonging. To be an original of a place or, more accurately, to have been there first seems to imply a primordial connection to land that takes precedence over other claims (Geschiere 2009: 2).[1] The relations between autochthons and allogénes, first-comers and latecomers, hosts and guests, indigenous and strangers, have been widely studied, especially as they relate to ethnicity (Boone 2017). Where migrants have gained access to land, often with the consent of those who were already in the area, the superior entitlements of the autochthons are often acknowledged by gifts or payments. The institution of the *tutorat* in Ivory Coast is a well-documented example of the patron-client relation between 'sons of the soil', who were there first, and migrants, who came from elsewhere to farm the land (Chauveau and Colin 2010).

Although widespread immigration is not so common in northern Uganda, the argument of autochthony certainly has weight, as we saw in the need to establish 'original owners of land' in Chapter 2. It is not only buyers who need to identify original owners but also those who wish to use land for a period. In Kaabong district, the Ik people were granted their own county in 2016 called 'Ik County', to signify that this land belongs to the Ik, according to the MP from the area. Most districts, counties and sub-counties in Uganda are given place names rather than ethnic names, but this was taken as an exceptional case, according to the MP, because of the special status of the Ik as indigenous people.[2] The name 'Ik County' and being considered 'indigenous' to the land means that the Ik, who are often considered of lower rank by surrounding ethnic groups, regard themselves as having authority to grant access to the territory. Two of the neighbouring groups, the Dodoth from Uganda and the Turkana from Kenya, are herders, who come to Ik County almost every year during the dry season to graze and water their animals in the lush Ik mountains when the Rift Valley turns too hot and dry. When the herders come, they are not only supposed to contact officials but also get in contact with the Ik owners or 'keepers of the land' to ask permission to stay, graze and water their animals. The Ik hosts are often reluctant to give their permission and say that they only 'half-trust' the guest herders, because even if the herders are friendly and offer goods for trading when they arrive, when they return home towards the rainy season, they often plunder Ik villages on the way (Gade, Willerslev and Meinert 2015). Yet, in the end, access is almost always granted by the Ik through this intimate friend-enemy relationship with the neighbouring groups. More serious problems arose when Dodoth herders had settled permanently in Ik County. This called for a large community meeting involving district as well as military leaders, and after long negotiations the Dodoth settlers were turned away based on autochthonous reasoning.

In the Ogul case, as in many others we heard, someone had given land to a friend from another clan or ethnic group long ago. The descendants of that friend had remained and multiplied, so that clan or ethnic belonging was mixed within a locality. Accounts of welcoming a friend or affine emphasize that some people were there first and were in a position to offer land to others. The role of the family of first-comers in performing rituals for the land confirms their special relationship to the place. As Ben's interlocutor put it: 'They belonged to the land because they did the ritual.' All over the Acholi sub-region, we heard stories of 'previously welcomed people' who had settled by invitation in an area dominated by members of another clan. When land becomes contentious for one or another reason, those who came later might be dismissed by some as not really belonging, of not having claims as strong as those who were there before (Adol 2021: 204–26). Yet continuous use of the land over many years compensates for later arrival, as was the case in Ogul. Yes, the Langi families came later, but the land had been given to them, and they had farmed it since the late 1930s. Continuous use without objection is recognized by Ugandan statutory law as entitlement (at least in the cases of freehold and Mailo land), but our impression is that another principle lies behind acceptance: the Langi belonged to the land because they had put themselves into it in the form of labour; their claims were based on a 'labor theory of property' (Lentz 2013: 211). And all the farmers of Ogul belonged to one another by virtue of what belonged to each.

Among the related Luo people of western Kenya, there is a similar contrast between belongers and strangers. A *wuon lowo* (master of the land) or *jalowo* (person of the land) is superior to a *jadak* (squatter, settler, visitor) by virtue of being a first-comer (Shipton 2009: 115). Not only are the land claims of Luo autochthons stronger, but their social status is higher; as in parts of West Africa they are accorded special respect, while late-coming *jodak* are assigned humiliating or polluting tasks. Yet this is not a caste relationship; marriages between belongers and settlers are common, as was the case in Ogul. Thus, cross-cutting ties are created, and one kind of belonging with its exclusiveness is balanced by the inclusiveness of another personal attachment.

Arguments of autochthony often relate to the rights of categories of people vis-à-vis other categories, whether ethnic or descent groups. However, at an individual level, claims to land are most commonly made on the basis of personal attachments to intimate others in the form of consanguinity or affinity. As we have seen in the foregoing chapters, belonging or attachment to other people mediates access to land. In Chapter 4, Daniel and his four brothers belonged to their mother, and she was attached to her brother, the one who married from her bridewealth. Through these attachments, they built houses and grew crops on his land. Atim and Awor and their sisters all belonged to their father, and therefore, as Atim said to her older sister, 'Do not think that this land belongs to you only. Our father's property must belong to all of us.' The intimate governance of land follows from the way that access is mediated through personal, often close, attachments.

Much as belonging in the sense of being attached to a place through people sounds positive, inclusion almost always implies exclusion in some form. Not only are some people belongers while others are not; even among belongers, some people belong more than others. Therefore, they maintain, their land claims are stronger. As Geschiere (2009) argued, there are perils to belonging in that it has a segmentary character. Distinctions are continually made concerning degrees of belonging. In Acholi, where the ideology of patriliny is strong, recognized paternal descent seems to be given greater weight than before in access to land. The term 'patrilineal fundamentalism' (Whyte et al. 2013: 294) is meant to capture the absolute significance given to agnatic belonging to the exclusion of other forms of attachment that might also mediate claims to land. Daniel and his brothers worried about their land access should their mother's brother, or more likely his sons, become strict patrilinealists. Attempts to dismiss the claims of 'formerly welcomed people' on the basis that they are not clan members are another example of patrilineal fundamentalism. Belonging through marriage is perilous as well. Separation and divorce have long been common in Acholi society (Grove 1919; Foster 1955–1959;[3] Girling 1960); in the wake of the war and encampment, when partnerships were not formalized, access to land through affinity became more uncertain. Given the perils of belonging, we must attend to the ways in which people seek to strengthen attachments that provide links to land.

Practising Attachments

Belonging is not simply a matter of attachment to a person or category. It must be practised. In some instances, it is explicitly performed as when Layika and Owor hugged each other after negotiating about their boundaries or when Agong and Kitenya were instructed to spend a night at each other's home to affirm their attachment as friends and neighbours. One of the most common and significant performances of belonging is burial and the funeral celebrations surrounding it. As we saw in Chapter 4 on Generations, burying parents and grandparents on ancestral land is an important component of generational relations to land. More than that, committing a corpse to the earth establishes belonging to the land quite literally. Geschiere (2009: 30) calls the funeral at home '... one of autochthony's major rituals, a veritable test of where one "really" belongs.... an occasion to link "soil" and "body" in all sorts of naturalizing ways.' Interment makes of the deceased a 'self of the soil'. In line with increasing concern about belonging and land in Cameroon, Geschiere suggests that burial 'at home' is becoming more significant, also for groups who did not necessarily practise it in former times. Shipton (2009: 96) as well as Geissler and Prince (2010) make the same argument for Luo people of western Kenya, suggesting that burial as the performance of belonging to a specific piece of land is increasingly important.

In Ik county in northern Uganda, burial practices and places have changed significantly since the 1960s. Before the 1966–1968 drought, Ik people used to bury the dead in the valleys, near streams, where the spirits were believed to hide. Through this burial practice, the attachment and belonging was to the territory in general. After the drought, people moved further up in the mountains, and transporting corpses to the valleys became difficult. Furthermore, missionaries visited and encouraged the Ik to bury their dead near the villages rather than in the bush. After the 1990s, the UPDF established detaches in the county and encouraged Ik families to bury their dead inside villages and homes as in other parts of northern Uganda (Meinert, Willerslev and Seebach 2017: 44), and consequently the attachment practices to land were further localized.

The burial of adult women is often more problematic than that of men. A woman should be buried at her husband's home on the land to which she gained access through marriage. But as we have seen, it is not always clear whether, or the extent to which, a woman was married. She may end up being buried at the home of her parents or brothers. Or she may be buried on the land where her children live, as in the case of Atim and Awor, who, together with their older sister, cemented their mother's grave to underscore that she belonged to the land and the land belonged to them. Marking the grave more permanently was a tactic on the part of the sisters, who wanted to reinforce their claim. But we should not think of burial only as instrumental. Burying a mother is infused with emotional attachment aside from considerations about land claims. In Susan Whyte's study of women's burials and belonging in eastern Uganda, burying a woman at the home of her children and their father was common even if he had never formalized the marriage with her. While 'arguments of culture' assert that a man may not bury his partner unless he has married her, there are countervailing 'arguments of affection' based on the principle that mothers belong to their children: 'We have a belief that children want to care for the grave and say "Mommy is buried here"' (Whyte 2005: 162). Mothers belong to their children, and having their mother's grave on their land is a powerful confirmation that the children belong to the land as the land belongs to them.

Aside from the explicit performances of belonging, such as burial or declaring reconciliation after a conflict, belonging is practised in mundane ways. It is realized when you are shown where to make a garden or build a house, when you borrow some fields for a season, or when you are given permission to dig clay for bricks. To be included as a user of land is to have an attachment to persons or groups. It is to be part of other people, and it confirms such belonging in a concrete material manner. Land entitlements that are embedded in social relations (as opposed to the ideal type of disembedded freehold) always involve some kind of belonging or attachment, usually to intimate others. Just as eating together or staying together creates relatedness (Carsten 2000), so sharing land is a way of practising belonging. Not only are attachments practised through access to land but accessing and using land shapes attachments. We have already mentioned that the farmers of Ogul created neighbourhood belonging through cultivating side by side. Shaping attachment through using land, one way or another, is particularly noticeable where a connection is somewhat fragile or there is doubt about someone's belonging. In Chapter 5 on Gender, we saw how women cultivated attachments by cultivating land: Awor farmed on the land of her former husband, thus confirming the belonging of her sons, who should use that land someday.

Attachments are practised in the activities of using the land: clearing bush, planting, weeding, harvesting, grazing, building, burying, quarrying. Even collecting firewood is usually an activity that demonstrates a kind of belonging, if only to the neighbourhood. In these activities, people leave marks on the land that can serve as evidence of use and thus of claims to land. More than that, they can be understood as ways in which people belong to land. They invest themselves by putting their labour into the land; we can say that they embody the land by their intimate work with it. Just as land transactions are embodied by seeing and walking the property (Chapter 2 on Transactions), land itself is embodied through transforming it. In the end, people belong to the land when they are buried in it. And in belonging to a given piece of land, they also belong to other people.

Attachments carry emotional loads from the past and expectations about the future. So, the practice of accessing and using land through attachments is not purely utilitarian, and conflicts over land are seldom only about land. Belonging is about feelings of recognition; attachments have affective dimensions of appreciation. That is why being excluded from using land can be hurtful beyond the practical concerns. Adol (2021) recounts the case of Jeje, whom he met during his fieldwork. Jeje's mother left her husband and came back to her parents with Jeje when he was just a year old. Jeje grew up with his mother's father, 'like a father to him'. He never went to his genitor's home and never tried to claim land there, knowing that the land was small and his father's other children were already struggling over it. The only parental home he knew during the 38 years of his life was that of his mother. As an adult, he buried two of his children there. But when a third child died, his mother's half-brothers directed him to bury her at the home of his 'real' father, adding that he should even plan to bury his mother there some day, since her bridewealth had not been returned and thus her marriage had not formally been dissolved. Nor would they allow him to use the land to build a house. Jeje and his mother were angry and hurt. By refusing to let him bury or build on the land, the uncles were also denying that he belonged. Jeje bought land nearby and declared he was cutting off close relations with his uncles.

The practice of belonging in specific situations is a matter of using the land and simultaneously strengthening or weakening relationships. Yet in every specific situation, social relations and practices of belonging are shaped by configurations of power and influence. In the case of Jeje, his position was weakened by the fact that his mother's father and her full brother had died. His mother herself declared that her half-brothers would not have been able to force Jeje off the land had her closest brother still been alive. In another case, which shows the strength of a land claimant, Adol writes of a widow whose land was being encroached by relatives of the man who had given her late husband land. They claimed she did not belong (her husband was of another clan). The original donor and his son, who would have stood by the gift of land, had died. Her position was weakened by these 'missing links', just as Jeje's was. But the widow had five sons, well-educated and employed in the Acholi sub-region. The resources they put into bringing the case to the Magistrates' court, and the respect they and their mother held in the neighbourhood, tipped the outcome in her favour.

Practices of belonging are carried out by actors whose past and present behaviours are evaluated by others. The widow with five sons had been a good neighbour; people were well-disposed towards her. Most of the cases we came to know were coloured by impressions of the actors' characters as revealed by past actions and general disposition towards others. The vignette about Broken Graves that opened Part II on Intimate Governance illustrates how important behaviour can be in practising belonging. The assertive demands of the young Oyo, his disrespectful objection to his patron's farming activity, and the outrageous act of destroying graves all together led to his exclusion from the land and the family.

The contrary and valued practices are those that promote social harmony, *ber bedo*. Maintaining attachments through respectful dialogue and negotiation, in land issues as in other matters, facilitates the civility that allows everyday life to run smoothly. The widow in Ben's case won her claim to the land given to her late husband. But she allocated two gardens to her opponents in the interest of compromise, thus taking a step towards the re-establishment of harmony. As we saw in the story of Ogul, peaceful co-existence requires emphasizing a dimension of belonging that is inclusive enough. The elders called upon people as Ogul farmers, not as Acholi or Langi. But they also limited that belonging by declaring that no new claims to land in Ogul would be allowed.

Conclusion

In this chapter, we have considered the meanings of belonging in relation to land. We have discussed principles of belonging – categorical identification with an ethnic group, autochthony as an argument in favour of first-comer groups, relational attachment to consanguines and affines, and the everyday attachments to neighbours. We suggested that belonging had to be practised by using land through performances such as burial or more commonly through the everyday activities of cultivation, harvesting, grazing animals, collecting firewood and using the soil for house building. Throughout we have shown how belonging mediates access to land and how using the land affects belonging. We have been primarily concerned with land that has been entrusted through inheritance, devolution, borrowing and gifting. The practices of land use involved were rural – mainly subsistence activities. Our reflections on belonging are most germane to these kinds of land claims and uses. The purchase of land, whether formal or informal, and its use for commerce and development raise other issues to which we now turn. But even in imagining development, notions of belonging and belongings are relevant.

Ben Adol Otto has a Ph.D. from the Institute of Peace and Strategic Studies at Gulu University and is currently the Programme Coordinator in ARiD – Advocates for Research in Development.

Michael Whyte, Ph.D., is Associate Professor Emeritus at the Institute of Anthropology, University of Copenhagen.

Susan Reynolds Whyte, Ph.D., is Professor at the Institute of Anthropology, University of Copenhagen.

Notes

1. Of course, it is not always the case that autochthons have a superior status, as we know from the situations of indigenous people around the world. But they are almost always considered to have a primordial, almost mystical attachment to the land.
2. Together with the Batwa and the Benet, the Ik are considered indigenous people of Uganda by organizations who work for indigenous people. In the national Constitution and the Land Act, these groups are not recognized as indigenous people, probably because this would grant them special rights to potential underground resources.
3. Foster, Paula Hirsch. 1955–1959. Field Notes. Deposited in Foster Archive, African Studies Library. Boston University.

References

Adol, Ben. 2021. 'Acholi Traditional Institutions and Post-War Land Governance in Pader and Agago Districts, Northern Uganda', Ph.D. dissertation. Gulu: Gulu University.

Boone, Catherine. 2017. 'Sons of the Soil Conflict in Africa: Institutional Determinants of Ethnic Conflict Over Land', *World Development* 96: 276–93.

Carsten, Janet. 2000. 'Introduction: Cultures of Relatedness', in Janet Carsten (ed.), *Cultures of Relatedness: New Approaches to the Study of Kinship*. Cambridge: Cambridge University Press.

Chauveau, Jean-Pierre, and Jean-Philippe Colin. 2010. 'Customary Transfers and Land Sales in Côte d'Ivoire: Revisiting the Embeddedness Issue', *Africa* 80(1): 81–103.

Cockburn, P. et al. 2018. 'Introduction: Disagreement as a Window onto Property', in Patrick Cockburn, Maja Hojer Bruun, Bjarke Skærlund Risager and Mikkel Thorup (eds), *Contested Property Claims: What Disagreement Tells Us about Ownership*. London: Routledge, pp. 1–20.

Edwards, Jeanette, and Marilyn Strathern. 2000. 'Including Our Own', in Janet Carsten (ed.), *Cultures of Relatedness: New Approaches to the Study of Kinship*. Cambridge: Cambridge University Press, pp. 149–66.

Gade, Christian, Rane Willerslev and Lotte Meinert. 2015. 'Half-trust and Enmity in Ikland, Northern Uganda', *Common Knowledge* 21(3): 406–19.

Geissler, Paul Wenzel, and Ruth Jane Prince. 2010. *The Land is Dying: Contingency, Creativity and Conflict in Western Kenya*. New York: Berghahn Books.

Geschiere, Peter. 2009. *The Perils of Belonging: Autochthony, Citizenship, and Exclusion in Africa and Europe*. Chicago: Chicago University Press.

Girling, Frank Knowles. 1960. *The Acholi of Uganda*. London: Her Majesty's Stationery Office.

Green, Elliot D. 2008. 'Decentralisation and Conflict in Uganda', *Conflict, Security & Development* 8(4): 427–50.

———. 2010. 'Patronage, District Creation, and Reform in Uganda', *Studies in Comparative International Development* 45(1): 83–103.

Grove, Captain E. T. N. 1919. 'Customs of the Acholi', *Sudan Notes and Records* 2(3): 157–82.

Lentz, Carola. 2013. *Land, Mobility, and Belonging in West Africa*. Bloomington: Indianapolis.

Lund, Christian. 2008. *Local Politics and the Dynamics of Property in Africa*. Cambridge: Cambridge University Press.

———. 2011. 'Property and Citizenship: Conceptually Connecting Land Rights and Belonging in Africa', *Africa Spectrum* 3: 71–75.

Meinert, Lotte, Rane Willerslev and Sophie Hooge Seebach. 2017. 'Cement, Graves and Pillars in Land Disputes in Northern Uganda', *African Studies Review* 60(3): 37–57.

Peters, Pauline. 2009. 'Challenges in Land Tenure and Land Reform in Africa: Anthropological Contributions', *World Development* 37(8): 1317–25.

Shipton, Parker. 2009. *Mortgaging the Ancestors: Ideologies of Attachment in Africa*. New Haven: Yale University Press.

Sjögren, Anders. 2015. 'Battles over Boundaries: The Politics of Territory, Identity and Authority in Three Ugandan Regions', *Journal of Contemporary African Studies* 33(2): 268–84.

Whyte, Susan Reynolds. 2005. 'Going Home? Burial and Belonging in the Era of AIDS', *Africa* 75(2): 154–72.

Whyte, Susan Reynolds et al. 2013. 'Remaining Internally Displaced: Missing Links to Human Security in Northern Uganda', *Journal of Refugee Studies* 26(2): 283–301.

Part III
Imagining Development

Case III

Claiming 'Their' School
Land Dispute between Two Churches over a Primary School

Catrine Shroff

We were sitting inside the Anglican church when the church chairman showed me the letter that they had sent to the school management committee in 2013. I could see the primary school through the windows and students playing football. Behind the school, on the other side of the football field, was the Catholic church. The school was in poor condition, and it looked squeezed in between the Anglican church and the Catholic church. During the conversation, I learnt that

Figure CIII.1. The two churches and the school © Mette Lind Kusk.

the deteriorated state of the school was indeed due to a battle between the two churches over the control of it.

The letter told the history of the school and its Anglican church, mentioning the key people and events. The founder, Mzee Alunyu, had schooled in Lira with the later president Obote and served in the King's African Rifles during the Second World War. He directed part of his clan to decongest the village by moving 5 kilometres south towards the Nile and to set up their homes, a school and a church. This was in 1956, and the area was a wilderness with leopards, elephants and buffaloes. Some former neighbours teased that the animals would kill them, phrased as *amati* in Lango, and the area became known as 'Amati'. The twenty-nine founding members built a mud-walled building, and the 'mother church', the nearby Kamdini St. Mathias Church of Uganda, provided a lay reader to teach reading, writing and arithmetic during the week and lead Sunday service. It was a subgrade school until the 1960s, when the Obote I government took over its administration as part of a nationalization of the church-based schools and with a government grant for the construction of four semi-permanent classrooms upgraded it to a primary school. The letter ends with a mention of the early catechists and subgrade teachers, priests, school leaders and people who donated the land.

Figure CIII.2. Wilderness
© Mette Lind Kusk.

Figure CIII.3. Letter © Mette Lind Kusk.

A few years after the upgrade to a primary school, local Catholics gained more numbers, and the chief allowed them to build a church, but instead of building their own school, the Catholics were to work with the Anglicans to further develop the government-run school.

By the mid-1970s, Idi Amin had ousted Obote, and the new regime played down the differences between Anglicans and Catholics, in part by abolishing the foundation body influence on primary schools, which reduced the importance of the church affiliation of a school. In this case, however, the collaboration between Anglicans and Catholics in one school is where the trouble began. Anglicans

Figure CIII.4. Meeting with the chief © Mette Lind Kusk.

claim that the Catholics *contributed* to the continuous construction by providing building materials and seats in the classrooms, whereas Catholics say that the Anglicans *gave the land* to the Catholic missionaries to build the school, making it a Catholic-founded school. The Anglican church had not registered the acquisition of the land for Amati primary school and Anglican church, as it was used to favouritism by the British regime. Moreover, the first president, Milton Obote, was an Anglican as well as an old school friend of one of the church founders. There is no written documentation of the claimed transfer of school land from the Anglican church to the Catholic church.

Figure CIII.5. Catholic missionaries © Mette Lind Kusk.

During the 1980s and 1990s, Catholic missionaries from Europe settled in the area, and many local leaders converted from the Anglican to the Catholic Church. The growth of the Catholic community had implications for the school management, as it listened more to Catholic views on government appointment of the head teacher and on issues related to religious education and worship practices. After the National Resistance Movement (NRM) came to power in 1986, the Ministry of Education introduced a practice where the head teachers would fill out the church affiliation of primary schools as part of the general reporting to the government. This is the second contestation in this land conflict; Anglican leaders claim that Catholic head teachers used this opportunity to change the foundation body to the Catholic Church.

At a meeting in 1996, the school auditor read aloud a letter to the School Management Committee and the Parent-Teacher Association stating that Amati primary school was founded by the Catholic Church. The Anglican community did not react, and the inter-church collaboration continued until 2001, when the education unit at the Catholic diocese of Lira approved a change in the man-

Figure CIII.6. Police interrogation © Mette Lind Kusk.

agement system that dismissed Anglican members of the School Management Committee and the Parent-Teacher Association. The Anglican lay reader and the Anglican diocese of Lira kept quiet. In 2003, the Anglican bishop laid the foundation stone of a new and much larger church on the southern side of the school. People from the Catholic community demolished the foundation stone, and in the following police interrogation the Catholic defence was that Amati Primary was a 'community school' – that is, a school founded by the community, not either of the two churches. The settlement as a community school was made official in 2004 by the sub-county chief and church representatives, and it was agreed that each church should have 15 acres of land on either side of the school.

The inter-church collaboration worked fairly well until a Parent-Teacher Association meeting in 2013, when the Catholic parish priest said that he was speaking on behalf of the foundation body. The Education Act of 2008 gave power to the foundation body to appoint six out of twelve members of the school management committee, including the chairman and the vice-chairman, and this policy led the Anglican church and the Catholic church to claim schools founded during the colonial era throughout Uganda. Amati Primary School came under fierce contestation, with violent encounters and police intervention to protect people and church property. A public hearing was organized for district authorities, clan elders, church representatives, the school management committee and community members to present evidence about the foundation body of the school.

Figure CIII.7. Community meeting © Mette Lind Kusk.

Figure CIII.8. A hindrance to development © Mette Lind Kusk.

Everyone was heard, but as the Chief Administration Officer at district level has not declared the foundation of the school, the matter remains unresolved. The deterioration is obvious: a drop from 1,500 students in 2001 to 1,000 students in 2015. There is no school management committee and no Parent-Teacher Association. As teachers' houses are parents' obligation, there are only three houses for the sixteen teachers; hence teachers rent outside the school, which makes the school an unpopular placement and affects the level of education. Within Amati vicinity, there is interest to use the 2004 settlement of a 'community school' to improve the school standard and unite the community, yet both churches at the diocesan level seem more focused on protecting church property. The inter-church conflict over the land exposes a dilemma between the interests of church property and community development. As one informant in Amati said: 'The close relations between church and school have become a hindrance to development.'

Catrine Shroff, Ph.D., was post doc at Aarhus University and is currently senior consultant at Nordic Consulting Group and Director of Mwangaza Light.

Chapter 7

Aspirations

Susan Reynolds Whyte and Catrine Shroff

Plotting Development

Daudi brought out a large brown envelope and extracted a letter as he tried to explain the details of his land case. The letter was recent – dated two months before Susan first visited him that day in March 2011 – but the story went back about fifty years and was part of the bigger picture of development in northern Uganda. The conflict was between an institution, the sub-county, and the descendants of a man who had earlier gifted land to the institution in the name of progress and community benefit. The sub-county chief had written to Daudi's lawyer in Gulu, where the case was pending in the Magistrates' Court. In his letter, the chief wrote that Daudi's father Abaci had given land to the sub-county in 1976 and that there had been no objection to the sub-county's use of the land until 2008. When the sub-county plotted this land to sell to developers, it included a small piece that should have remained with Daudi's family; to compensate, the sub-county had promised to plot and survey the rest of Daudi's family land within the planned Town Board 'for the family future development'. The letter asserted that all this had been agreed in a meeting that included the family members, local leaders and elders. It denied Daudi's allegation that the sub-county had acted without his knowledge or that of the family members.

Daudi remarked dismissively that his father had already been dead five years by the time he was supposed to have given land to the sub-county. He kept repeating that the sub-county 'did everything by force' instead of informing him properly and discussing plans. 'I can't disagree with the development issue, but they're not taking the right steps.'

Daudi's father Abaci was a soldier. One of his nephews explained that he was an enlightened and visionary man. He had served in the Second World War and had travelled and seen new things. He wanted development for his home area, and his Palwa clan had plenty of land in and around the trading centre of Pacuk. So, in the 1960s, Abaci gave some land for a community hall; the building was used as a sub-county office and now is rented out as a video hall. In 1976, when new administrative units were delineated, his family gave more of their land to the Division, which later became the sub-county government. It may well be that Abaci himself was dead by then; Daudi said he was killed by Amin's soldiers in 1971. But people often refer to descendants by the name of a recently dead man. Abaci gave the land, according to several older people, by which they may have meant that some members of his family agreed to allocate land for the newly established Division.

Daudi was a child at the time. After his father died, he went to stay with his father's sister in Pader and grew up there, though he kept his ties to Pacuk. He came to visit from time to time; he had a hut on his father's land. Although he was the only son of his father, he had many lineage brothers who remained on Palwa land in the area. In the years he was away, the trading centre/sub-county headquarters became an IDP camp, and displaced people put up huts on his land. At one point, he received a phone call from the Salvation Army requesting permission to build two Early Child Development Centres (nursery schools) on his land for the many children in the camp. The condition was that the buildings would be his when the camp closed. So, when he finally moved back in 2008, he and his wife and seven children were comfortably accommodated in one of the large, well-built structures, while the other served as a store and shelter for his poultry and rabbits. The sub-county chief who took over from the one whose letter Susan saw in 2011 also took on responsibility for the case. In 2013 he showed Susan a thick file with letters from lawyers about the Abaci claim for 100 million shillings in damages. With irritation and some disdain, he remarked of Daudi: 'That boy has not grown from here, but from Pader. He came back here because he was attracted by the resources, the two ECD buildings on his land.'

Daudi, the man whom this (unpopular) chief called a 'boy', was referred to respectfully as *Ladit* or *Muzee* (elder, var. *Mzee*) by others. His lineage was large, influential and well-connected – even to members of the sub-county council with whom they were in conflict. One of Daudi's lineage brothers, Polycarp, came back to Pacuk in 2010 after working in Kenya for thirty-seven years; he must have left about the same time as Daudi did. Polycarp too declared his wish to see development and his resentment that he was not being compensated. He said that he had told the sub-county: 'We don't want you to leave. We also want to be developed. I may build a house or buy land for the young ones.'

What Daudi and Polycarp were struggling for was recognition and specific benefit from the development process in Pacuk. From our early visits to the sub-county offices in the trading centre in 2010, we had been aware of the plans to transform the trading centre from an IDP camp with a few schools and churches to a Town Board with modern amenities, business opportunities and storied buildings. We had seen the impressive technical drawings, with prospective new roads lined with plots for commercial and residential use. The plans were afoot as the camp was closing in 2008, and by the end of 2009, the district had recommended the elevation of the trading centre to the status of Town Board. Pacuk was fortunate in having land on which to realize development and at the same time generate some revenue. Not all sub-county headquarters were in that position. But the sub-county land was encumbered in two ways: there were still displaced people – living and dead – whose huts and graves had to be removed before development could proceed; and there were claims on the land by the Abaci family.

There were three aspects of the development plans to which Daudi and his Palwa brothers objected: the new market, the new roads and the sale of plots. These were all located in the trading centre close to where Daudi and other Palwa lived. The market structure was inaugurated in September 2010; building must have started in 2008 or 2009. It was financed by USAID under NUTI (Northern Uganda Transition Initiative). It was to replace the old market in a cool grove of mango trees (ownership of that land turned out to be contentious as well, but that is another story). Daudi and Polycarp complained that the new market was on Palwa land and that no one had asked their permission. Polycarp told Susan: 'Why not discuss? We also want development. Government should give us something and we transfer. I went to the lawyer and said I'll collect the market fees. They are using my land while I'm sleeping hungry. Development I get from where? From them? I want money to construct a house.' By the time Susan talked to Daudi and Polycarp, they could see that the market was a solid fact; they could not reclaim the land upon which it stood. But they wanted compensation at least. They thought their historical family rights over the area should have been recognized and that they should have a specific benefit by virtue of their descent, not just the general benefit that the new market might provide for everyone.

The opening of the new roads affected Daudi and other members of his lineage who had huts and graves in the roadway. Others had to move as well, but they did not have good grounds for objecting, since they were staying on sub-county land in the aftermath of displacement. In May 2010, a grader appeared to make two parallel roads that ended at the new market. Although the sub-county authorities claimed they had given notice in good time, the people we interviewed were bitter that they were not able to prepare properly. Exhumation required the sacrifice of a goat, which many people needed time to acquire. Daudi said: 'The grader did things on force without informing people.' He was unable to remove the bones of four of his brothers before the grader passed. It was not until August and September that he acquired the necessary goats and reburied them on nearby Palwa land where his father's brother lives. One of his lineage sisters, a widow with six children, recounted how she returned from Gulu with the body of her child who had died in hospital there to find that her hut had been knocked down and her brother (a lineage brother to Daudi) had urgently removed the bones from two graves just before the grader passed over them. It was only afterwards that they killed a goat on the spot where the grave had been.

One of the new roads was named Abaci, and the other was named after a member of the sub-county council who had been instrumental in developing the plan. Polycarp remarked that 'roads are also development'. He wanted money to build a house on the second one and change its name to Palwa Road. For what was important about the new roads in the trading centre was that they were to be lined with plots for commercial and residential buildings. The sub-county marked off twenty-five plots and offered them for sale at 1 million UGX each. The condition was that owners must develop their plots by putting up permanent commercial or residential buildings. By 2012, all twenty-five plots had been spoken for, although not all buyers had completed payment. The sub-county informed them that they would have to pay 1.5 million if they did not finish paying by a certain deadline.

By early 2015, none of the buyers had been shown their plots. The court case brought by Daudi had not been settled, and there was an injunction on further development of the plots. The LC3 chairman was considering whether the uncontested plots might be given out at least. The plot buyers had formed a committee to pressure the sub-county to hand over their plots. The District Physical Planner pointed out another problem: the contractor with the grader had not followed the plan, so the roads were in the wrong place. By that time the new roads were overgrown in any case and were mere paths. The Secretary of the Sub-county Court Committee bemoaned the fact that a new road would have to be opened and the sub-county could not afford to hire a grader.

The matter of the case brought by Daudi had not been resolved. Many deplored the situation and the escalation involving lawyers and the district court. Lawyers were expensive, and the only way forward was to negotiate and agree locally. On that there was consensus. One of the potential plot buyers, who had given up and bought a plot from another family, said: '*Ladit* is stopping development. It needs to talk to him slowly slowly to make him understand.' Several senior men expressed their intention to talk to Daudi or to his lineage brother Polycarp. In 2013 the sub-county had organized a meeting with the Abaci family where it was decided to form a committee to work out a solution. But no meeting had been held by early 2015. The sub-county chairman claimed that Daudi and his brothers had come to him to say they wanted mediation rather than pursuing the case in court.

Polycarp complained about the poor communication: 'The politicians are the problem. The councillors are our neighbours. They are selling plots without talking to us. They should give us a map for the township – give me half or something. But they cannot hear what I'm saying.' He blamed the sub-county for not inviting them to discuss the matter: 'They fear to call us. They are the beggar; we are not the beggar. We don't want this lawyer issue; we don't have money . . . We will only withdraw the case if the sub-county sits with us. But if we withdraw now, the sub-county wins.' Polycarp was also concerned that his brother Daudi was sick with tuberculosis; 'maybe he is affected by too much thinking.'

A visit to Daudi confirmed that he was indeed weak. He looked very ill as he lay on a sofa. His wife brought out his medical forms, which showed he was on standard treatment for TB and weighed 43 kg. He said that nothing had changed regarding the case; it was still with the Magistrates' Court. His lawyer had gone on study leave but assured Daudi that he could ring if anything happened. We did not stay long. Daudi had a friend visiting, a man who had earlier worked for the UN. On the table between them lay a book entitled *7 Ways to Financial Success*.

By the end of October 2016, nearly ten years after the original division of plots, six or eight people had been shown their plots, and one person had put up a building. The court case was still pending, which inhibited distribution of plots in the disputed area. The chair of the sub-county council was certain that they could win. After all, the district lawyer would represent the sub-county for free, while Daudi and his family would have to waste their own funds to fight the case in court. But the chairman did not want to pursue the court case while Daudi was so ill, perhaps not long for the world. The major protagonist on the side of the Palwa clan seemed now to be Polycarp, and he had been invited to join the new sub-county council on the seat reserved for the elderly. The council chairman was hopeful that Polycarp would convince Daudi and his lineage mates to reach an agreement for the sake of development. 'If you are a member of council and are against development, it's not good.' Other council members and a parish chief speculated that Polycarp's idea of development included improvement of his own family circumstances and that he would demand financial compensation. The chairman remarked that they could budget for that if the amount was reasonable. In other words, they could buy their way to a compromise so that the plot owners could finally undertake their commitment to develop their plots.

Three months later, in January 2017, the main change in the situation was that Daudi's health had improved after three months in hospital. His wife was expecting their tenth child ('and this will be the last', she asserted firmly). With his renewed strength, he was still pursuing the case. His wife remarked that Daudi's brothers supported him with words but not with money. She thought he might have to sell more land to pay the lawyer, as he had done initially.

A meeting had just been held about the allocation of the twenty-five plots. Daudi attended and expressed his bitterness. The Amin regime had grabbed his land, he said, and now his brothers were betraying him, wanting to settle with the sub-county. Perhaps he was thinking of Polycarp, now a member of the sub-county council. Certainly, none of his brothers were present, so there was no support for him when the sub-county chief asked him to cool down and leave the meeting. The chief spoke calmly, inviting him to come to his office later to discuss the matter.

Of What Is This a Case?

The plotting of development in Pacuk, and the conflict that hindered the process, is one particular version of a story that was common in the Acholi sub-region in the decade that followed the closing of the IDP camps. With its details of surveys and plot divisions, graders and new roads, historical land gifts and current court cases, it is an illuminating extended case. We suggest that it is a specific instance of two more general interrelated phenomena. Daudi was making a claim on some land that his dead father had given to the local government long ago. The pattern of claiming land that forebears had given over to an institution is found generally in northern Uganda. At the same time, his claim is entangled with the efforts of local government to divide and sell plots of land in this small urban centre. So, this is also a specific case of the more general phenomenon of division and commercialization of land in urbanizing areas. Moreover, the case is a concrete example of some abstract principles. The concrete criticism that Daudi was blocking development is founded on an abstract principle that development is an absolute value, an ideal that must be pursued. The sub-county is promoting development through encouraging the sale of plots, while Daudi and his family also declare their belief in development. The case invites us to consider what development might mean generally and specifically. And when we ask the obvious question 'development for whom?' we may be led to intangible matters like trust.

This Land *Is* For Sale

When fighting broke out in the Acholi sub-region during the late 1980s, people in affected areas took refuge at churches, health facilities and local government headquarters. These were mostly located in small urban centres. Later, when government forced the entire population into internment, the IDP camps were established in trading centres, often the very places where people had already fled spontaneously. Once an IDP camp had been gazetted, all landowners, not only institutions, had to allow displaced people to build houses and stay on their land. They were not allowed to charge rent, although some who had agricultural land in the immediate periphery of the camp did realize some kind of gain from allowing displaced people to use it. Small trading centres like Pacuk (a pseudonym) underwent forced urbanization, as thousands were concentrated in a constrained space. To the service institutions already located there were added facilities provided by humanitarian relief, such as the Early Child Development buildings put up on Daudi's land.

After the end of hostilities in 2006, and as the camps were decommissioned around 2008, displaced people were urged to 'return to where the war had found them'. Most left, but some preferred to stay on for various reasons (Whyte et al. 2013a). Thereafter, landowners could charge them rent, and the impetus towards commodification of land was thus encouraged. More important in that respect was the move by many centres that had hosted IDP camps to upgrade their status to Town Board or Town Council. Also, Gulu Municipality, where thousands had fled though it was never recognized as an IDP camp, upgraded to City status as its suburbs expanded considerably. These moves meant that land in urban and semi-urban areas increased in value (Büscher, Komujuni and Ashaba 2018). As in Pacuk, plans were made, plots were delineated and a lively market in land developed. Therefore, those with family land in or adjoining the centres found themselves in an advantageous position. One person remarked: 'A plot on the road is worth three acres in the village [rural area].' Likewise, institutional land, which very often lay in or near the growing centres, began to look more attractive.

Land sales were increasing throughout Acholiland, in part because the loss of livestock before and during the war left people with little else that could be exchanged for money. Land became a form of wealth (*lim*), like livestock, that had a potential monetary value. This commodification of land ran against the fundamental ideal of entrustment in Acholi culture. Ancestral land (*ngom kwaro*) is to be kept in stewardship for future generations, not sold. Money realized in land sales disappears quickly, while land remains as a basis for subsistence and belonging (Kusk 2018: 78). When people were being encouraged to leave the camps and return to their rural homes, leaders urged them to go back and secure their ancestral land and to avoid selling it. One announcement we heard even added that those who wanted to buy and sell land should do so in urban centres. There was no question that many political leaders saw the market in urban plots as desirable and necessary if small and larger urban centres were to develop (Meinert and Kjær 2017; see Lentz 2013: 223ff for a description of the tensions around division into plots in small urban centres in Burkina Faso). Thus, a contrast emerged between the ideals of entrustment and development. In urbanizing areas, land was most definitely for sale. The two ideals also implied a distinction between the near and the far future (Guyer 2007). The potential of urban plots for development gave them value within a more immediate time frame – a foreseeable future for yourself and your children. Entrusted stewardship of ancestral land was about a foreseeable future too, but it was also a matter of long-term value for generations yet to come (See Chapter 2 on the temporalities of transactions).

Claims on the Land of Institutions

When people today speak of how land was given away in the past (not sold, but nevertheless handed over) to new institutions, they attribute it to the desire for development. Daudi told how his father, who had travelled as a soldier and lived in southern Uganda, wanted development for his home area. A former sub-county chairman said wistfully, 'In those days our parents gave land for development.' A man involved in a boundary conflict with the local church said: 'Our grandfather gave this land for development. We have no problem with that ... They were Christians. They thought if the church was here and the school was here it was good. Things like knowledge and land will help people after you die.' The case that opened Part III of our book shows this early commitment to development by way of the link between churches and schools. It also illustrates the desire to 'own' development; each party to the conflict wanted to control the school and the land upon which it stood.

People who have given land to institutions in more recent times also formulate their generosity in terms of appreciation of development. A man who gave land in 2013 for teachers' use at the neighbouring senior secondary school remarked that he gave land so the teachers could stay at the school. There was no written agreement; he gave it in the same spirit in which his grandfather had done so. It brought development close to hand. 'If development is coming, you need not be rigid. Instead of boarding a bus [going to the city], development is near.' It is noteworthy that in Adjumani and Lamwo Districts, where locals have given land for refugees to settle (for unspecified periods of time), they explain their willingness in two ways: first, the refugees from South Sudan are humans like us and we know what it is like to flee from war; second, the refugee settlement will bring development to our area. The chairman of Palabek Refugee Settlement told Susan that the Acholi Ugandans requested a refugee settlement because they saw the development that refugees had brought to neighbouring Adjumani District.

In a sense, the donation of land to institutions that will serve the community involves imagination of the near future – development should come here and soon – just as it does for those buying plots to build shops. The difference is that the benefit envisioned is for the more general good, not only for the advancement of one individual or family. While land is still donated, especially in rural areas where some kin groups have extensive holdings, it is extremely rare in growing urban centres today. Instead, the opposite is occurring; land once given is being reclaimed. It is as if the gift of embedded land could not be final; family members felt that they still retained some entitlements, just as Chauveau and Colin (2010: 98) showed that a land sale could be considered incomplete and challenged by a descendant of the seller in Côte d'Ivoire. Land disputes between institutions and local people occur all over Uganda, but the recent history of northern Uganda has provided especially fertile ground for this type of conflict, with the radical changes that have occurred in the wake of the IDP camps (Whyte et al. 2014). The claims on institutional land are one important part of the story of plotting development in growing urban areas.

In some cases, the institutional land at issue was considered public or government land. It could be land upon which stood a public market, a health centre, a community hall or a local government building. In the case of Pacuk, the sub-county authorities claimed that local government owned an area within the trading centre. On this land, they had overseen the construction of a new market, and they wished to subdivide and sell another portion to generate income. Before doing so, they had to clear the land of displaced persons and the graves of those buried there during the war.

In other cases, land is held by non-government institutions such as churches and mosques. The Church of Uganda (Anglican) and the Catholic church have been landholders since the time of the Protectorate. They have constructed churches, health centres and schools on their land. During the war, they provided refuge for many displaced people, some of whom have remained.

The simple division between government and non-government institutions is more complicated when it comes to schools, as the case of 'Claiming "Their" School' demonstrates. Many schools were founded by Catholic or Anglican missions and churches on land they considered theirs. When the government took over the schools in the 1960s, it provided and paid the teachers and mediated donor funds for the building of new classrooms. It acknowledged the role of the church by recognizing 'the foundation body' and giving it the privilege of appointing half the members of the school management committee, including its chair. Thus, while the government provided the software (teachers and curriculum) and often some classroom blocks, the church provided the hardware in the form of land and the original buildings.

Generally, the conflicts over institutional land were of three types:

1. Descendants of men or families who donated land for projects of common good were asserting that the institution had taken more land than it was originally given.
2. People who settled on, or were using, land claimed by institutions refused to vacate or to acknowledge institutional claims.
3. Institutions disagreed between themselves over rights to a piece of land and the facility that was located there.

The conflict between Daudi and the sub-county officials was clearly of the first kind, as were other cases in Pacuk, including a dispute between the Anglican church and the families whose forefathers gave land to the church. Mostly these were boundary disputes; the claimant was seldom demanding all the land. Many of the second type were conflicts over timing; the settlers claimed they needed to stay longer because they had nowhere else to go. But sometimes, as in the case of a leprosy facility no longer in use, they asserted their rights as settlers who had lived on the former institutional land for many years. The last type of conflict was illustrated by the case 'Claiming "Their" School', which opened Part III of our book. Because of the history of church-state relations around education, and the fact that the recognition of the foundation body had been withdrawn and then reintroduced, there were a good many cases of schools and school land that were claimed by both the Anglican and Catholic churches. As of 2018, in the Lango sub-region, there were conflicts over twenty schools, while another twenty had been settled.

Of course, there are other kinds of land conflicts between families and powerful organizations, some of which have been discussed in earlier chapters. In these too, the ideal of development is brought into play to justify land claims. National parks, an important source of tourism income, constitute very large land areas and are subject to several varieties of conflict (Chapter 9). Businesses such as the mining company in Karamoja (Chapter 8) or the wind turbine enterprise in Kaabong (Chapter 2) or Madhvani Sugar Ltd (Serwajja 2012; Mariniello 2015) acquire, or attempt to acquire, both large and smaller areas, in the name of economic development.

The cases to which we draw attention here differ in that they are located in urban centres and involve protagonists who know one another. Service institutions like schools, churches and health facilities are used by people in the locality, staffed by persons who usually live in the neighbourhood and with whom the disputants interact on an everyday basis. Daudi and his lineage brother and their families were well-connected with members of the sub-county council. In other instances, people refusing to vacate church land are members of the congregation, who pray together with those who are asking them to leave.

Land obtained by companies for business tends to be registered as freehold or leasehold. Forest reserves and national parks are gazetted by government, so their boundaries are formalized and publicized. In contrast, the claims against local institutions concern land that is often not titled. In many cases, there are no papers, no surveys and no mark stones to formalize ownership of institutional land. It was given at a time when land was abundant, and surveying was uncommon. Until the Constitution of 1998, land belonged legally to the government, so there seemed no need to register the land of government institutions. Most land held by the Church of Uganda, like the land in the case of 'Claiming "Their" School', was not registered, perhaps because the Anglican church had been close to government. (The Catholic church, in contrast, tended to formalize its landholdings.) Because of the many conflicts, district governments in northern Uganda have been encouraging both government and non-government organizations to survey and register their land (Whyte and Shroff 2017).

'Development Cannot Stand on Air – It Must Stand on Land'

This assertion, which we heard many times, underlines the perceived necessity of land for development. It also reveals the image of development that is foremost in the minds of most people. Development is material. It consists of roads, markets and, most of all, buildings. In Pacuk, and in other growing small urban centres, the physical plans for development were posted in a public place where residents could study them. The drawings showed streets lined with delineated plots for commercial and residential buildings. In Pacuk, twenty-five of these plots were offered for sale by local government. But much of the land along the streets was owned by families, like that of Daudi. They too were encouraged (some said, required) to mark off plots and develop them. The demand that land in urban centres be developed figured as well in the case of Atim and Awor (Chapter 5). If they could not afford to do so, they were advised to sell off some plots in order to develop the remaining ones. Ideally, plots should be surveyed and identified with mark stones. But surveying and registering a plot as freehold is a costly and cumbersome process (Kusk 2018) – so much so that plotting and surveying Daudi's family land within Pacuk Town Board was the compensation offered for the land he claimed. Most plot sales were not formally registered, and plots were not surveyed. But they were committed to paper and signed by witnesses. One man who was selling plots of family land within the Town Board emphasized that sales were not secret: 'Land is sold by day, not at night.'

Land must be cleared in order to build. As one resident of Pacuk put it: 'When development comes, those mangos at the old market will be cut down. Whether we like it or not, the trees will be cut. That is money. Development will cut them.' Trees would be replaced by buildings. A man operating a vocational school in a prospective Town Board decried the lack of good permanent buildings. 'In rural areas, it's worse. We should also develop – put up structures, open schools like this.' The structures envisioned were of fired bricks; evidence of brick production was everywhere. Indeed, the very land that hosted a new building might be the source of soil for making the bricks. A man making bricks on land he and his local church both claimed said: 'Structures must be there for development. Whether it is for the church or not, structures must be built.'

Those structures are rectangular, in contrast to the round huts of the IDP camps and the circular Acholi houses that are still by far the most common after people moved back to their rural homes. Round houses have thatch roofs, while rectangular ones have corrugated metal (*mabati*) roofs. One spokesman for development in a Town Board dismissed poverty as a justification for thatched roofs: 'Even a poor man can make a semi-permanent house of mud bricks and buy *mabati* so structures are not grass thatch like a village. Urbanisation cannot be there if people are living in thatch houses' (Whyte et al. 2014: 612).

Plotting the Future

It was striking in Pacuk how often the word development was used in connection with land plans. The sub-county wanted to sell plots to those who could develop them. And it encouraged others who already had land within the projected Town Board to divide it into plots and develop it. If they could not develop it themselves, they should sell or lease it to someone who could. Daudi and his brother Polycarp both declared that they too wanted development, while many criticized Daudi for impeding it by filing a court case that dragged on and on. In the case of the claims on the school in Amati, the interest of the two churches in asserting claims to the land upon which the school stood had become 'a hindrance to development'. Development is invoked as an ideal, a goal, a motivation and a justification. At a general level, it is irrefutable; no one wants to be seen as against development. This unanimity is possible because 'development', its implementation and its beneficiaries are not specified, a point to which we will return. But for the moment we emphasize that development is seen as a significant value that should move people in connection with the disposition of land.

Development points towards a desired future. Whereas claims on ancestral land are often formulated in terms of past use, the keen interest in land is future oriented:

> ... when I talk to people about *why* land is important for them, the future potentials are central in informing their decisions and guiding them in their attempts to claim land, as are the negative potentials related to the enmity generated by wrangling. Therefore, a perspective on the future of land as people perceive it is highly relevant. (Kusk 2018: 53)

In order to unfold the cultural conception of development as orientation towards the future, we may borrow three concepts from Appadurai (2013): Imagination, Anticipation and Aspiration.

Imagination as an element of the everyday, Appadurai suggests, is fundamental in producing locality.

> ... especially in the lives of ordinary people, the personal archive of memories, both material and cognitive, is not only or primarily about the past, but is about providing a map for negotiating and shaping new futures. While state generated archives may primarily be instruments of governmentality and bureaucratized power, personal, familial, and community archives – especially those of dislocated, vulnerable, and marginalized populations – are critical sites for negotiating paths to dignity, recognition, and politically feasible maps for the future. (Appadurai 2013: 288)

In the Acholi sub-region, memories and remains of the conflict and displacement are fundamental for how people imagine land. Displaced people were forced to leave their land; landowners in the IDP camps were obliged to accept settlers on theirs. Deserted IDP huts and 'graves in the wrong soil' (Jahn and Wilhelm-Solomon 2015) are the material reminders of land assumptions negated. People could no longer expect to bury their dead on their own land; they could be forced off their land and not even allowed to farm it. They could be crowded together on the land of institutions or other families. This kind of living provoked imaginations of moral decline and depravity (Mergelsberg 2012). Fears and suspicions emerged about whether their land might be taken by powerful outsiders. Then when security returned, land wrangles with intimate others added to the anxieties about land. So, part of the imagination with which people faced the future was unease about land.

Another part was visions of a different kind of life. For much as existence in the camps was a kind of 'social torture' (Dolan 2009), for some people at least it was a learning experience. Humanitarian workers and foreigners brought new ideas and practices: '. . . such vast, foreign presence influence[d] local ideas about "what it is worth having", and what a good life could look like' (Kusk 2018: 86). There were Early Childhood Development Centres, playgrounds, water systems, vocational schools and video halls. Small businesses and trade existed, despite the stringent restrictions. The camps were city-like spaces with 'innovating frameworks', but this was an 'incomplete, unfinished form of urbanity' characterized by waiting and liminality (Agier 2002: 337).

With the closing of the camps, the era of liminality and waiting seemed to fade as horizons of development opened. The efforts to achieve new urban status, the technical drawings of streets and plots, even the graders and the construction of new market buildings and local government headquarters sparked the imagination of a locality transformed. These memories of the camps and visions of urbanity and development constituted the personal, family and community archives that provided maps for the future.

Imagination provided grounds for anticipation – that is, figuring probable short-term futures. Anticipatory moves included making plans for the use of land, speculating on the value of land in favourable locations, preparing land for construction and taking steps to safeguard land. In Pabbo, which had been the largest IDP camp in the Acholi sub-region, landowners were keen to develop their land as upgrading to Town Council status proceeded. The displaced people had left, but the graves of those buried in the camp remained (Meinert and Whyte 2013; Seebach 2016). Landowners wanted to put up new buildings in the growing urban centre but were loath to construct on graves because the spirits of the dead might disturb the families of the landowners. Development and graves did not fit together. Efforts to persuade families to exhume and remove the bones left 'in the wrong soil' anticipated development in Pabbo (Jahn and

Wilhelm-Solomon 2015) just as it did in Pacuk. A contrary example appears in the story of Atim and Awor (Chapter 5), whose sister paid to cement their mother's grave on their plot in Pader centre in order to protect the land from development.

Land in an urban centre or on a road close to a centre assumed greater value. Owners of such land anticipated possibilities. A family with a piece of land on the outskirts of Gulu near the university main campus was struggling to keep it. They hoped to build a hostel so they could rent rooms to university students. Despite the unresolved conflict, they began to cut down trees on the land as fuel to burn bricks for the anticipated building (Kusk 2018: 181, 276). Daudi sold some of his agricultural land in order to fight the court case about land that could be plotted and sold in the new Town Board. Sylvia (Chapter 3) disputed fiercely with her brother-in-law about a piece of land on the road. Away from the road, there was plenty of land for common family use. Only the land along the road was divided and contested (see also Anying and Gausset 2017: 366). In another case, Kusk (2018: 276) sums up neatly: 'The disputed land is very small, maybe ½ an acre. It's not good for cultivation, now his father just lives there. It is next to the roadside, so it is a good area. If development comes, they can sell it or construct something.' Anticipation here is based on imagined development.

Appadurai asserts that aspirations towards a good life in future are just as much a part of any culture as are traditions and values rooted in the past. Wants, hopes, expectations and preferences may differ from one society to another, and he urges us to attend to images of the good life and the 'politics of hope' that mobilize towards its achievement. The catch is a point developed in an earlier work but neglected in *The Future as Cultural Fact*: the capacity to aspire is unevenly distributed. Capacity is like a muscle that must be exercised: 'capacity to aspire, like any complex cultural capacity, thrives and survives on practice, repetition, exploration, conjecture, and refutation' (Appadurai 2004: 69). People with more resources have more opportunities to try out pathways to future aspirations; poor people, those in difficult circumstances, have fewer: 'part of poverty is a diminishing of the circumstances in which these practices occur' (ibid.).

For nearly twenty years, as the LRA war dragged on, circumstances did not permit most residents of the Acholi and Lango sub-regions to pursue their aspirations for development. When peace came and the IDP camps were closed, the ideal seemed more reachable. But there were differences in capacity to aspire. The sub-county office in Pacuk exhibited beautiful drawings of the future Town Board; they negotiated with donors for electricity and new roads. They were able to draw on support from the District Planner and from the Faculty of Technology at Makerere University (Whyte et al. 2014: 610–11). Daudi and his family had resources too. They sold land to hire a lawyer and file a court case with the District Magistrate. They had visions of development, and they were able to pursue their aspirations. Most residents of the centre shared the aspirations, even though it meant that they had to leave the land they had been occupying. However, only a minority of them had the capacity to practically pursue the goal of development. They had neither the resources to buy plots and put up buildings, nor past experience of successfully pursuing aspirations for development. It was striking that many of the plots being sold went to people originally from the area but currently living and working outside of the growing centre. Two of the plots sold by a family with land in the centre of Pacuk were bought by soldiers who were serving in Somalia. In the same way, the sister of Atim and Awor, who was working in Soroti, felt that she should have the land in Pader Town Council because she had the money to develop it by constructing a permanent building and had gone to court to fight for the land (Chapter 5). Her capacity to aspire was greater.

The case of Stephen Langole, which opens Chapter 1, is a frank example of imagination, anticipation and capacity to aspire. He imagines the post-conflict condition of land sales and insecurity of tenure. He anticipates that acquiring private land in different locations will provide insurance against land greed. He has the capacity to aspire to personal development through land purchases, in terms of financial resources, connections, knowledge and experience – even though his pursuits are dogged by conflicts and obstacles. His plot in Gulu town (Land 3), for example, was an anticipated investment, which he wanted to develop by putting up a structure. The effort was partly hindered by the development plans of Uganda Railways Corporation, but if URC takes his land by compulsory acquisition and pays compensation, his investment will prove sound. The many land wrangles in which Langole is involved suggest that although his capacity to aspire is strong others have aspirations that may clash with his. There may be coincidence or contradiction between individual and collective development plans as the matter of the Uganda Railways land survey reminds us.

Conclusion

Development is a general ideal that has nearly unanimous support in post-war Acholiland. But the particulars are problematic. Development how? Development for whom? In Pacuk, Daudi and his brother Polycarp put it clearly. They were not against development for the community, but they also wanted it for themselves and their own children. As Polycarp said to the sub-county council: 'We don't want you to leave [the land]. We also want to be developed. I may build a house or buy land for the young ones.' Simply speaking, development may be for the individual, the family or 'the community' – although community always means some and not others (M. Whyte and S. Whyte 1998). Often development of an individual brings growth to a family; at least that is the family's hope. A community development project initiated by a family may advance both. One man in Pacuk, who was running a vocational training school on (what he claimed was) family land, asserted that his target was to help the community but added that it would also help his family.

Often enough, community development is at odds with family and individual development. If institutions such as schools, health centres and local government are considered communal, then the many cases of reclaimed formerly donated land show such contradictions. Community institutions can also oppose one another in their aspirations, like the Catholic and Anglican church communities in Amati; this hindered development of the local community and thus children's education suffered.

Our TrustLand project has assembled a multitude of cases where families oppose families and individuals oppose intimate others. Sometimes both parties to a land wrangle have aspirations for development; sometimes one wants to develop (construct a building) or sell a piece of land while others want to keep it in trust for children and grandchildren. In the case of 'A Disputed Land Sale', which opened Part I of this book, Elisabeth declared that the plot on the outskirts of Gulu town was to be kept for her grandsons, but her daughter Grace sold the land without her knowledge and used the money for a permanent structure on the land where she was staying.

That an individual's development can be impeded by family needs or aspirations is abundantly illustrated in Stephen Langole's case. He declares that he wants 'to possess private land free from any other claims even from people who are intimately close to me like my wife and children'. Yet there are family entanglements on five of the six pieces of land he claims. He got the land through kinship connections – through inheritance or on the recommendation of a relative. He allowed family members to use the land – to live, to run businesses, to graze livestock and even to build a house. He concludes that private landholding is almost impossible in practice; constant negotiation and accommodation are necessary. He cannot rely on anyone: 'My experience, based on the way people who are intimately connected to me contest my ownership and control of land, demonstrates the difficulty in trusting anybody on matters of land.'

Trust is obviously a necessary element of entrustment; stewards must be reliable, responsible and faithful to the common agreement that land should be protected for future generations. But trust turns out to be a key issue in development of land as well. Do people keep their word when they promise to vacate land should the owner want it for development? Can a buyer trust that the seller is the legitimate representative of the owners? Will money allocated for a development project be misused?

We have argued that trust cannot be taken for granted in northern Uganda. It is tentative and must be proposed and reaffirmed over time. It is through consultation and communication that this can happen, as was clear in the case that opened this chapter. Daudi and his brother Polycarp repeatedly complained that they were not recognized; that the sub-county did things without their knowledge. They wanted discussion, they wanted to be appreciated through compensation, to be acknowledged and included in the plans for Town Board development.

Communication and consultation do not in themselves create trust but are a step in the right direction. Including Polycarp in the sub-county council was a positive move that at least proposed some kind of trust. The opposite, lack of communication, provides fertile ground for mistrust, as Kusk (2018) has shown in her study of land wrangles with intimate others. Even in conflicts about larger development projects, such as the Madhvani sugar cane plantation, the mining project in Moroto, and the wind turbine in Kaabong, complaints are made that investors did not consult and negotiate directly with local people. Development as locally imagined, as anticipated, and as an aspiration must be specified, discussed and debated continually if a modicum of trust is to be ensured.

Susan Reynolds Whyte, Ph.D., is Professor at the Department of Anthropology, University of Copenhagen.

Catrine Shroff, Ph.D., was post doc at Aarhus University and is currently senior consultant at Nordic Consulting Group and Director of Mwangaza Light.

References

Agier, Michel. 2002. 'Between War and the City: Towards an Urban Anthropology of Refugee Camps', *Ethnography* 3(3): 317–41.
Anying, Irene Winnie, and Quentin Gausset. 2017. 'Gender and Forum Shopping in Land Conflict Resolution in Northern Uganda', *The Journal of Legal Pluralism and Unofficial Law* 49(3): 353–72.
Appadurai, Arjun. 2004. 'The Capacity to Aspire: Culture and the Terms of Recognition', in Vijayendra Rao and Michael Walton (eds), *Culture and Public Action*. Stanford, CA: Stanford University Press, pp. 59–84.
———. 2013. *The Future as Cultural Fact: Essays on the Global Condition*. London: Verso.
Büscher, Karen, Sophie Komujuni and Ivan Ashaba. 2018. 'Humanitarian Urbanism in a Post-conflict Aid Town: Aid Agencies and Urbanization in Gulu, Northern Uganda', *Journal of Eastern African Studies* 12(2): 348–66.
Chauveau, Jean-Pierre, and Jean-Philippe Colin. 2010. 'Customary Transfers and Land Sales in Côte d'Ivoire: Revisiting the Embeddedness Issue', *Africa* 80(1): 81–103.
Dolan, Chris. 2009. *Social Torture: The Case of Northern Uganda, 1986–2006*. New York: Berghahn Books.
Guyer, Jane. 2007. 'Prophecy and the Near Future: Thoughts on Macroeconomic, Evangelical, and Punctuated Time', *American Ethnologist* 34: 409–21.
Jahn, Ina, and Matthew Wilhelm-Solomon. 2015. '"Bones in The Wrong Soil": Reburial, Belonging, and Disinterred Cosmologies in Post-Conflict Northern Uganda', *Critical African Studies* 7(2): 182–201.
Kusk, Mette. 2018. 'On Uncertain Ground: Intimate Wrangles over Land and Belonging in Northern Uganda', Ph.D. dissertation. Aarhus: University of Aarhus.

Lentz, Carola. 2013. *Land, Mobility, and Belonging in West Africa*. Bloomington: Indianapolis.
Mariniello, Giuliano. 2015. 'Social Struggles in Uganda's Acholiland: Understanding Responses and Resistance to Amuru Sugar Works', *The Journal of Peasant Studies* 42(3–4): 653–69.
Meinert, Lotte, and Anne Mette Kjær. 2017. '"Land Belongs to the People of Uganda": Politicians' Use of Land Issues in the 2016 Election Campaigns', *Journal of Eastern African Studies* 10(4): 769–88.
Meinert, Lotte, and Susan Reynolds Whyte. 2013. 'Creating the New Times: Reburials after War in Northern Uganda', in Dorthe Refslund Christensen and Rane Willerslev (eds), *Taming Time, Timing Death: Social Technologies and Ritual*. New York: Ashgate, pp. 175–95.
Mergelsberg, Ben. 2012. 'The Displaced Family: Moral Imaginations and Social Control in Pabbo, Northern Uganda', *Journal of Eastern African Studies* 6(1): 64–80.
Seebach, Sophie Hooge. 2016. 'The Dead Are Not Dead: Intimate Governance of Transitions in Acholi', Ph.D. dissertation. Aarhus: Aarhus University.
Serwajja, Eria. 2012. 'The Quest for Development Through Dispossession: Examining Amuru Sugar Works in Lakang-Amuru District of Northern Uganda', *International Academic Conference on Global Land Grabbing II, October 17–19, 2012*. New York: Cornell University.
Whyte, S. R., et al. 2013a. 'Remaining Internally Displaced: Missing Links to Security in Northern Uganda', *Journal of Refugee Studies* 26(2): 283–301.
———. 2013b. 'From Encampment to Emplotment: Land Matters in Former IDP Camps', *Journal of Peace and Security Studies* 1: 17–27.
———. 2014. 'Urbanization by Subtraction: The Afterlife of Camps in Northern Uganda', *Journal of Modern African Studies* 52(4): 597–622.
Whyte, Susan Reynolds, and Catrine Shroff. 2017. 'Institutional Land Conflicts'. Gulu: Institute of Peace and Strategic Studies, Trustland Policy Brief. https://trustlanddotme.files.wordpress.com/2018/05/policy-brief-4.pdf.
Whyte Susan Reynolds, and Michael A. Whyte. 1998. 'The Values of Development: Conceiving Growth and Progress in Bunyole', in Holger Bernt Hansen and Michael Twaddle (eds), *Developing Uganda*. London: James Currey, pp. 227–44.

Chapter 8
Inside-Outsiders
Marianne Mosebo and Lotte Meinert

Middlemen for Marble Miners

Peter sat in the front seat next to the driver of the four-wheel vehicle who diligently manoeuvred the potholes in the murram road at a great speed. Peter turned to the back seat to explain to Marianne:

> Minerals cause a lot of conflict because they have a lot of value. When I joined [the civil society organization], we were seeing latent conflict and intervened before it turned violent. The locals did not build on knowledge, just speculations. [They said things such as]: 'This one . . . the RDC [Resident District Commissioner] . . . the CAO [Chief Administrative Officer] . . . this *mzungu* [white person] they are in with the investors. We saw him riding in a car with the investors'. We [the CSO] accessed people and explained that they have rights. You cannot lock out the investors, because we [the Karamojong] don't have the capacity to mine these things. The investors can benefit us with roads, health centres, royalties . . . . The bad thing with investors is that they are business-minded. They give promises, but they are not concrete. When people want their rights, the investors go to the government, who put their soldiers. At the mining site, there are those barracks just to intimidate people from coming. The elders are saying: 'Why are they intimidating us in our own land?' If you move with soldiers, it means you are guilty . . . people get annoyed because the land belongs to the people yet the minerals belong to the government. They don't see the logic.

Peter was a young man who had been appointed by the civil society organization (CSO) to lead the communication with miners on behalf of the civil society network in Moroto, which is the regional headquarters of Karamoja. He was meant to be the focal point for dialogue with site landowners, who also worked as artisanal miners. Peter explained that he considers himself lucky because even though he was orphaned in the armed cattle raids of the 1990s together with so many other Karamojong children, he still got a chance to go to school on a government grant. The grant meant that he did not become a 'school drop-out' but became part of the small, educated elite in Karamoja who often play the role of middlemen between the mining industry, other outside elites and local landowners.

On this dry and hot morning in 2015, Marianne had been allowed to tag along to a marble mining site with Peter. They had set off on a murram road that slithered through the landscape like the pythons after which Moroto is named. Pythons used to be here in abundance, said Peter, but as the trees and bushes decreased through the previous century, animals went away as well. It was a drought year, so the few crops in the fields had withered; mainly scrub and thorny, dry bushes grew along the way. Peter commented on how the Karamojong are used to living in an environment marked by erratic rainfall patterns. Historically, pastoralism and flexible mobility in the vast region have been the most reliable means of survival. The mining site was located in a mountain area known for its dryness. Marianne and Peter discussed how some people in town say that the locals from this area are lucky because they have the minerals and can get an income. Others say that this community is unfortunate because they are likely to lose their land in the end. The windows of the car were closed to avoid the dust blown about by the strong and playful Karamoja winds. Peter made the common joke in Karamoja that the winds are the 'Karamoja allowance' because the wind is the only blessing that the Karamojong ever gain from outside.

During the drive, Marianne asked about the use of the word *elite*, and Peter reflected:

> Some [feel] guilty when you use that word. It's those ones with a business mind. They can go and manipulate their own people, buying people's land, not even following the right procedure . . . *Elite capture* has become a common phrase in meetings . . . Elite capture . . . is when you just capture something for yourself. . . . It is when the educated take advantage of communities, who are illiterate, to buy land and sell to investors. These days, people want to acquire wealth very fast in the wrong way.

The car was nearing the mining site at the foot of a mountain, and at the bottom of a small hill there was an enclave of thin trees and small simple huts for soldiers. A pole had been placed across the road, and when the car stopped, a soldier stood up from a small stool in the shade and lazily walked over to the car. Peter told the soldier that they were here to talk to the artisanal miners about some tools they had provided them with a while ago. The soldier nodded, and the pole was removed to let the car through. Where the road bent to the left, the car passed a metal gate. It was the sole entrance to a walled compound serving as the mining company's quarters. A bit further along was a drinking place serving local brew, *ngaagwe*, for the artisanal miners. After the drinking place, a site appeared with a building under construction. It was a factory, which was becoming an increasingly difficult part of the mining story, according to Peter. Further along still, the artisanal mining site appeared, and the car stopped.

An older woman, with a colourful head scarf, came to greet Marianne and Peter. She was the chair of the artisanal miners. Marianne explained her research on the relationship between the different stakeholders in mining, and the chair replied:

> The relationship with the investors is not stable. They said they only wanted the blocks [of marble], and then the small rubble was for the community to benefit from. So, we became surprised that they changed they minds and picked an interest in the small stones. . . . They put the factory without consulting the people. The factory doesn't employ local people, only a few women for cooking. Some were employed at first, but they didn't pay them . . . . Back when they first came, two years ago, they came without talking to people. We just heard the sound of the machine and found soldiers there. We were surprised. They then held a meeting with the investors and authorities at district and sub-county level and made the agreement of small stones versus the big blocks.

Peter explained that this mine was one of the few in the Karamoja region holding a full mining lease. Explorations for mining can happen without the involvement of the local community, but when they have a full mining lease, the company and authorities must involve the local community in the development of the site. However, in the case of the factory, the local stakeholders had not been involved, according to the chair, but woke up one morning surprised by the sound of machines. The artisanal miners saw the factory as an infringement of the deal they thought they had with the mining company when the company first arrived. The factory would undermine their business of breaking and selling the small stones to truck drivers, who drove the rubble to factories outside Karamoja for producing a powder used in paint and other products.

The discussion with the chair turned to focus on the relationship with the CSOs, and she explained how the organizations had taught them about their rights in land issues. She said that people from the organizations were 'our voices' (*ngiporotoi*). 'So these ones are not the elites?', Marianne interjected, and the chair responded with a laugh: 'No! They came and helped us form groups, and they gave us tools. It's not like those ones who came and grabbed the land. The investors come to meet elites. When they come to the community [the deal] is already finished.'

When asked about the NgaKarimojong word for elite, the chair said: 'We call them *ekokolan* – thieves', which made Peter laugh. Marianne and Peter spent some time at the mining site talking to some of the artisanal miners. One of the young miners pointed out that the artisanal miners wanted to go to the training sessions and meetings about mining. They did not want other people to go and then later be trained by them. They wanted investors to talk to the miners directly rather than to go through elites and others in town. The mediators were not regarded as necessary by the artisanal miners, who believed they could speak for themselves. The discussions were good, but the soldiers at the site seemed keen to have the visitors leave sooner rather than later, so after a while Marianne and Peter thanked the people they had talked to, climbed into the car and headed back to Moroto town.

The conversation about the term 'elite' continued with other stakeholders after the visit to the mining site, and the negative connotations of the term were confirmed by many locals, who also pointed out that 'if you are seen as someone who helps the locals, you are not called an elite'. Some of the NgaKarimojong words they used for elite mean 'someone who is business minded' or 'someone who has knowledge and takes advantage of other people's lack of knowledge'. Some would simply translate elite as *ngikasiomak*, 'someone who is educated', while others translated it more negatively as *ngikaothok*, 'someone who claims to be knowing more' – that is, someone who claims to be smarter than others and benefits from it. None of the participants in the discussions self-identified with being 'business-minded elites' but 'educated elites', as they all worked for NGOs and CSOs. They did recognize how elites were often not appreciated for their efforts. A CSO employee said that elites continuously face local landowners who 'accuse everybody of conniving with the investors', while the CSO employees and other local educated people saw themselves as 'trying to help'.

A young man who had co-founded a research and advocacy organization explained that they started their work because they saw a lack of coordinated effort in regard to mining in Karamoja: 'The mining sector is still young. It will grow. And it will have to have an impact on our lives. We need to embrace it. But we need to get organized. We are not experts in mining, so we hope for training so we can pass the information to the communities.' His words confirmed those of another young advocate who had been appointed to a coordinator role amongst the CSOs working with mining: 'The CSOs have become mediators.' The young advocate explained that they had instated themselves as a necessary link between the local landowners and the powerful others to close the knowledge gap in the mining processes: 'There is a missing link. Who knows what when? The link is not there. The backdrop to it is: What the government wants with the region, what the CSOs want with the region, what the communities want with the region, and what the local government wants with the region.'

At the mining site, this position is exactly what the young artisanal miner had opposed when he said that the artisanal miners wanted investors to talk to them directly rather than go through elites in town, and that they wanted to go to trainings themselves. The young, educated people who saw themselves as necessary mediators were not regarded as such by the artisanal miners. The young advocate was aware of these opposed positions and made it clear that they were aware of their own role and that it was not always congruent with what all locals want.

Many of the young mediators point to the traditional land authority structure and land ownership as a problem. In Karamoja, most of the land is communally held, but according to Peter the tenure is divided into two types: *communal customary* tenure, which focuses on user rights to grazing areas and access to traditional religious sites according to clan belonging. The other type is *individualized customary* tenure, where home settlements and garden ownership are more closely bound to families and household heads through the patrilineal system. Elders hold the knowledge and authority on land issues as the custodians of land. Some of the young mediators believed this way of governing and relating to the land was perceived by outsiders as 'lacking organization', and this led to wrangles over access to land.

The young coordinator said that the organizations were trying to harmonize the traditional system with the formal one. The modern, formal system means instating Area Land Committees, in which a number of people are assigned to discuss and deal with land issues in their areas: 'The council of elders might be powerful in Karamoja, but it cannot omit state law', as he pointed out. This pertains particularly to mining because while the people might own the right to use the land, it is the government that owns what lies underground. The coordinator explained that the local government representatives were working on integrating the council of elders with what he called 'the modern system'. Marianne discussed this with an employee at an international NGO, who was affectionately called 'conservationist' amongst his friends because of his love of the traditional way of life in Karamoja. He said: 'The law recognizes the customary land ownership but not the customary traditional governance system. Karamoja is facing an existential threat. . . . We're between a rock and hard place . . . . We're dealing away with traditional ways. The future comes with conditionality.'

With these words, he expressed the dilemma of NGOs and elites of how to secure benefits for the Karamojong people. The elites felt that they had to share information, educate, link up various stakeholders and organize and harmonize traditional with modern systems, and in the process, they were 'dealing away with traditional ways'. The 'conservationist' was educated and had never been a pastoralist himself, so he and other educated Karamojong were often called *arieng* – strangers – by Karamojong, who in return were called 'indigenous'. They were inside-outsiders, put in a position as betwixt and between their home region and 'the outside world'. They were continuously faced with being categorized by insiders as the type of *elites* who were betraying their fellow Karamojong in their efforts to help and make beneficial links to outsiders.

Weeks after these discussions, at a hotel in Moroto town, Marianne ran into one of the central outsiders in this mining story: the foreign director of communication from the mining company, who was happy to have a chat with another outsider. The director was accompanied by his Ugandan driver, who also seemed to be a kind of bodyguard. The director explained that they were building factories at their various mining sites and that they had a local Karamojong spokesperson who took care of the CSR (Corporate Social Responsibility) issues. The local spokesperson was studying law in Kampala and was not present in Karamoja at the time, so Marianne talked to him on the phone. He emphasized that the factories would help the local Karamojong in important ways: they would provide job opportunities and with far better working conditions than the artisanal mining work of breaking small rocks in the hot sun and strong winds. The spokesperson explained how the company had carried out environmental and social impact assessments, and legally everything was in order between the mining company and the Directorate of Geological Survey and Mines in the Ministry of Energy and Mineral Development. The company had worked to ensure the surface rights holders' interests in three ways: consent from all stakeholders, a corporate social responsibility plan and payment of royalties. They had even held cultural rituals where bulls were sacrificed because the mountain used to be a religious site where elders met.

The director grandly invited Marianne to return to the mine and factory she had been to with Peter. When Marianne started organizing for her translator to come along, the director pointed out that there was no need to bring one because the workers were on holidays and there would be no one to talk to. The visit to the mine with the director did not happen, but it was clear that both the director and his spokesperson believed the factory had always been part of the mining lease deal dialogue with the local landowners, which was considered part of the company's Corporate Social Responsibility towards the local community.

This is the same factory that the artisanal miners had experienced as suddenly appearing on their land without any notice and that they felt was a threat to how they were making a living. In the view of the artisanal miners, the building of the factory breached the deal they had made through the middlemen with the company – a deal that would allow them to earn cash directly from the minerals under their land outside the royalties system.

When the factory was built, middlemen tried to mediate and explain that the artisanal miners eventually would get jobs in the factory, but as local people were not employed in the building process, the artisanal miners called the middlemen 'bad elites', engaging in 'business mindedness' and 'corrupt actions to gain money on the backs of poor people'. Peter explained that they had tried to organize meetings between the artisanal miners and the company, but the company director and his spokesperson never accepted the invitations for the meetings.

Of What Is This a Case?

The case of artisanal marble miners in Karamoja is a specific example of a resource extraction enterprise on the part of investors (or development actors) from outside the local community threatening landholding and land rights. While this is one common type of 'development' activity, there are many other types where land rights are at issue. In Chapter 2 on Transactions we saw how when a private company or national government or international donor initiates plans that require land, the relationship to local landholders and land users must be mediated. Land acquisition cases raise conceptual issues concerning the 'inside-outsiders' who so often broker the relationship between the external actors and the various stakeholders within the affected local community.

Inside-outsiders may be considered a kind of elite with special qualities. They have inside knowledge and experience of the local language and land situation, the social structures and tensions, as well as 'inside sensitivity' in relation to religious practices, cultural ways of doing things and how to evoke trust and understanding. At the same time, they have outside knowledge of international languages such as English and the languages of development, rights and Corporate Social Responsibility. They have various types of outside experience with education, business enterprises, organizations and the political system. They have the cultural capital of exposure to the outside world and the social capital (Bourdieu 1986) of having outside 'connections'; they are cosmopolitans who have lived in cities such as Kampala and Nairobi. They are seen as having both positive and negative potential because they can 'bring something good home from the outside' but also bring bad connections and 'give away what is good at home' to outsiders for their own benefit. These inside-outsiders often do not hold any formal authority in the local society, where elders are traditionally at the top (Dyson-Hudson 1963), and they do not hold a formal position in relation to the investors or development actors. They occupy an important and yet tricky betwixt and between position as middlemen.

There are a range of inside-outsiders. Some may better be called outside-insiders, depending on the degree to which they are based in the local society with family, land and an occupation. Their intimacy with (other) locals varies, and their interests in land and development differ. Roughly, they tend to be categorized as either 'business-minded' elites who try to connect companies or development projects to landowners, or as 'rights-minded' inside-outsiders who try to ensure that locals are protected. Both kinds of inside-outsiders are, in some way or other, trying to benefit individually as well as contribute to the collective.

Inside-outsiders who are political actors may hope to help their region develop and at the same time benefit personally. Middlemen from CSOs or NGOs see themselves as actors who on the one hand must help the locals defend their rights against the investors, the officials and elites, who are suspected of pursuing their own interests, and on the other hand advise locals to welcome development, which almost always is thought to require input from outside. In addition to working for the greater good, the CSO representatives are trying to make a career for themselves by being in-between.

In the remaining part of this chapter, we first give some background to the specific case of mining in Karamoja. We then use the concrete case of artisanal marble miners to consider three more abstract aspects of inside-outsider dynamics in relation to development and land. We discuss the ways that inside-outsiders imagine potentials for development. Then we turn to the mistrust that so often accompanies attempts to build development on land. Finally, we reflect on some of the dilemmas through which inside-outsiders must navigate.

Mining and Land in Karamoja

The overall livelihood and food security situation in Karamoja in the past decades has been deeply affected by cattle raiding, climate change, disarmament and attempts to settle and 'modernize' pastoralists (Gray and Sundal 2017; Nakalembe, Dempewolf and Justice 2017; Hopwood, Porter and Saum 2018; Stites 2020; Abrahams 2021). The artisanal mining practices and brokerage we describe take place in communities that have been and are in serious livelihood crises because pastoralism is not respected and supported by authorities but considered 'backwards' and less valuable than agriculture, even though the ecosystem is more fit for pastoralism (Gabbert 2021; Galaty 2021; Little 2021). For most of the population in Karamoja, pastoralism has become near impossible, and food security is at a point where it could be described as a protracted crisis of ongoing hunger, arguably man-made (Stites and Marshak 2016). In this context, artisanal mining is for some the only available source of livelihood.

The literature on mining and natural resource extraction in Africa is vast and covers issues of exploitation (Ballard and Banks 2003; Nem Singh and Bourgouin 2013), politics, conflict and law (Bruunschweiler and Bulte 2008; Ali, Sturman and Collins 2018; Nalule 2020), relationships between artisanal and industrial mining (Pedersen et al. 2019), gender and mining (Ranchod 2001), environmental impacts (Pretty and Odeku 2017), privatization and indigenization (Kragelund 2012). Lately, there has been a growing interest in the issue of elite agency (Gilberthorpe and Rajak 2016) and elite capture (Buur and Monjane 2017; Buur et al. 2019). It is the discussion of elite agency that we turn to in this chapter, with a focus on the situation of inside-outsiders as illustrated in the mining sector in Karamoja.

The Karamoja region has not been surveyed as thoroughly for minerals and oil as other parts of Uganda due to insecurity in connection with cattle raiding and disarmament. Yet gold has been mined by artisanal miners for a long time, and the cement industry has been extracting limestone in the southern part of the region for two decades. Now marble and other stones and minerals are also being explored for and mined (Rugadya 2020).

The online map of concessions in the Karamoja region looks like a nearly finished puzzle, but the relatively late start of mining means that the majority of concessions in Karamoja are at an exploratory stage.

The national government has rights over underground resources and grants exploration licences to businesses wishing to survey mining potential as well as licences for various stages of mining processes. There are four types of licences in Uganda: retention licence, exploration licence, location licence and mining leases. Negotiation with local landowners is only required in the case of application for an actual mining lease. The direct consequence of this is that companies holding an exploration licence may surprise local people by placing demarcation stones on their land without informing or consulting them about their activities. However, when a company applies for a full mining lease, customary owners and stakeholders are required by law to be included as part of dialogues with mining companies and with the local representatives of the political system of Uganda. The differences in processes, and lack of transparency and communication, often create tensions between outsiders (both nationals and foreigners) and local people, as well as those who claim to represent them (Rugadya 2020).

The Ugandan legal framework prevents companies from buying land directly from the landowners. In order to be granted a lease, they must enter into a contract with the Ugandan state regarding underground resources and negotiate access through the 'surface rights holders'. This means that mediators at various levels are needed to make these negotiations between the foreign company and state structures in Kampala, authorities in the regional headquarters in Karamoja, the local government structure at village level and finally the local landowners. The local communities need someone who speaks the language of the outsiders, both literally and figuratively; thus, they need middlemen. In this chapter, we mainly focus on the elites mediating between local landowners and outside actors. Other mediators, the outside-outsiders or outside-elites, who are never or rarely seen in Karamoja but figure mainly in statements, are another story.

The development of a social class of 'local elites' who get involved as middlemen in mining in Karamoja has a long history but also testifies to recent changes in the community. The 'young warriors' in the pastoral societies were an important part of the social structure as herders and as warriors during cattle raids, but their status position was below the elders, and they were dependent on the older generation's ritual initiation of their age-set to be able to progress in the gerontocratic system (Dyson-Hudson 1963; Thomas and Asch 1966). Schooling and formal education first came with the missionaries, whose religion, teachings and presence local power holders resisted vehemently (Mirzeler and Young 2000). Thus, the first people to receive formal education were those marginal to the gerontocratic power centre of Karamoja. While formal education gained a larger and larger presence and acceptance over the years, many Karamojong still struggle to pay the fees, and the region continues to score abysmally in national education statistics. For a few young people, there were education opportunities beyond primary school in Karamoja, which gave a new status. They attended educational institutions in other regions of the country. These elites with their position as inside-outsiders have come to play important mediating parts in outsiders' access to underground resources through the land and locals.

Potentials and Inside-Outsiders

'Uganda cannot wait for Karamoja to develop'. This saying is usually attributed to the first president of Uganda following independence, Milton Obote, and it is often understood in the sense that Karamoja was so 'underdeveloped' that the region had to be left behind while the rest of Uganda steered ahead. Yet there is a different interpretation available among the inside-outsiders that speaks to the potential of underground resources as representing a promise, not only for Karamoja but for the whole nation. In this latter understanding, the potential of underground development needs to be realized by insiders as well as outsiders. The two need to be connected to release the potential because outsiders may have the perception that Karamoja is resource scarce and hostile, while insiders may believe cattle and the pastoral way of life is the only important kind of wealth and growth. Middlemen are needed to expose the middle ground.

During colonial times, Karamoja was indeed considered 'resource scarce', and the land and people were considered 'hostile' by outsiders (Barber 1968). The region was marginalized socially and economically, as the British saw no benefit from investing in it. Demarcation of nations and regions limited the semi-nomadic lifestyle of the Karamojong, and conflicts were concentrated within new national and regional boundaries. The introduction of automatic weapons by outsiders escalated the conflict, and the area was declared a war zone (Mirzeler and Young 2000). Years of insecurity, marginalizing, detrimental state policies, livestock diseases and drought, which also led to poor agricultural production, meant that the region continuously experienced crisis-level food insecurity (Iyer and Mosebo 2017). The lack of alternative livelihoods meant that resilience levels were low. It is in this environment that mining represents itself as an opportunity; for certain people, it is the only opportunity.

The region's environment has probably been fragile for a long time, and it did not help that the colonial government exploited it for grazing and cattle, which contributed to environmental deterioration (Mamdani 1982). After government disarmament programmes ended around 2010, the outsiders' discourse on Karamoja changed from being one of resource scarcity to resource abundance (underground) (Mosebo 2017). Inside-outsiders who were development-minded played an important role in imagining development (see Chapter 7). They promoted the image of underground wealth, which could be extracted, and played a part in connecting mining companies from outside.

For insiders in Karamoja, the environment was probably always considered abundant but in a variety of other ways. Wealth in most parts of this pastoral region has for long been livestock: cattle, goats, sheep, which can be grazed and watered in large territories. Livestock are considered 'ground projects' of central value for life itself and for the potentials of marrying, having a family, having a life worth living (Evans-Pritchard 1940; Thomas 1966; Dyson-Hudson 1972; Hutchinson 1996; Mosebo 2017). Yet apart from the central value of cattle herding, there were always other important and supplementary ways of increasing the quality of life – agriculture, hunting for wild game, gathering honey and wild fruits and trading arms and other goods over long distances. The importance of these not alternative but mainly supplementary sources of income and livelihood were considered of particular value in times of difficulty, and those who had 'something on the side', besides cattle, were regarded as wise. Others who were looking to make a life in other ways apart from herding sought job opportunities in the public or private sector. These insiders often became a kind of insider-outsider with crucial knowledge about what the pastoralists considered of potential value. When mining came up as a possibility after the relative peace, inside-outsiders knew that cattle herding would still be one of insiders' 'ground projects', but they also knew how to evoke people's experience of the importance of having 'something on the side' – they could 'talk up' the potential of tapping into the resources underground and convince insiders that the new or current 'something' might be mining.

Inside-outsiders tried to convince the pastoralists that mining carried too good a potential to let outsiders run with it all. When development – or potentials of development – comes from outside, from foreign investors or 'big people' (nationals) who are investing in Karamojong land under the auspices of development, some of the inside-outsiders advise local people not to critique or question these development investments. They say: 'If you speak against it, you are accused of being against development as the typical Karamojong you are.' As we saw in Chapter 7, development is an irrefutable ideal; everyone wants it in principle. However, both local people and inside-outsiders are often aware that the resource potential can also turn into a resource curse (Auty 1993), and the curse scenario is often linked to elite exploitation and extraction. It is thus difficult to imagine a potential resource curse scenario or any mining adventure without the presence of a predatory elite (Nem Singh and Bourgouin 2013), even if only in discourse. With promises and potentials not always realized as imagined, the risk of disappointment and mistrust among different actors increases.

The role of elites in imagining the potential of natural resources and anticipating development in their 'home' areas is not restricted to mining. From eastern Cameroon, Geschiere describes elites' part in brokering relations between their communities of origin and logging companies. He notes that elites often have prior contact with the companies and are aware of the increased value of forest resources. They know the laws and procedures regarding the establishment of community forests, and they take initiatives to constitute them in the name of development. Yet their role evokes suspicion:

> this increased interest from the side of elites seems to elicit an equally increasing distrust on the part of villagers. The same people who used to reproach the elites for not taking any interest in the village were the first to denounce their secret dealings with logging companies or the ways in which elites from the area . . . try to claim promising parts of 'their' ancestral forest. (Geschiere 2009: 88–89)

As in Karamoja, the inside-outsiders are aware of the potential value of what is on or under the land. They are in a position to introduce companies that can realize that value on the world market and at the same time (claim to) protect and bring development to their communities of origin.

Mistrust, Invisibility and Elite Extractions

In the case of the artisanal marble miners, Peter explained how 'elite capture' refers to the situation in which people with advantages exploit their position to benefit individually and forget about securing benefits for their communities. As the region receives increasing attention from outside, elite capture is a growing problem that creates increasing mistrust between local people and inside-outsiders. In Chapter 6 on Belonging, the suspicion of inside-outsiders was aimed at the High Court judge, who came from Kampala to mediate the land conflicts at Ogul. Although this was not a development initiative but an attempt to contain violence, rumours circulated about the judge's motives. Some even accused him of wanting to take over the disputed land in order to mine minerals.

The extraction industry in Africa (Buur et al. 2019) is shrouded in stories of elite capture and suspicions of people 'mining their own business'. Mistrust and suspicion seem to thrive particularly well in the vicinity of mineral extraction due to high expectations of profits and invisibility or non-transparency.

The case from Karamoja provides insight into how the processes around mining are received and managed in a setting where underground extraction is a relatively new phenomenon – there are many expectations which are not yet realized. It shows how unintelligible and complex processes are when a lot takes place in offices far from the mining sites, leaving so much that is invisible to the people directly affected by them. Invisibility and disembedded transactions (see Chapter 2) leave room for explanations based on speculation and half-witnessed events, such as seeing a government official in a car with an investor and drawing the conclusion that the government official is not a neutral mediator anymore. The invisibility of the deals combined with the very visible changes in the landscape tend to create mistrust. Big equipment arrives, buildings shoot up, trucks drive out with minerals, outsiders in suits speaking foreign languages are present. When there is sparse communication, people start speculating: Who is benefitting? Are the insiders who connect with outsiders extracting something for themselves?

Peter, the CSO representative in the case, pointed to the problem of elite capture and implied that high up officials actively withheld knowledge so they could continue taking advantage of the situation in various ways. The CSOs wished to intervene to provide transparency and to 'close the knowledge gaps' so that elites could not take advantage of the local communities. In their view, the novelty of mining in Karamoja had been a window of opportunity for the elites, who had knowledge from outside. As the quote at the beginning of the case reveals, the community resistance to what they viewed as elite capture was barred from turning into violent conflict by the local mediators. The CSOs provided the locals with more knowledge, making their rights visible to them and hoping they could use this information to secure their rights. The CSOs saw this path as opening up a way for the positive development that mining could bring for the region. Many locals, such as the chair of the artisanal miners, were grateful for the training and involvement by the CSOs. Yet for some of the locals, both elite capture and well-meaning CSO involvement were considered confusing, and they suspected that both of these inside-outsiders were involved in the extraction of resources.

Confusing processes were also considered a problem for outside investors. For investors, the local modes of land governance and land ownership seemed disorganized, and it is likely that the local communities maintained the confusion and lack of transparency on their side to retain some power. The local mediators worked to make these processes transparent on both sides, so it was like a game of tug of war with the CSOs caught in the middle. Paradoxically, where elites are concerned, it is the confusion and invisibility of processes on both sides that provide a space for them and give them a role to play in land processes or else they would have no stake in the mining, because they are not landowners. They have no authority in providing access and no position to directly influence processes. They have identified a problem and a solution, and they have instated themselves to bring the solution to the problem – as local development mediators.

When Human Rights Watch raised a critique of the marble mining company, the spokesperson responded that the company had held meetings with the district council, area members of parliament, other stakeholders and 'indigenous people' (Business & Human Rights Resource Centre 2017). From their perspective, they had 'followed the rules'. Yet the process of drawing in representatives of the so-called indigenous people often creates mistrust. People who represent 'the locals' are not necessarily the same as those who consider themselves rightsholders of the land. As we saw in Chapter 2 often several local groups make claims to the same land, and when outsiders do not know this, they make mistakes and buy land from people who do not have the authority to sell.

The artisanal miners were upset that the deal that meant they could earn cash directly from the rubble in the mining site, outside the royalties system, did not come to pass. The agreement the company highlighted was the CSR plan of building a factory and of paying royalties. The company paid the obligatory 3 per cent of royalties to the surface rights holders, while, according to the rules, the state keeps 80 per cent and 17 per cent goes to the district and local government.

Marilyn Strathern (2011) has provided a way of thinking about sharing processes in her essay 'Sharing, Stealing and Borrowing Simultaneously' which might help highlight the double relation between doing everything lawfully and still being considered a thief. Strathern suggests that we look for co-presence in all social configurations: what is also always there or potentially there, apart from the obvious or visible. Strathern points out that the same range of behaviour that can be called borrowing can also be called stealing. Perhaps what turns the one into the other are the limits of people's tolerance for one another's intentions (2011). The mining company followed the rules, and from their point of view they were borrowing access to the land, and they were sharing the benefits through royalties and the CSR plan. Yet from the perspective of the artisanal miners, the company never intended to discuss the building of the factory, and thus their extractions were classed as stealing. This ended any tolerance people had for the company. The woman who was chair of the artisanal miners expressed this diplomatically: 'Our relationship with the investors is not stable.'

When people start doubting the intentions behind development from outside, stories and mistrust thrive. The artisanal miners said that during a meeting the company had made people sign an attendance list, which later appeared as a formal signed document of agreement with the mining company. The story – whether true or not – shows that people felt cheated and that their limits of tolerance for the company's intentions had been transgressed. With the appearance of the factory, the artisanal miners knew that the company was no longer interested in sharing – that is, leaving smaller stones for the miners to sell. The ethos of sharing in Karamoja is explicit (Mosebo 2015), also in relation to land and underground resources. It is considered bad form not to share if you have plenty of something. If you have plenty of pasture and water, you must share with other herders and their herds who are in need. If you have plenty of marble in your mountains, you should share this with people who come to ask for it. This principle of sharing responds to the needs of the recipient, and in this understanding, people are obligated to share their wealth with people who demand a share (Woodburn 1998). If they do not, they are depriving someone of receiving, and in a sense that is stealing (Mosebo 2017). Thus in Karamojong logic, the factory changed the company's actions from sharing to stealing, even if the company saw it as part of their CSR strategy. The idea that the outsiders did not come with good intentions was underscored by the presence of the soldiers who guarded the mining site. They increased mistrust of the company's intentions: 'The elders are saying: "Why are they intimidating us in our own land? If they come in a good way, why should they need soldiers? If you move with soldiers, it means you're guilty."'

Even though the company did everything they were legally required to, it was not enough to guard them from gaining a bad reputation. This was not simply a matter of giving the right amount of money, employing enough local people, letting people work the mine for a profit (Mosebo 2017). Their actions surrounding the mining needed to show intentions towards positive development for local people. While the mining company had a legal licence to operate, there were still questions about their social licence to operate (Prno 2013). Were they mainly borrowing, sharing or stealing land? These are questions that are not only relevant for mining but for land issues more generally across northern Uganda.

Dilemmas and Development Brokers in Land Issues

Even though inside-outside mediators raise mistrust, they can play crucial roles for realizing potentials of development (Buur and Monjane 2017). Local development mediators regard mining as an opportunity for the communities to benefit from the wealth in the region, and they regard the outsiders, the investors and the mining professionals in Uganda as necessary partners towards this. As the young CSO representative said: 'We do not have the capacity to mine these things.'

Much as mediators are needed, they also pose dilemmas, in large part because of their in-between positioning. Mediators are actors who have a capacity to go between positions; they have knowledge, know-how, experience and insights, motivation, interest and social standing across spheres to bring together actors, knowledge and ideas from inside and outside (Buur, Baloi and Tembe 2012). They can be brokers between insiders and outsiders because of their unique position.

The concept of *brokerage* in anthropology has a long history of focusing on actors working in the space between communities and political elites (Lindquist 2015). The local elites in the mining case were working exactly between the local communities and the political and economic systems outside the region, which have a direct effect on the region. Brokers, more generally, are actors with a capacity to connect the local to the larger whole by pulling together elements from various social systems, as described early on by Lévi-Strauss (1966) and Wolf (1956). The broker figure is often characterized by moral ambiguity because she/

he crosses social boundaries and is suspected of gaining from this individually (Boissevain 1974; Lindquist 2015). In relation to land and mine development, we see how brokers are often questioned morally as 'business-minded' people who are selling land unscrupulously, forgetting about traditions and values of the land, and they are suspected of conniving with the investors.

There was no evidence that any of the local mediators in the mining case (except the spokesperson who was employed by the company) was actually conniving with the investors. Nor did they appear to have ulterior motives of extracting resources on the backs of the local communities solely for their own benefit. The mediators were aiming at securing development for the region as well as securing personal development. They wanted the opportunities that development presents and to be regarded as citizens on par with other Ugandans with the rights that this is seen to provide (Mosebo 2015). If a development process is successful and accepted within a socio-economic system, it creates a space for an educated elite within that system, and the middlemen become insiders rather than strangers. In Karamoja, they therefore 'hunted' for opportunities to instate themselves in the development processes and become representatives of the Karamojong but also looked to become 'someone' in the eyes of the people. This connects them to societal development, but it also risks placing them in new dilemmas, since the implementation of any land intervention is likely to benefit some of the local community while excluding others.

Rugadya (2020: 6) describes how local elites in the Karamoja region helped miners' associations to obtain royalties from marble and limestone companies. According to the Mining Act of 2003, these royalties were meant for the landowners who held surface rights, but the artisanal miners were better organized, causing resentment among the landowners. In the same way, the middleman in the case of the wind turbine in Ik County (Chapter 2) put himself in a dilemma when he identified some families and not others as 'original owners' of the land.

Outside entrepreneurs and development projects also need brokers, to get access to local people and resources, and to be able to claim that local populations have been heard and represented. In the words of Bierschenk and colleagues, local development brokers are key:

> In the case of the development project . . . brokers represent the project's local social carriers, at the interface between the people (the 'target group') aimed at by the project and the development institutions. They are supposed to represent the local populations, express its 'needs' to the structures in charge of aid and to external financiers. In fact, far from being passive operators of logic of dependence, development brokers are the key actors in the irresistible hunt for projects carried out in and around African villages. (Bierschenk, Chauveau and De Sardan 2002)

Brokers are out to hunt for projects, but projects are also hunting for brokers. Yet brokers, as we have seen in our cases, do not only go between already-established positions. They also create new positions and meanings themselves. Brokers do not merely negotiate between reified formations such as 'the global' and 'the local' but embody several such formations and are active in producing meaning, categories and identities (James 2011).

Local mediators carve out a space for themselves, as a way of life, but they often find themselves in dilemmas on two interconnected but separate levels: the personal level and the societal level. To be part of the community, the elites must contribute towards the survival and well-being of the local people. In Karamoja, sharing is essential for social belonging. The local mediators are thus expected to contribute to the local communities with their knowledge, resources and access to the outside. Yet, those capacities are exactly what make them stand out as strangers or outsiders, and the processes they engage in continuously reinforce this outsider position. They must balance their involvement and carefully communicate what they are doing in order not to face existential threats.

Conclusion

Development, in the sense of growth, almost always involves land in some way. It also very often involves resources and actors from outside, and in some cases, as we have seen in this chapter, there is a gap between actors and intentions from outside and actors and intentions from inside. Development brokers insert themselves into this gap and mediate between insiders and outsiders, as a kind of inside-outsider themselves, who speak both local and international languages of development. They seldom live from pastoralism as the local communities do, but they identify as Karamojong. The local communities, however, regard some of these inside-outsiders with scepticism as elites who are interested in capturing riches for themselves (though seemingly on behalf of the locals). Other elites and inside-outsiders are considered useful in negotiating with outside business people. Inside-outsiders are often seen by outsiders as key to the realization of development potentials in a region, and sometimes deals are made with representatives that do not seem transparent to local communities. This creates suspicion, mistrust and disagreement, as we have also seen in other cases in the book – some are suspicious of outsiders who buy land for development purposes, while others are keen on this kind of investment and development from outside.

Marianne Mosebo, Ph.D., was post doc at the Department of Anthropology, Aarhus University, and is currently Assistant Professor at the Emergency and Risk Manager Education program at University College Copenhagen.

Lotte Meinert, Ph.D., is Professor at the Department of Anthropology, Aarhus University.

References

Abrahams, Daniel. 2021. 'Land is Now the Biggest Gun: Climate Change and Conflict in Karamoja, Uganda', *Climate and Development* 13(8): 748–60.

Ali, Saleem H., Kathryn Sturman and Nina Collins. 2018. *Africa's Mineral Fortune: The Science and Politics of Mining and Sustainable Development*. Boca Raton: Routledge.

Auty, Richard M. 1993. *Sustaining Development in Mineral Economies: The Resource Curse Thesis*. London: Routledge.

Ballard, Chris, and Glenn Banks. 2003. 'Resource Wars: The Anthropology of Mining', *Annual Review of Anthropology* 32: 287–313.

Barber, James. 1968. *Imperial Frontier: A Study of Relations Between the British and the Pastoral Tribes of North-East Africa*. Nairobi: East African Publishing House.

Bierschenk, Thomas, Jean-Pierre Chauveau and Jean-Pierre Olivier de Sardan. 2002. *Local Development Brokers in Africa: The Rise of a New Social Category*. Working Papers of the Department of Anthropology and African Studies 13. Mainz: Johannes Gutenberg University Mainz.

Boissevain, J. 1974. *Friends of Friends: Networks, Manipulators and Coalitions*. Oxford: Basil Blackwell.

Bourdieu, Pierre. 1986. 'Forms of Capital', in John G. Richardson (ed.), Handbook of Theory and Research for the Sociology of Education. New York: Greenwood Press, pp. 241–58.

Bruunschweiler, Christa N., and Erwin H. Bulte. 2008. 'Linking Natural Resources to Slow Growth and More Conflict', *Science* 320(5876): 616–17.

Business & Human Rights Resource Centre. 2017. 'Uganda: Human Rights Watch Report Says Mining Firms Not Consulting Karamoja Indigenous People – Includes East African Mining & DAO Marble Responses'. Business & Human Rights Resource Centre website. Retrieved 08 May 2017 from https://business-humanrights.org/en/uganda-human-rights-watch-report-says-mining-firms-not-consulting-karamoja-indigenous-people-includes-east-af-rican-mining-dao-marble-responses#c79549.

Buur, Lars, and Celso Marcos Monjane. 2017. 'Elite Capture and the Development of Natural Resource Linkages in Mozambique', in Melanie Pichler, Cornelia Staritz, Karin Küblböck, Christina Plank, Werner Raza and Fernando Ruiz Peyré (eds), *Fairness and Justice in Natural Resource Politics*. London: Routledge, pp. 200–17.

Buur, Lars, Obede Suarte Baloi and Carlota Mondlane Tembe. 2012. *Mozambique Synthesis Analysis: Between Pockets of Efficiency and Elite Capture*. Copenhagen: Danish Institute for International Studies.

Buur, L., et al. 2019. 'Understanding the Three Key Relationships in Natural Resource Investments in Africa: An Analytical framework', *The Extractive Industries and Society* 6: 1195–204.

Dyson-Hudson, Neville. 1963. 'The Karimojong Age-System', *Ethnology* 2(3): 353–401.

———. 1972. 'Pastoralism: Self-image and Behavioural Reality', *Journal of Asian and African Studies* 7(1–2): 30–47.

Evans-Pritchard, Edward Evan. 1940. *The Nuer: A Description of the Modes of Livelihood and Political Institutions of a Nilotic People*. Oxford: Clarendon Press.

Gabbert, Echi Christina. 2021. 'Introduction: Futuremaking with Pastoralists', in Echi Christina Gabbert, Fana Gebresenbet, John G. Galaty and Günther Schlee (eds), *Lands of the*

Future: Anthropological Perspectives on Pastoralism, Land Deals and Tropes of Modernity in Eastern Africa. New York, NY: Berghahn Books, pp. 1–38.

Galaty, John G. 2021. 'Modern Mobility in East Africa: Pastoral Responses to Rangeland Fragmentation, Enclosure and Settlement', in Echi Christina Gabbert, Fana Gebresenbet, John G. Galaty and Günther Schlee (eds), *Lands of the Future: Anthropological Perspectives on Pastoralism, Land Deals and Tropes of Modernity in Eastern Africa*. New York, NY: Berghahn Books, pp. 41–58.

Geschiere, Peter. 2009. *The Perils of Belonging: Autochthony, Citizenship, and Exclusion in Africa and Europe*. Chicago: Chicago University Press.

Gilberthorpe, Emma, and Dinah Rajak. 2016. 'The Anthropology of Extraction: Critical Perspectives on the Resource Curse', *The Journal of Development Studies* 53(2): 186–204.

Gray, Sandra, and Mary B. Sundal. 2017. '"Milk Has Gone": Dietary Change and Human Adaptability in Karamoja, Uganda', *American Anthropologist* 119(4): 662–83.

Hopwood, Julian, Holly Porter and Nangiro Saum. 2018. 'Resilient Patriarchy: Public Authority and Women's (in)security in Karamoja, Uganda', *Disasters* 42(1): 140–58.

Hutchinson, Sharon E. 1996. *Nuer Dilemmas: Coping with Money, War, and the State*. Berkeley: University of California Press.

Iyer, Padmini, and Marianne Mosebo. 2017. 'Looking for Work: Wage Labour, Employment and Migration in Karamoja'. Report. USAID/Tufts University/Karamoja Resilience Support Unit.

James, Deborah. 2011. 'The Return of the Broker: Consensus, Hierarchy, and Choice in South African Land Reform: The Return of the Broker', *The Journal of the Royal Anthropological Institute* 17(2): 318–38.

Kragelund, Peter. 2012. 'Bringing "indigenous" Ownership Back: Chinese Presence and the Citizen Economic Empowerment Commission in Zambia', *The Journal of Modern African Studies* 50(3): 447–66.

Lévi-Strauss, Claude. 1966. *The Savage Mind*. Chicago: University of Chicago Press.

Lindquist, Johan. 2015. 'Brokers and Brokerage, Anthropology Of', *International Encyclopedia of the Social & Behavioral Sciences* 870–74.

Little, Peter D. 2021. 'Global Trade, Local Realities: Why African States Undervalue Pastoralism', in Echi Christina Gabbert, Fana Gebresenbet, John G. Galaty and Günther Schlee (eds), *Lands of the Future: Anthropological Perspectives on Pastoralism, Land Deals and Tropes of Modernity in Eastern Africa*. New York: Berghahn Books, pp. 78–98.

Mamdani, Mahmood. 1982. 'Karamoja: Colonial Roots of Famine in North-East Uganda', *Review of African Political Economy* 25: 66–73.

———. 2013. *The Contemporary Ugandan Discourse on Customary Tenure: Some Theoretical Considerations*, MISR Working Paper 13. Kampala: Makerere University.

Mirzeler, Mustafa. K., and Crawford Young. 2000. 'Pastoral Politics in the Northeast Periphery in Uganda: AK-47 as Change Agent', *Journal of Modern African Studies* 38(3): 407–29.

Mosebo, Marianne Bach. 2015. 'Enhancing Well-Being: Urban Karimojong Youth Between Security and Development in Uganda', Ph.D. dissertation. Copenhagen: University of Copenhagen and Danish Institute for International Studies.

———. 2017. 'The Value of Pastoralism and Mining: Balancing Futures in Karamoja, Uganda', *The Extractive Industries and Society* 4: 539–47.

Nakalembe, Catherine, Jan Dempewolf and Christopher Justice. 2017. 'Agricultural Land Use Change in Karamoja Region, Uganda', *Land Use Policy* 62: 2–12.

Nalule, Victoria R. 2020. *Mining and the Law in Africa: Exploring the Social and Environmental Impacts*. Cham: Palgrave.

Nem Singh, Jewellord, and France Bourgouin. 2013. *Resource Governance and Developmental States in the Global South: Critical International Political Economy Perspectives.* London: Palgrave Macmillan.

Pedersen, Rasmus Hundsbæk, Mutagwaba, Willison, Jønsson, Jesper Bosse, Schoneveld, George, Jacob, Thabit, Chacha, Maisory, Weng, Xiaoxue and Maria G. Njau. 2019. 'Mining-Sector Dynamics in an Era of Resurgent Resource Nationalism: Changing Relations between Large-Scale Mining and Artisanal and Small-Scale Mining in Tanzania', *Resources Policy* 62: 339–46.

Pretty, Makua, and Kola O. Odeku. 2017. 'Harmful Mining Activities, Environmental Impacts and Effects in the Mining Communities in South Africa: A Critical Perspective', *Environmental Economics* 8(4): 14–24.

Prno, Jason. 2013. 'An Analysis of Factors Leading to the Establishment of a Social License to Operate in the Mining Industry', *Resources Policy* 38: 577–90.

Ranchod, Sarita. 2001. *Gender and Mining: Workplace. Input to MMSDSA Regional Research.* Birnam Park: African Institute of Corporate Citizenship.

Rugadya, Margaret A. 2020. 'Land Tenure as a Cause of Tensions and Driver of Conflict Among Mining Communities in Karamoja, Uganda: Is Secure Property Rights a Solution?', *Land Use Policy* 94: 1–11.

Stites, Elizabeth. 2020 '"The Only Place to Do This Is in Town": Experiences of Rural-Urban Migration in Northern Karamoja, Uganda', *Nomadic Peoples* 24(1): 32–55.

Stites, Elizabeth, and Anastasia Marshak. 2016. 'Who Are the Lonetia? Findings from Southern Karamoja, Uganda', *The Journal of Modern African Studies* 54(2): 237–62.

Strathern, Marilyn. 2011. 'Sharing, Stealing and Borrowing Simultaneously', in Veronica Strang and Mark Busse (eds), *Ownership and Appropriation.* Oxford: Berg, pp. 23–41.

Thomas, Elizabeth Marshall, and Timothy Asch. 1966. *Warrior Herdsmen.* London: Secker & Warburg.

Wolf, Eric R. 1956. 'Aspects of Group Relations in a Complex Society: Mexico', *American Anthropologist* 58(6): 1065–78.

Woodburn, James. 1998. 'Sharing is Not a Form Exchange: An Analysis of Property-Sharing in Immediate-Return Hunter-Gatherer Societies', in Chris M. Hann (ed.), *Property Relations: Renewing the Anthropological Tradition.* Cambridge: Cambridge University Press, pp. 48–63.

Chapter 9
Conservation

Lioba Lenhart and Lotte Meinert

Human-Wildlife Conflicts over Land

Lioba met Christopher Olum in July 2014 at Purongo sub-county headquarters. They had attended a meeting with the sub-county chief on human-wildlife conflict, and the chief had introduced Christopher to her as 'an interesting person to talk to about stray elephants'. Christopher was fifty years old and married to two wives with whom he had nine children. He was the head of one of the families that lived in Lawaca village, which borders the northern part of Murchison Falls National Park (MFNP), but he had moved to Purongo trading centre along with other families because of ongoing crop raids by elephants.

Christopher narrated that in 2007, when people returned home from the IDP camps, he and his family went back to Lawaca to resettle and farm their ancestral land, produce food for their daily consumption and sell some of the surplus on the local market to pay for the children's education and medical bills. 'We had a good start', he remembered, 'but this did not last for long'. About two years later, wild animals began to frequent the place, destroyed crops, damaged huts and granaries where stocks were kept, and sometimes attacked, injured and even killed people. 'We were in trouble and had to decide what to do', he said. So, they moved back to Purongo trading centre where they had lived in the IDP camp. Christopher rented a place to stay with his family and started to work for other people. He loaded heavy goods on trucks and did occasional work in the market to get money for rent and food but could no longer afford to support the children in school. When one of his wives was knocked by a motorcycle in the trading centre and admitted to hospital for three months, it was extremely difficult to provide care for her. 'My life was torn apart, and sometimes I felt like leaving this world', he said.

Two years later, Christopher's life had not changed much, and he had become even more desperate and bitter. He talked about his 're-displacement' and lamented about the fate of his children, who were 'born in the camp, grew up in the camp, went back home shortly only to be displaced again to this trading centre' where they had learnt a lifestyle 'which is not in line with my family's norms'. He blamed the government for having ignored people's problems right from the mid-1980s until today.

Christopher remembered that before the war 'there were many animals, maybe more than what we have today in the park – elephants, hyenas, buffaloes and many others', but at that time wildlife had not been 'stubborn like this current elephant generation'. His family had planted cassava, maize, sesame, millet, groundnuts and many other crops. Only smaller animals such as squirrels and edible rats had sometimes ravaged groundnuts and millet. 'There were no food shortages in our homes, and we could even take food crops [surpluses] from Lawaca to Pakwach using the train', he recalled. He, his brothers and all male youths of Lawaca had paid bridewealth with money raised from farming crops. Money had still been enough for paying school fees. However, during the war between the LRA and government, they were given an ultimatum to leave their fertile land within only 24 hours. 'So, we hurriedly had to depart for imprisonment in the IDP camp and to behave like beggars, something I had not thought of at all', Christopher remembered. Here, while living in fear of rebel attacks and abductions, and seeing children and adults dying because of diseases and lack of medical services, they experienced serious shortages of food for the first time because handouts from World Food Programme were not enough.

During one of his discussions with Lioba in 2016, Christopher concluded that people had been left alone with their plight, and he painted a very gloomy picture of the future, saying:

> UWA [Uganda Wildlife Authority] staff, central and local government, and our political representatives from Local Council to Parliament have always turned a blind eye to our problems and appeals. They are eating well, can pay for the schools of their children and are looking at us as fools . . . I should be staying in my home. I feel displaced for so long . . . I fear I will die without having a stable home and my children will not inherit my land or be able to marry wives [cannot afford paying bridewealth] but become slaves in people's farms and houses instead.

Border Troubles
It was a hot and windy day in late December 2014 when several people were sitting in Mr Kidega's hut near the border of Murchison Falls National Park. The

group included two *rwodi kweri* (village chiefs in charge of communal agricultural activities), several elders and youths – most of them men and all of them farmers – Lioba and her research assistants. Christopher was part of the group.

The group intended to walk along the border of the park to witness what had challenged the people since their return from the IDP camps. They had been full of hope for a better life; they had land to return to that was fertile and so they expected good harvests. But their hopes and initial successes in farming were soon dashed. They had not foreseen the amount of destruction that would be caused by big game, particularly elephants and buffaloes, crossing the park border and destroying people's crops.

Although the sun was already high in the sky, the group had not yet set off, because they could not agree whether or not to walk together with a UWA ranger. People stressed that 'UWA cares more about animals than us, who have to abandon our land because of elephants'. They also feared that the ranger could spot somebody from their village 'who is hunting his food' and 'accuse him of poaching'. After a lengthy discussion, they finally agreed that they would need the ranger not only for protection from potential attacks by wild animals but also to avoid being mistaken for poachers and shot. As the local chairman had explained to Lioba some days earlier, crossing the park border always poses a risk; people had disappeared in the park.

So, they linked up with the ranger, whom they met close to the park's Wangkwar Gate, and started their walk in the midday heat, first on footpaths and then cross-country through tall spear grass. Not surprisingly, on the way the ranger indeed spotted an old man about to place a trap. They requested that the ranger 'just forgive him' instead of taking legal action, arguing that they were walking for a different purpose. The ranger insisted on cautioning the old man and confiscated his *panga*, spear and snares. Along the way, elephants' footprints and paths were unmistakable, and so was the destruction of crops caused by them.

During the walk, the participants continuously discussed what they observed and finally drew a map to indicate physical features of the land, vegetation, land use patterns and occurrence of wild and domestic animals, and – most important – they noted problems and made recommendations. The major problems identified were wildlife, water and the UWA. Wildlife, in particular elephants, but also buffaloes and warthogs, were destroying people's crops with the effect that people had lost interest in farming and were therefore facing food shortages and a lack of money needed for satisfying other basic needs. People experienced water scarcity but were not allowed to use water from streams demarcating the park border. They were also not allowed to fish or to collect firewood or grass in the border area. The UWA's approach to dealing with so-called 'problem animals', such as digging trenches, planting chilli or smearing repellents made from chilli on ropes put around the fields, did not help. Rangers did not respond in time to 'problem animal' attacks, and there was no compensation for losses.

A heated discussion evolved around how to address these problems. An elder proposed that 'government should redistribute some elephants to other parks or sell them to other countries'. Another man recommended the provision of licensed guns to people and allowing them to kill one elephant, 'which would help to chase away others for 50 years'. A woman suggested the UWA should revise the park's management plan so that it provided for resource sharing (water, grass, fish, firewood). Others proposed to put up an electric fence around the park and suggested that rangers should not stay in their detach close to Wangkwar Gate but with the community so that they could quickly react to wildlife attacks. The UWA should facilitate trained scouts from the community, and government should pay compensation for losses. The ranger stressed, however, that elephants cannot be relocated to other parks; people cannot be allowed to kill elephants, because Uganda is a signatory to conventions for the protection of wildlife; and compensation cannot be paid, because it is not provided for by any legal Act. However, he said that resource sharing could be negotiated for special occasions, for instance funerals. He also stressed that rangers could not always respond as quickly as expected if called by people to chase away 'problem animals', because of lack of transport. By that time, they had only one motorbike and one car at their disposal.

Human-Wildlife Conflict, the Park and Development
When asked about human-wildlife conflict, one of the UWA rangers whom Lioba frequently met in Purongo explained that 'this is not a new thing, it started a long time ago, actually from Sudan', hinting at the Luo migration of about 1400–1500 AD. He stressed that 'what was initially a conflict between humans and animals has quickly become a conflict between humans' and referred to the widely known myth of the spear and the bead, which concerns a feud between the two brothers Labongo and Gipir, who became the founding fathers of the present-day Acholi and Alur. Their dispute started with an elephant raiding their garden that was chased away by Gipir, who had taken his brother's spear, and culminated in the separation of the Luo.

This was the beginning of the Acholi's repeated displacement, Lioba was told during a meeting with elders at the chief's place in March 2015. One elder recalled that already one hundred years ago the Acholi in this area were forced into camps by the colonialists. The reason given was the outbreak of sleeping sickness spread by tsetse flies. However, there were speculations that people actually had been displaced to pave the way for the development of a game reserve (Bunyoro-Gulu Game Reserve), which was indeed established in 1928, when people were still in the camps, and became Murchison Falls National Park in 1952. After their return, the park had become an unalterable fact that people had to accept – an area imagined and designed as an uninhabited, pristine wilderness and no longer a place for human settlement and farming and hunting activities. During the war between the LRA and the government, which started in the mid-1980s and lasted until 2008, people had to stay in camps for years. And only a few years after their return from the camps they were displaced again by elephants.

The nearly 80-year-old Lajul Hely felt privileged to have been employed at Paraa Lodge in the park as early as 1959. He had worked in the Department of Housekeeping for almost 30 years and remembered that during colonial times most tourists had been Whites – British, Americans, Europeans – with a few Indians. He recalled the visit by the British Queen Elizabeth in 1954 and remembered that her daughter Princess Anne had also come. Lajul Hely explained: '[The park] was too expensive for Africans, who only started to come during the time of [president] Obote and Amin.' Obote promoted exclusive big game trophy hunting safaris for rich white professional hunters who were interested in killing leopards and huge tusker elephants. Amin's soldiers were after ivory and therefore killed thousands of elephants, but being army officers, they were not held accountable. It was the park, Lajul Hely told Lioba, that had paved the way for development. When the park was created, the trading centre developed. His father built the first house in the centre in 1952, which he used as a shop. In 1954, there were already seven buildings. The colonial government contracted people to build a road to connect Purongo with Pakwach, the next trading centre at that time. Ocaya Matino Martin was the first to use a pickup for business. In 1965, Ocan Lagoro bought a tractor. His son Ocan Jovan became the first miller and also opened one of the two big farms. The second one was owned by Oryema, then Inspector General of Police. However, with President Amin development stopped and only gained momentum a few years ago, after the end of the LRA war. 'Now, there are many farms and tractors in this area, and a lot of tourists are visiting the park, but who owns them [the farms and tractors], who benefits from them [the tourists]?' Lajul Hely asked. 'These are a few, but the majority has remained poor, despite the park or the big farms.'

During the time when people stayed in the IDP camps, the human population had nearly doubled and so did the elephant population, which had been seriously decimated at the time of Amin. Population growth had resulted in fierce competition between humans and wildlife over limited living space and resources. 'People's war was elephants' peace' – as one of Lioba's interlocutors put it; 'nobody disturbed them when they came to people's gardens and homes, and now they have become accustomed to the land that was vacant for so many years'.

Yet during a meeting in October 2016 at Purongo sub-county headquarters, the UWA warden stressed the value of wildlife protection for the sake of biodiversity and for attracting international tourists. He condemned poaching and illegal trade in wild animal meat, fur, body parts and ivory. However, he acknowledged that stray elephants and other big game had posed a problem to local people, and highlighted various methods to address it, such as scare shooting, digging trenches, blowing whistles, keeping bees or burning bricks made from chilli and cow dung. He stressed that UWA had trained community volunteers, so-called UWA scouts, to assist the rangers in observing elephant movements and chasing away stray elephants. He advised that people should grow crops of no interest to elephants and marketable, such as chilli, garlic, ginger, okra or sunflowers, and to buy millet and other crops for their daily needs from the profits. This meeting had been one of a series of meetings to look for solutions to human-wildlife conflict, during which the same things were repeated again and again without producing tangible results. Besides these conventional approaches, the UWA had also endeavoured to make the local people benefit from conservation through a community tourism project. An 'Acholi Culture and Tourism Centre' was built from park entrance revenue sharing. It was intended to house a museum and restaurant and offer guided tours, thus providing livelihood alternatives to agriculture and at the same time being conducive to the protection of wildlife. However, the centre had not opened until years after the completion of the construction work; it had become an arena of competing interests and displays of power among sub-county and district officials and potential investors.

In December 2016, the Acholi Paramount Chief blamed stray elephants for continued poverty in those parts of the Acholi sub-region that border protected areas. In his view, the UWA had not done anything effective against stray elephants, so he suggested the Acholi people should deal with the problem themselves and kill the animals. However, some of the displaced people from Lawaca, about ten kilometres away from Purongo Trading Centre, had already taken matters into their own hands, although not in the way anticipated by the Chief and without asking for support from the UWA.

Self-Help

When visiting Lawaca in mid-August 2016, the first thing Lioba and her research assistants saw was a deserted homestead overgrown with grass. The open door of one of the dilapidated huts allowed a look at a simple mat on the floor, some clothes and blankets, a clay jug, a small jerry can, a cup, a basin, pots and plates. 'This is Mr Omony's home, which we now use for shelter when safeguarding our crops and harvests', Omony's nephew Simon Ocan explained. In 2010, Omony had moved to the trading centre together with his extended family after a group of elephants had destroyed all his crops in one night and nearly killed his wife when they tried to enter the hut where part of the produce was stored.

Simon, however, could not get used to life in the centre, the daily struggle for badly paid casual work and dependency on the goodwill of others. In 2015, he decided to engage in farming again and convinced a few relatives and friends, who were stranded in the trading centre like him, to return to their ancestral land. The idea was simple: people putting their adjacent fields together and growing the same crops in blocks – mainly marketable produce but also some crops for subsistence needs – while patrolling in shifts and taking other coordinated measures against elephant invasions. 'During daytime, when elephants can be seen from far', he explained, 'it often helps to blow the *vuvuzelas* or beat jerry cans'. They also protected the crops with bells on pesticide-treated ropes around the blocks. However, at night one had to be alert. 'We are sleeping in makeshifts to wait for the elephants, we make fire and sit around and wait; one, three days, one week they are not coming, but you have to be ready any time', he said. They began experimenting with burning cow dung, tires and plastic materials and found that wild animals feared the smoke and smell. They also tried to use solar light to illuminate the fields at night, which turned out to be effective but rather expensive. Finally, they encouraged herdsmen from western Uganda to graze their cattle in the area, after having discovered that elephants do not like the natural smell and dung of domestic animals, nor the smell of cattle sprayed against ticks.

In the first year, the group had only seven members. In the second year, the number had increased to twenty households, and in early 2017, thirty-six households participated. The second year's harvest of sunflower, groundnuts, rice and watermelons was good, but marketing of produce was still a problem. The herdsmen's cattle had increased to 300 head, and they were allowed to stay longer, since cattle presence seemed to help. Although most of the farmers were still commuting between their homes in the trading centre and their makeshift shelters, they were optimistic that their model would work and allow them to come home one day.

Having heard about their successes, other people joined the group. One of them was Christopher Olum.

Of What Is This a Case?

Christopher Olum and the people of Purongo sub-county bordering Murchison Falls National Park, who shared their experiences with Lioba, are among many others living in the vicinity of protected areas who have to bear the costs of conserving Uganda's rich biodiversity in ten National Parks, numerous Wildlife Reserves and Sanctuaries and 506 Central Forest Reserves. The people from Ik County to which Timu Forest Reserve belongs and which borders Kidepo Valley National Park told Lotte similar stories. Underlying themes of these narrations are: the competition between people and wildlife and flora over land; disagreements over conservation goals, processes and procedures; and the close link between the practice of conservation and economic development.

Fortress Conservation

Uganda, with 18,783 recorded species of flora and fauna, is one of the most biodiverse countries in the world (NEMA 2016). The country's rich biodiversity is related to its location, where several ecoregions with their typical communities of plants and animals in high altitude, forested, moist savannas and dryland and wetland biomes converge (Pomeroy et al. 2002: 7). However, Uganda lost an estimated 50 per cent of its overall biodiversity value between 1975 and 1995 (Pomeroy, Tushabe and Loh 2017: 1) and has shown a fairly constant loss rate of 1 per cent per year thereafter (NEMA 2016: 8). Main threats to biodiversity include over-harvesting and an unsustainable use of resources; habitat degradation and loss due to conversion into commercial land uses, particularly agriculture, logging, charcoal burning and mining; the recent discovery and exploration of oil and gas in the Albertine Rift; the introduction of alien species; and diseases and pollution. Many of these threats are caused by demographic pressure and poverty, leading to pressure on land. In addition, the effects of climate change have negatively impacted on biodiversity, as demonstrated by the increasing frequency of droughts, floods and mudslides. Additional concerns are encroachment on protected areas, human-wildlife conflicts and illegal wildlife trade (NEMA 2016: ix–x, 25–37).

To counter these threats to biodiversity, Uganda has adopted, among other measures, what has been called 'fortress conservation' by critics and a 'protectionist approach' by supporters, with protected areas managed by government agencies. This state-centric top-down approach aims to protect nature by excluding local people, who are suspected of using natural resources in irrational and destructive ways, thus causing biodiversity loss and environmental degradation (Doolittle 2007: 705). Fortress conservation is typically enforced by armed guards patrolling the borders of protected areas, imposing fines, arresting trespassers and in cases of poaching sometimes executing a shoot-on-sight policy.

Uganda's wildlife conservation legislation and policies vest ownership of wildlife in the government 'on behalf of, and for the benefit of, the people of Uganda' (Government of Uganda 2019: 12). Forest reserves are likewise held in trust by the government 'for the common good of the citizens of Uganda' (Government of Uganda 2003: 8). National laws regulating wildlife and forest conservation include the Ugandan Constitution of 1995, the Uganda Wildlife Statute of 1996, the National Forest Policy of 2001, the National Forestry and Tree Planting Act of 2003 and recent legislation such as the Uganda National Land Policy of 2013, the new National Environment Act of 2019 and the new Uganda Wildlife Act of 2019. Uganda joined the Convention on International Trade in Endangered Species of Wild Fauna and Flora (CITES) in 1991 and signed and ratified the Convention on Biological Diversity (CBD) in 1992 and 1993 respectively.

The Uganda Wildlife Authority (UWA), a government agency under the Ministry of Tourism, Wildlife and Antiquities, is responsible for the protection and sustainable development of wildlife populations within and outside protected areas. Wildlife laws and wildlife trade conventions are enforced by militarily trained game rangers, who vigorously pursue highly organized criminal poachers and subsistence hunters from communities neighbouring protected areas (UWA 2020).

The protection and sustainable development of forests gazetted as Central Forest Reserves (CFRs) is the responsibility of Uganda's National Forestry Authority (NFA) under the Ministry of Water and Environment. The NFA is mandated to '[m]anage Central Forest Reserves on a sustainable basis and to supply high quality forestry-related products and services to government, local communities and the private sector' (NFA 2020). NFA enforcement officers and police officers from the Environment Protection Police Unit, often with support of army personnel, are tasked with ensuring proper demarcation of forest reserves and the eviction of encroachers (Lumu 2017).

The UWA and NFA stress that the enforcement of the fortress or protectionist approach to the preservation of natural landscapes and endangered animal and plant species has been massively undermined by rural people living near protected areas in search of livelihoods and by illegal activities. Despite the remarkable increase in wildlife populations such as buffaloes, zebras, elephants and giraffes since the establishment of the UWA in the mid-1990s (UWA 2018: 15), wildlife is still threatened by people's encroachment into national parks and wildlife reserves and poaching for game meat, killing of elephants for ivory and pangolins for their scales, or pastoralists' poisoning of lions, leopards or hyenas in revenge for killing their livestock (UWA 2020). The condition of the forests is even more dramatic because the NFA has not always managed the forest reserves well; and in some areas according to neo-patrimonial practices (Petursson and Vedeld 2018). As a result, since 1990, Uganda has lost 400,000 hectares of its forest cover; and in 2017, nearly 98 per cent of the Central Forest Reserves had been encroached into by farmers and loggers involved in illegal cultivation, timber trade and charcoal production (Lumu 2017).

Competition between people and protected area authorities over land and natural resources is the main source of conservation conflicts. Internationally, there has been a paradigm shift from fortress conservation to 'new conservation'; this adds the goals of poverty alleviation and economic development to the conservation agenda and calls for decentralized, community-based approaches to be put in practice under an array of labels including Community Conservation, Integrated Conservation and Development Projects and Community-based Natural Resource Management. But Uganda has been largely untouched by this shift. Decades of violent conflict meant that rethinking conservation was not a political priority. With the establishment of the UWA in 1996 and NFA in 2003, and the formulation of new policies since the early 2000s, wildlife and forest conservation and management were no longer considered the responsibility of government alone. They were to be accomplished in partnership with district authorities, communities and the private sector (UWA 2020; NFA 2020). The fortress approach has been softened to a certain extent by bringing 'conservation *with* the people', as Murphree (2000: 2) puts it, into play under the new hallmark of 'community participation', as stipulated in the new Wildlife Act of 2019 and the National Forestry and Tree Planting Act of 2003, not least because of the authorities' lack of management and enforcement capacities.

These new policies, however, do not imply that people and park and forest authorities have become equal partners. Uganda's approach to conservation has not reached the stage of 'community-*based* conservation' or 'conservation *by* the people' (Murphree 2000: 3, 5–6), which would imply collective management, use and controls on use of common pool resources and equitable benefit sharing at local levels by communal groups. Wildlife and central forests have remained the property of the state, are held in trust by the state for the people of Uganda, and UWA and NFA have the lead in wildlife and forest conservation and management within protected areas and, in the case of UWA, also on people's land, where a vast number of wild animals are found.

Displaced in the Name of Conservation

State-induced fortress conservation can be traced back to the 1872 establishment of the world's first national park, Yellowstone, which was imagined as a pristine wilderness to be preserved for future generations and ages (Brockington, Duffy and Igoe 2008: 18–19). For this to happen, the native Americans of the area were forcibly relocated, and the park was placed under the management of the US federal government, which hoped for investment and tourism.

The Yellowstone model of state-controlled and state-managed conservation, which is inevitably linked to the displacement of the local people, has greatly influenced conservation all over the world (Brockington and Igoe 2006). There are no statistics showing the overall number of people evicted from protected areas. However, estimates indicate that by the mid-2000s tens of millions of people, including up to fourteen million people in Africa (Agrawal and Redford 2009: 4), had become 'conservation refugees' (Dowie 2009). In Sub-Saharan Africa, conservation is the second most prominent and widespread reason why indigenous groups experience land alienation (Laltaika and Askew 2021: 104). Displacement in the name of conservation, like other forms of displacement, has taken the form of forceful eviction of local people from their land and dwellings and economic displacement through depriving them of their livelihoods by restricting access to or excluding them from certain areas (Cernea 2005: 48; Brockington and Igoe 2006: 425). Besides material loss of land, houses and livelihoods, conservation refugees have decried their symbolic obliteration from the landscape: 'their removal from its history, memory and representation' and loss of power and control over their environments (Brockington and Igoe 2006: 425).

European colonialism brought the model of protected areas with all its repercussions to Sub-Saharan Africa, where it has been adopted and remained largely unchanged by postcolonial governments (King 2010: 17–19). However, even in pre-colonial times, certain areas were set aside for various uses, including chiefs' hunting activities and 'conservation' purposes. Access was typically administered by chiefs and clan leaders on behalf of the communities (Bere in Girling 1960: 230–32; Gombya-Ssembajjwe, Abwoli and Bahati 2001). Animals were respected, and those that were considered as clan totems could not be killed by clan members (Roscoe 2015 [1911]). Specific trees regarded as sacred became places for performing rituals and sacrifices (Okello 2002). It was largely during the colonial and postcolonial periods that protected areas were separated from human settlement and people were displaced in the name of conservation (Banana, Nsita and Bomuhangi 2018; King 2010).

The first national park in Africa, Albert National Park (now Virunga National Park), was created in 1925 in Belgian Congo, followed by Kruger National Park in 1926 in South Africa under British colonial rule. Uganda's first national parks were established in the 1950s, when Uganda was a protectorate of the British Empire. One of the main drivers of early wildlife conservation efforts was the influence of powerful aristocratic big-game hunters. Their wish 'to preserve suitable specimen for their sport from the alleged depredations of Africans' (Brockington, Duffy and Igoe 2008: 47) marked the beginning of demarcating certain localities. Another important driver was the intention to preserve landscapes and protect 'the wilderness' from human interference 'to ensure that there is a "Big Out There" other to ourselves' (Brockington, Duffy and Igoe 2008: 48) – an oasis of peace and healing and a counterpoint to civilization with its supposed restlessness and destructive forces. In contemporary conservation discourses in Africa and elsewhere, the 'three particular obsessions of colonial views of nature' – the notion of wilderness, the issue of hunting and the desire to separate nature in protected areas from human interference – have endured (Adams 2003: 19). Protected areas have remained as much a place as an idea not only for the sake of biodiversity conservation but also because of the rich opportunities of marketing 'wild' spaces, things and experiences. The international hunting fraternity is still a powerful force behind conservation (Brockington, Duffy and Igoe 2008: 47–48). International environmental non-governmental organizations such as the World Wide Fund for Nature, which has been frequently associated with violent evictions, or the African Wildlife Foundation and the Wildlife Conservation Society do not only 'proselytise Western ideals of wilderness, people-less landscapes' but also control huge funds for conservation and therefore have great influence in local contexts (Brockington and Igoe 2006: 443).

The creation of forest reserves is a slightly different story compared to national parks and game reserves. At the advent of colonialism, the state became the master of forests, which were divided into protected areas and reserves (Barrow et al. 2016: 136). In Uganda, the British colonial administration declared most of the land, including large areas of woodlands and forests, as Crown Land, from which people could be evicted any time, and which could only be accessed for subsistence by people with so-called 'privileges'. Some of the forest dwellers such as the Batwa, Ik and Benet were allowed to continue residing in the forests, but only as a privilege, not a right (Banana, Nsita and Bomuhangi 2018). Furthermore, because of epidemics such as sleeping sickness, rinderpest and smallpox, communities were resettled to other places (Banana, Nsita, and Bomuhangi 2018). In the areas they left behind, the number of wild animals increased, and the vegetation spread, and some of these areas were then declared reserves. Consequently, the displaced people could not return. Forests were mainly maintained to produce timber, and the 1947 Forest Act confirmed the local people's 'privileged access' to the reserves for collecting dry wood and water but denied them rights to other resources or to settlement. In some areas, the boundary delineation of private land, game and forest reserves led to violent displacement of small-scale farmers. Upon independence in 1962, the Uganda Land Commission took over the management of former Crown Land and the forest reserves were managed by the Forest Department.

Striking examples of forcible evictions of local people from forests and parks in postcolonial Uganda are the Benet, the Batwa and the Ik, many of them now living in abject poverty on the fringes of national parks and nearby towns. The Benet were displaced from Mount Elgon Forest in 1983, when Mount Elgon National Park was created, and had to face repeated expulsions between 1990 and 2004 (MRG 2014). The Batwa were expelled from their ancestral land in the early 1990s to make way for Bwindi Impenetrable Forest National Park, Maghinga Gorilla National Park and Semuliki National Park (MRG 2020) created to save the mountain gorillas. Apaa in northern Uganda is another case that repeatedly made the headlines. After the local Acholi people left the IDP camps following twenty years of war, they returned to what they claimed to be their customary land; but the UWA considered it to be part of East Madi Wildlife Reserve gazetted in 2002 when people were still displaced. Continuous violent evictions by the UWA and national army that cost many lives were met with fierce resistance and accusations that the UWA and investors were grabbing the people's ancestral land (Lenhart 2013; Otto 2017).

There are many less spectacular, less known and less documented cases of uncounted conservation refugees in Uganda, including the case of Christopher, his fellow farmers and their forefathers from Purongo. Another case is Ik subsistence farmers, hunters and gatherers and Dodoth pastoralists, who were evicted from Kidepo valley in 1958, when the area – which after independence became Kidepo Valley National Park – was gazetted as a game reserve by the colonial government (Turnbull 1972). Their displacement implied that all Ik had to live in the Morungule and Timu mountains and farm the steep and ecologically fragile mountain slopes (Meinert, Willerslev and Seebach 2017). They became extra vulnerable to hunger during the dry season and during years of prolonged drought because they were left with very few options for collecting wild fruits and honey and hunting game meat that would have provided them with sufficient vitamins and proteins. Their practice of small-scale hunting and gathering was now considered poaching and transgressing, and members of the Ik community often tell stories of how people who entered the national park were killed by park rangers. Not only were the Ik displaced from Kidepo valley when the park was established, but so were the pastoralist Dodoth, who from then on were prevented from grazing their animals and engaging in small-scale hunting in this area. Some Dodoth began to take their cattle, goats and sheep to the Morungule and Timu mountains, which the Ik considered their home and territory for subsistence farming, hunting and gathering, but not suitable for grazing large numbers of animals. Other Dodoth took their cattle further south and clashed with other pastoralist groups over access to water and pasture. Thus, the displacement caused by the establishment of Kidepo Valley National Park increased inter-ethnic tensions and contributed to the escalation of cattle conflicts between various Karamojong pastoralist groups in the following decades. Today, the Ik and Dodoth live as neighbours and in some areas in mixed communities in a precarious harmony that can easily be disturbed due to competition over land and natural resources (Gade, Willerslev and Meinert 2015).

Conservation and Development

In Uganda (and elsewhere), excluding local people from protected areas, depriving them of their livelihoods and denying them viable aspects of their identity related to land goes hand in hand with letting others in. In the case of national parks and game reserves, these are photo safari tourists, trophy hunters and private investors building and running lodges or organizing tours. In the case of forest reserves, they are concessionaires planting trees, logging and cultivating inside forest reserves; as well as tourists and tour operators in some of the forests. Wilderness – be it landscapes and 'wilderness experiences' or 'wilderness products' such as wildlife, timber, charcoal, medicinal herbs and the like – is something that sells and has proven to be a key driver of Uganda's economy.

The Ugandan government strongly woos solvent tourists and hotel and tour operators who have shown interest in national parks and wildlife reserves (Musoke 2019), as tourism is the country's fastest growing economic sector, leading foreign currency earner and important source of employment. In 2018/19, 1.5 million people visited Uganda, spent US$ 1.6 billion in the country and contributed 7.7 per cent to the gross domestic product (Wadero 2019). Of them, 325,000 were 'leisure tourists' attracted by scenic landscapes and iconic wildlife species and interested in gorilla or chimpanzee tracking, game drives, bird watching, boat cruises on the Nile or sport hunting (UBOS 2019: 105–6).

In the case of forests, tourism also plays a certain, albeit minor, role. Some of Uganda's remaining natural forests such as Kibale Forest and Bwindi Forest have become national parks managed by the UWA, where tourists have the chance to observe gorillas and chimpanzees in their natural habitat (UWA 2020). Other forests managed by the NFA as Central Forest Reserves (CFRs) also attract tourists, including Mabira Forest, Budongo Forest and Mpanga Forest, where activities such as forest walks, mountain biking or bird and butterfly watching are offered. These forest-tourism sites have been developed in collaboration with the private sector (NFA 2020). However, only a few CFRs have a significant proportion of natural forest stands. The majority consist largely of forest plantations, mainly of pine and eucalyptus species for commercial timber production, which are exploited by the NFA and private investors to be sold on domestic and international markets. The same applies to other wood and non-wood forest products such as fuel wood, charcoal, rattan and honey, as well as to cash crop plantations inside CFRs (UBOS 2019: 115).

Wildlife and trees that have been turned into commodities as 'renewable resources' (UWA 2018: 45) attract domestic and foreign investment and are integrated into global value chains with support from key global players including the World Bank, World Trade Organization, World Wide Fund for Nature and others. They are considered a promising path to economic development while simultaneously paying for the costs of conservation. However, the local population has played only a marginal role in such a vision of development. Some provisions for them are made in the Wildlife Act of 2019, which affords not only public-private partnerships but also 'community conservation' in the form of sharing of revenue generated from national parks and game reserves with local communities, as well as wildlife use rights on communal and private land, including hunting or ranching of wildlife, trading in wildlife and wildlife products, and using wildlife for tourism and recreation (Uganda Wildlife Act 2019: Sections 22, 35, 51 and 65). The Act also states the new provision of compensation for damages including death, injury, destruction of crops and property caused by certain wildlife species outside protected areas (Uganda Wildlife Act 2019: Sections 82, 83, 84 and Fourth Schedule). Similarly, the National Forestry and Tree Planting Act of 2003 provides for collaborative management of central and local forest reserves by 'a responsible body and a forest user group'; and for issuing licences to interested persons or entities for 'cutting, taking, working or removing of forest produce from a forest reserve or community forest' (National Forestry and Tree Planting Act 2003, Part II, Section 5, Part IV, Section 41 and Part V).

In the case of national parks and wildlife reserves, at present, community conservation mainly takes the form of sharing of revenue from park entrance fees and from the use of wildlife outside protected areas, mostly sport hunting.

Usually, the 20 per cent revenue of park entrance fees is spent on local infrastructure – e.g. solar panels for schools, classroom blocks, health centres, roads or bridges – as well as community projects intended to offer an alternative to agriculture in areas highly affected by human-wildlife conflict, such as bee hive projects for honey production or community-based eco-tourism projects. However, our research among communities neighbouring Murchison Falls National Park and Kidepo Valley National Park and studies carried out in the border areas of Bwindi Impenetrable National Park in south-western Uganda (Ahebwa, Van der Duim and Sandbrook 2012; Tumusiime and Vedeld 2012) show that the benefits of the 20 per cent revenue do not at all outweigh losses from physical and economic displacement, nor do they compensate for crop raiding by hungry elephants and other wildlife. The findings also reveal that prior to 2012, the revenue sharing policy had not been implemented. This only changed with UWA's concerted awareness-raising of new Revenue Sharing Guidelines (UWA 2011) at that time, which focused on putting the responsibility for selecting projects funded through UWA's Revenue Sharing Fund in the hands of the people by setting up Parish Development and Parish Procurement Committees tasked with planning and managing the money. However, despite the UWA's intention to decentralize 'decision making and action to the lowest levels possible' and minimize 'Revenue Sharing Fund dissipation' (UWA 2011: 2), the 20 per cent – a rather minimal amount compared to the total revenue from park tourism – has often not reached the targeted people. This may be due to the fact that projects have to be approved by the UWA, and local government officials are in charge of receiving funds and allocating the money. In Purongo and Bwindi (Tumusiime and Vedeld 2012; Lenhart 2023), people lamented that the authorities would only pay lip service to people's participation in decision-making and did not actually want to relinquish power and lose control. They accused UWA personnel on the ground and members of local government of misappropriating funds and blamed them for corruption, nepotism and fraud.

In the case of forests, local people's views and needs are seldom given priority; or local people are not even considered as partners, as demonstrated by the case of the Ik living in the area of Timu forest. In 2017, the private company 'Inspire Africa' – a 'human capital organisation', as the organization calls itself, with the mission 'to create and empower fresh generations of African entrepreneurs with practical entrepreneurial experience, while extending to them practical business exposure and mentorship' (Inspire Africa 2017) – started a coffee plantation project inside Timu Forest Reserve with funding from the Northern Uganda Social Action Fund (NUSAF 3). Groups of local young people were given coffee seedlings to plant between the trees, where they were expected to thrive, and were promised benefit from the future harvest. The idea behind the project, according to one of the coordinators, was to replace illegal subsistence farming in the forest reserve with coffee production, thus contributing to preserving the forest while simultaneously creating a cash crop livelihood alternative for the youth. However, the farmers who had their gardens taken over by the coffee project obviously felt threatened. Moreover, ploughing the fields with a tractor, compared to the farmers' way of digging between the trees with hand hoes, reshaped the forest scape rather than protecting it. The NFA had not approved the coffee plantation inside the forest reserve but shared the logic of the implementers that it followed national development plans for modernization of agriculture by transforming subsistence agriculture into commercial farming. At the same time and place, the NFA ran a reforestation and tree planting programme, which was also not well received locally, because the trees were not only planted by prisoners from the district prison and not by locals but were also planted in people's gardens. These two attempts to promote 'conservation through development' were, to some extent, doomed to fail from the beginning because the implementers had not actively involved the local people, who depended on the land for their livelihoods. In contrast, Budongo forest in western Uganda is a more promising example. Here the forest authorities successfully changed their management strategy by combining the conventional protectionist approach with the conservation through development approach to focus on multiple-use forest management involving local people (Babweteera et al. 2018).

Just Conservation: A Conclusion

Christopher Olum and the people of Purongo, the Ik and many others affected by wildlife and forest conservation conflicts in Uganda are questioning the state's top-down approach, with protected areas at its centre, and with government deciding on conservation affairs and its agencies UWA and NFA having the lead in implementing programmes and projects and enforcing conservation laws in cooperation with other security organs. The Ugandan authorities argue that they have a mandate as custodians of wildlife inside and outside national parks and game reserves and of trees and other forest products inside Central Forest Reserves. On the one hand, they are tasked with protecting the country's rich biodiversity for present and future generations; on the other hand, they are obliged to contribute towards driving forward Uganda's economic development by selling wildlife experiences in the savannah landscape to tourists, and trees and other forest products to concessionaires.

Having realised that communities and individuals will only protect wildlife and forests when they also benefit from conservation, the state has recently expanded its approach to include 'community conservation' mainly in the form of sharing revenue from park entrance fees. However, our case studies, as well as research conducted among communities neighbouring national parks and forest reserves in other parts of the country, reveal that the introduction of 'community conservation' has not changed the relationship between the local people and the conservation agencies, which has remained tense and characterized by mistrust. In large part, this is because people lost their land and houses, access to vital livelihood resources, family homes and cultural space in the name of conservation. Some were forcefully evicted from their land to create national parks and forest reserves, as in the case of the Ik, Batwa and Benet. Others were displaced 'first by the colonialists and now your [UWA's] elephants', as the people from Purongo used to complain to the UWA rangers and wardens from Murchison Falls National Park. Revenues largely remain with government and private investors, who obtain concessions for running lodges and operating tours within national parks and opening plantations within Central Forest Reserves. The local people were not compensated for their losses and received limited, if any, economic returns from this marketing of the 'wilderness'. They experienced food insecurity, psychological stress and social and economic downward mobility – a fate they share with people who have undergone other forms of development-induced displacement (Cernea and Schmidt-Soltau 2003; Cernea 2005; Agrawal and Redford 2009; Laltaika and Askew 2021).

Christopher and the people of Purongo repeatedly emphasized exactly these points (Lenhart 2023). Being neighbours of a national park, they said they felt neglected by a government 'that cares more about animals than us' and that has chosen to rigorously protect wildlife, not least because of the benefits accruing from conservation and the selling of 'wilderness experiences' to tourists in collaboration with their private sector allies. They stressed that they had to bear the brunt of conservation, facing hunger and poverty caused by crop raiding of hungry elephants crossing the park border and being accused of poaching when hunting in their customary hunting grounds in the border area of the national park. They were sometimes subjected to arbitrary arrests and mistreatment, and even murder and disappearances were reported. However, unjust outcomes and unfair treatment were not their only concern. They also emphasized that their voices were not heard, not even when they tried to involve higher authorities, including their elected representatives in parliament. They bemoaned the lack of recognition and exclusion from decision-making on issues that fundamentally affect their lives.

The grievances of Christopher and many other people in Purongo, Ikland and elsewhere in Uganda concerning land and land use, trust and governance in the context of conservation point to the violation of the three intertwined dimensions of social justice: outcome justice, or the fair sharing of resources, benefits and costs of conservation; procedural justice or ways of achieving a fair outcome based on participation in and the fairness of decision-making processes; and recognition or respect for difference and avoidance of domination (Martin 2017). Conservation in Uganda has to a greater or lesser extent undermined not only existing livelihoods but also lifeworlds, which have been moulded over centuries through specific ways of living on, from and with the land. The long-established 'fortress' or 'protectionist' approach has turned local hunters into 'poachers' and gatherers of firewood, fruits and berries into 'thieves'. It has also disregarded the social and spiritual dimensions of land as a source of identity, belonging, generational succession and locus of ritual acts. The more recent 'conservation as development' paradigm – contrary to its intention – has perpetuated some of the negative distributional effects on the communities. People like Christopher – who were largely excluded from decision-making in the context of 'community conservation', lost trust and confidence in the conservation agencies and withdrew from any dialogue with their representatives on the ground – finally took matters in their own hands – in some cases, as happened in Lawaca, with some success. However, generally, withdrawal of an affected population makes it even less likely that their voices will be heard and their needs recognized, which will further worsen their position in terms of distribution.

A decisive factor for just conservation is conservation governance. In Uganda, the top-down approach of state-controlled and state-managed conservation has reduced community participation largely to the state's sharing of a rather small amount of revenue with neighbours of protected areas to be invested in community projects, instead of making it a community demand-driven approach with activities planned and developed in a participatory process. This would have required devolution of certain rights and obligations to the communities, which has not happened. The local people at the end of a chain of vertical power and interests related to wildlife and forests – central government with its agencies UWA and NFA, local governments at the district and sub-district levels, private investors and communities – have remained the ones least involved in decision-making processes. They receive the smallest share of profits, even though they are the ones who suffer disproportionately from the negative impacts of conservation. Rather, in a context of 'neo-liberally inspired commoditization of natural resources' (Bollig 2016: 771), government has courted the private sector interested in tourism and trade as partners. These actors have created and maintained an image of conservation intended to make it a market hit. They are the ones in control of conservation affairs, driven by influential international conservation actors such as the World Wide Fund for Nature and supported by global economy key players including the World Bank.

Thus, some thorny questions concerning the practice of conservation in Uganda and elsewhere remain to be answered. Who should benefit from conservation and who will be at the losing end: the state and tourists, the local people and rural poor, or animals and trees? How can social justice be achieved for those who are most affected by potentially negative repercussions of conservation? What are best practices in devolving conservation rights and obligations from the state to local communities so as to realize social justice and foster economic development, without compromising the welfare of wildlife and forests? Can this be achieved in the context of global capitalism, which transforms nature into commodities of trade? Finding answers to these questions is not an easy endeavour, and answers will differ depending on whether it is the protection and preservation of wildlife and landscapes or interventionist forest resource management. However, the insight that just conservation cannot only be about doing justice to people but must include doing justice to nature to achieve ecological sustainability applies to both.

Our case studies on conservation conflicts show the fierce competition between humans and wildlife and trees for land. All need access to land for survival and suffer from displacement. Land is a place of close relationships. Plants, animals, humans, minerals and water are important to each other and interdependent. They constitute a 'biotic community', as Leopold put it in his essay on land ethics (Leopold 1987 [1949]: 204). In the context of conservation, striving for justice for people, particularly the most disadvantaged groups, should be a matter of course. However, we also experience the tremendous loss of biodiversity, alarming degradation of ecosystems and destruction of landscapes in Uganda and worldwide (WWF 2018) with their severe consequences for mankind. Thus, if justice for people is at the expense of the non-human, neither social nor ecological justice will be achieved. However, a transformed self-conception of people as part of the land's biotic community would not only lead to a greater acceptance of nature conservation but would also encourage greater political efforts to ensure that nature conservation benefits the well-being of all – non-human and human – parts of this community.

Lioba Lenhart, Ph.D., was Associate Professor at the Institute of Peace and Strategy Studies, Gulu University (2009–2021) and is now Programme Advisor for Participatory Transformation of Land Conflicts in Northern Uganda, Civil Peace Service Programme, German Federal Ministry for Economic Cooperation and Development (BMZ) and GIZ.

Lotte Meinert, Ph.D., is Professor at the Department of Anthropology, Aarhus University.

References

Adams, William M. 2003. 'Nature and the Colonial Mind', in William M. Adams and Martin Mulligan (eds), *Decolonizing Nature: Strategies for Conservation in a Post-Colonial Era*. London: Earthscan, pp. 16–50.

Agrawal, Arun, and Kent Redford. 2009. 'Conservation and Displacement: An Overview', *Conservation and Society* 7(1): 1–10.

Ahebwa, Wilber Manyisa, René van der Duim and Chris Sandbrook. 2012. 'Tourism Revenue Sharing Policy at Bwindi Impenetrable National Park, Uganda: A Policy Arrangements Approach', *Journal of Sustainable Tourism* 20: 377–94.

Babweteera, Fred, Christopher Mawa, Caroline Asiimwe, Eric Okwir, Geoffrey Muhanguzi, John Paul Okimat and Sarah Robinson. 2018. 'Budongo Forest: A Paradigm Shift in Conservation?' in Chris Sandbrook, Connor Joseph Cavanagh and David Mwesigye Tumusiime (eds), *Conservation and Development in Uganda*. London: Routledge, pp. 104–22.

Banana, Abwoli Yabezi, Steve Nsita and Allan Bomuhangi. 2018. 'Histories and Genealogies of Ugandan Forest and Wildlife Conservation: The Birth of the Protected Area Estate', in Chris Sandbrook, Connor Joseph Cavanagh and David Mwesigye Tumusiime (eds), *Conservation and Development in Uganda*. London: Routledge, pp. 16–44.

Barrow, E. G. et al. 2016. 'Who Owns Africa's Forests? Exploring the Impacts of Forest Tenure Reform on Forest Ecosystems and Livelihoods', *Forests, Trees and Livelihoods* 25(2): 132–56.

Bollig, Michael. 2016. 'Towards an Arid Eden? Boundary Making, Governance and Benefit Sharing and the Political Ecology of the "New Commons" of Kunene Region, Northern Namibia', *International Journal of the Commons* 10(2): 771–99.

Brockington, Daniel, and James Igoe. 2006. 'Eviction for Conservation: A Global Overview', *Conservation and Society* 4(3): 424–70.

Brockington, Dan, Rosaleen Duffy and Jim Igoe. 2008. *Nature Unbound: Conservation, Capitalism and the Future of Protected Areas*. London: Earthscan.

Cernea, Michael M. 2005. 'Restriction of Access is Displacement: A Broader Concept and Policy', *Forced Migration Review* 23: 48–49.

Cernea, Michael M., and Kai Schmidt-Soltau. 2003. 'The End of Forcible Displacement? Conservation Must NOT Impoverish People', *Policy Matters* 12: 42–51.

Doolittle, Amity. 2007. 'Fortress Conservation', in Paul Robbins (ed.), *Encyclopedia of Environment and Society*. Thousand Oaks: SAGE Publications, p. 705.

Dowie, Mark. 2009. *Conservation Refugees: The Hundred-Year-Conflict Between Global Conservation and Native Peoples*. Cambridge: The MIT Press.

Gade, Christian B. N., Rane Willerslev and Lotte Meinert. 2015. 'Half-Trust and Enmity in Ikland, Northern Uganda', *Common Knowledge* 21(3): 406–19.

Girling, Frank Knowles. 1960. 'Appendix D: Land Tenure and Methods of Hunting by R. M. Bere', in Frank Knowles Girling and Wielka Brytania, Colonial Office (eds), *The Acholi of Uganda*. London: Her Majesty's Stationery Office, pp. 230–33.

Gombya-Ssembajjwe, William S., Abwoli Y. Banana and Joseph Bahati. 2001. 'Case Study – Property Rights: Access to Land and Forest Resources in Uganda', in Alain de Janvry, Gustavo Gordillo, Elisabeth Sadoulet and Jean-Phillippe Platteau (eds), *Access to Land, Rural Poverty, and Public Action*. Oxford: Oxford University Press, pp. 151–62.

Government of Uganda. 2003. *The National Forestry and Tree Planting Act, 2003*. Kampala: The Republic of Uganda.

———. 2019. *Uganda Wildlife Act, 2019*. Kampala: The Republic of Uganda.

Inspire Africa. 2017. 'Background'. 2017. Inspire Africa website. Retrieved 20 April 2020 from: http://www.inspireafrica.co.ug.

King, Brian. 2010. 'Conservation Geographies in Sub-Saharan Africa: The Politics of National Parks, Community Conservation and Peace Parks', *Geography Compass* 4(1): 14–27.

Laltaika, Elifuraha, and Kelly M. Askew. 2021. 'Modes of Dispossession of Indigenous Lands and Territories in Africa', in Echi Christina Gabbert, Fana Gebresenbet, John G. Galaty and Günther Schlee (eds), *Lands of the Future: Anthropological Perspectives on Pastoralism, Land Deals and Tropes of Modernity in Eastern Africa*. New York: Berghahn Books, pp. 99–122.

Lenhart, Lioba. 2013. 'Alleged Land Grabs and Governance: Exploring Mistrust and Trust in Northern Uganda: The Case of the Apaa Land Conflict', *Journal of Peace and Security Studies* 1: 64–85.

———. 2023. 'Justice Dilemmas in Conservation Conflicts in Uganda', in Michael Bollig, Selma Lendelwo, Alfonso Mosimane and Romie Nghitevelekwa (eds), *Commodifying the 'Wild: Conservation, Markets and the Environment in Southern and Eastern Africa*. Martlesham, Suffolk: James Currey.

Leopold, Aldo. 1987 [1949]. 'The Land Ethic', in Aldo Leopold (ed.), *A Sand County Almanac*. Oxford: Oxford University Press, pp. 201–26.

Lumu, David. 2017. 'Over 400 Forest Reserves in Uganda Encroached on', *New Vision*. Retrieved 20 April 2020 from: https://www.newvision.co.ug/new_vision/news/1449205/400-forest-reserves-uganda-encroached.

Martin, Adrian. 2017. *Just Conservation: Biodiversity, Wellbeing and Sustainability*. London: Routledge.

Meinert, Lotte, Rane Willerslev and Sophie Hooge Seebach. 2017. 'Cement, Graves, and Pillars in Land Disputes in Northern Uganda', *African Studies Review* 60(3): 37–57.

MRG. 2014. 'Eviction of Indigenous Benet in Uganda Risks Conflict', MRG – Minority Rights Group International website. Retrieved October 2021 from: https://minorityrights.org/2014/11/06/eviction-of-indigenous-benet-in-uganda-risks-conflict/.

———. 2020. 'Uganda: Decades of Displacement for Batwa, Uprooted in the Name of Conservation', MRG/ Minority Rights Group International website. Retrieved October 2021 from https://minorityrights.org/uganda-decades-of-displacement-for-batwa-uprooted-in-the-name-of-conservation/.

Murphree, Marshal W. 2000. 'Community-Based Conservation: Old Ways, New Myths and Enduring Challenges', *African Wildlife Management in The New Millennium Conference, Mweka, 13–15 December 2000*. Mweka: College of African Wildlife Management.

Musoke, Ronald. 2019. 'Uganda Softens Stance on Investing in National Parks', *The Independent*, 26 July. Retrieved 20 April 2020 from https://www.independent.co.ug/uganda-softens-stance-on-investing-in-national-parks/.

NEMA – National Environment Management Authority. 2016. *National Biodiversity Strategy and Action Plan II (2015–2025)*. Kampala: NEMA.

NFA. 2020. 'About NFA'. NFA – National Forestry Authority website. Retrieved 20 April 2020 from https://www.nfa.org.ug/.

Okello, Benson. 2002. *A History of East Africa*. Kampala: Fountain.

Otto, Irene Abalo. 2017. 'Tracing the Roots of Apaa Land Conflict', *The PML Daily*, 10 June. Retrieved 20 April from https://www.pmldaily.com/news/2017/06/tracing-the-roots-of-apaa-land-conflict.html.

Petursson, Jon Geir, and Paul Vedeld. 2018. 'Lost in the Woods? A Political Economy of the 1998 Forest Sector Reform in Uganda', in Chris Sandbrook, Connor Joseph Cavanagh, and David Mwesigye Tumusiime (eds), *Conservation and Development in Uganda*. London: Routledge, pp. 206–25.

Pomeroy, Derek, Herbert Tushabe and Jonathan Loh. 2017. *Uganda Biodiversity 2017 Report*. Kampala: Department of Environment Management College of Agricultural and Environmental Sciences, Makerere University.

Pomeroy, D. et al. 2002. *Uganda Ecosystem and Protected Area Characterisation*. Kampala: Makerere University Institute of Environment and Natural Resources (MUIENR) and Washington D.C.: The International Food Policy Research Institute (IFPRI).

Roscoe, John. 2015 [1911]. *The Baganda: An Account of Their Native Customs and Beliefs*. London: FB & C Limited.

Tumusiime, David, and Pål Vedeld. 2012. 'False Promise or False Premise? Using Tourism Revenue Sharing to Promote Conservation and Poverty Reduction in Uganda', *Conservation and Society* 10: 15–28.

Turnbull, Colin. 1972. *The Mountain People*. New York: Simon and Schuster.

UBOS – Uganda Bureau of Statistics. 2019. *2019 Statistical Abstract*. Kampala: Government of Uganda.

UWA – Uganda Wildlife Authority. 2011. *Guidelines for Revenue Sharing between Wildlife Protected Areas and Adjacent Local Governments and Communities*, March 2011. Kampala: UWA.

———. 2018. *State of Wildlife Resources in Uganda 2018*. Kampala: UWA.

———. 2020. Uganda Wildlife Authority website. Retrieved 20 April 2020 from http://www.ugandawildlife.org.

Wadero, Arthur Arnold. 2019. 'Tourism Revenue Hits Shs5.8 Trillion', *Daily Monitor*, 20 September. Retrieved 20 April 2020 from https://www.monitor.co.ug/uganda/news/national/tourism-revenue-hits-shs5–8-trillion-1848830.

WWF – World Wide Fund for Nature. 2018. *Living Planet Report – 2018: Aiming Higher*. Monique Grooten and Rosamunde E. A. Almond (eds). Gland: WWF and ZSL– Zoological Society of London.

Afterword
Who Belongs Where, and What Belongs to Whom?

Christian Lund

> There is no image, no painting, no visible trait, which can express
> the relation that constitutes property. It is not material,
> it is metaphysical; it is a mere conception of the mind.
> —Bentham, Theory of Legislation, 1874

This Land Is Not For Sale is about land and conflicts in northern Uganda and the institutional transformations engendered in part by war, conflict, violence and displacement. It investigates how claims and transactions shape the governance of the resource upon which most people in northern Uganda depend for their livelihood: land. However, the book has a broader reach and a significant epistemological ambition. First, the contributions show that for every question we ask about land and property in Africa, we get one answer and two new questions in return. The collection demonstrates that when we ask a simple question such as *Who belongs where, and what belongs to whom?* a series of interconnected questions emerge about the social contracts of property. We, therefore, have to ask about identity and rights subjects and their meaningful forms of visibility, about the relevant institutions of public authority, about the nature of property, and about the representations of rights. To be a rights subject – to be visible to the law as a person with legal standing and rights – may seem self-evident to the privileged. However, historically, virtually all societies have treated large portions of their members as legal minors with less than full rights. Women, serfs, children, immigrants and the poor are just the beginning of a long line of human beings for whom the concern is far from redundant. And 'attributes such as gender, race, and caste, as well as class, creed, and conviction have different valences allowing for more or less punch in the property claim' (Lund 2020: 8).

Second, the book's focus on a period of post-conflict reconstruction demonstrates with clarity that it is not simply people's homes and schools that undergo reconstruction; all the elements of how people see and understand actors, institutions and norms are equally reassembled in known and new ways. The chapters therefore demonstrate that the key concepts must remain objects of our enquiry as much as the empirical reality we see through them. They are correspondingly at stake and constantly under construction. Let us briefly shine a light on some of the most significant ones: actors, institutions, rights and representations.

When people talk about 'us' and 'them', or those who are entitled and those who are not, it is more than a simple grouping of people here and there. People are classified according to attributes that give them a particular social identity and quality and therefore different abilities to possess, to own or to be entitled. These attributes render people visible to institutions and society in particular ways. Ethnicity, nationality, gender, kinship position, marital status, age and attachment to a specific area frequently crop up as qualifiers. In the post-war situation, the importance of social position was amplified. In relation to land, 'war victims' emerged mainly as 'nephews' – young men who had lost their father and paternal link to access land. While some seem perennial, others appear more fluid, and as the chapters show, their relative importance varies over time. In fact, the significance of the different attributes changes, and it is the reproduction and change of the *contingent significance*, rather than change in some essence of the attributes, which is at stake. People often refer to these identity attributes – gender, age and belonging and so on – as if their significance was permanent and transcendental. Ironically, people often determine the significance of identity in the act of invoking it and thereby make up what they believe to be already there. However, it is when states invest such difference with political meaning, when difference is institutionalized with privilege and exclusion as a result, that the ground is prepared for envenomed and enduring conflict (see Mamdani 2020).

The stakes are unbelievably high for people who depend on recognition of their identity to validate their claims. This particular post-conflict moment makes the social construction of status and rights, of rights subjects and institutions, particularly intense. The chapters make clear that everybody acts in the face of uncertainty. Claims are made to the best of people's ability to read the situation, the dangers and opportunities, as well as their ability to knit together a plausible and persuasive narrative about their interests (Rose 1994). Not in a completely random or opportunistic fashion, but people rework the institutional debris from before the war with one of the important hard-earned norms that has survived the conflict: peaceful and harmonious living, something that the painful atrocities have made an explicit virtue. People reinterpret, reinvent and recycle the available repertoires; something old, something new, something borrowed, something blue . . . This leads to questions of recognition.

Institutions or groups of actors are simultaneously actors and arenas and manifestations of power relations. All three aspects are important for an understanding of the political processes involving institutions. First, as an actor, a politico-legal institution defines and enforces collectively binding decisions and rules – or, rather, *attempts* to define and enforce them because this capacity is rarely fully accomplished and is often challenged. Second, an institution is also an arena where competing social actors struggle to influence the way rulings are made. Third, as arenas, institutions are also manifestations of power relations (Lund 2008: 9).

Statutory institutions – that is, institutions that make up part of the official constitutional governance structure in society – are designed to administer statutory law, but the cast of institutions is usually much bigger, and Uganda is no exception. Government and rebel groups have taken turns in controlling different areas. Institutions of more intimate land governance such as families', clans' and elders' fora also crowd the picture, as do religious institutions and NGOs of different stripes. Statutory institutions are supposed to be 'blind' to gender and ethnicity, whereas these attributes are highly visible – sometimes even defining – to chiefs, elders, families or other local institutions engaged in the more intimate governance of access to land. In practice, however, the vision of institutions is more muddied and incidental. Accordingly, the range of potential authorities and their internal relations and hierarchies are brought into play in land conflicts, making some actors visible and invisible as rights subjects in recombinant ways. Rights subjects and institutions are all reworked: who is entitled, and by what institutions are rights protected and enforced? And, not to forget, rights subjects are not only individuals; families, clans and other congregations of people may have legal standing according to law, lore or political opportunity.

The dialectics of recognition between rights and authority can play out between many different institutions. Post-conflict settings like northern Uganda demonstrate that. The rupture of war makes different combinations possible simultaneously. While government empowers certain institutions to exercise authority, ordinary people's claims sometimes breathe life into entirely different entities of authority (Ubink 2008). However, it is not the mere availability of institutions which concerns the contributors to this book but the trust people are willing to place in them. The wake of war has affected all institutions in society, and people's trust in the different institutions is tentative, at best. Trust is built by increment and depends on the observance of decisions and rulings. It tends to take time. The construction of functional institutions and social contracts requires stamina, but they can be destroyed in a brutal moment of war. What institution will have the legitimate authority to decide what specific rights are bestowed on whom, and to which institutions are different claimants visible and eventually beholden? Northern Uganda's recent history does not encourage resolute predictions about what kind of authority will prevail when and how. The research in this book demonstrates that it depends.

The ongoing construction is not just institutional but equally concerns the rights themselves, or the nature of property, if you like. If we ask to whom does the land belong, the chapters in this book quickly show us that it is difficult to answer before we also examine *how* land belongs to people. And even this question immediately splits into several queries. In legal scholarship, there is a classical division between *ownership* of a resource and *rights* to it (Singer 2000; Underkuffler 2003). Ownership, or freehold, is often regarded as having all the powers over a particular resource. The power to use it, the power to exclude from it, and the power to transfer it at will without any interference from relatives, neighbours or government are firmly in the hands of the owner. There is, at the base of 'ownership', a rather absolutist assumption of the sovereign *concentration* of powers and a presumption about their *clear simplicity*.

An alternative view to ownership is often presented as a bundle of rights. The totality of rights constitutes a proverbial bundle where each stick represents a particular distinguishable right, so to speak. In different societies, these elements are conceived differently according to cultural norms, institutional history and production systems. For example, some may have a right to farm the land, but others hold a right to graze it or glean from it. Are the grazing rights as strong as the farming rights, for example, or is the momentary right of gleaning as real as the more enduring right of farming? Does the *certainty* of a right correspond to its *extent*, so to speak? Such perceptions of how (much) something belongs to somebody are not merely academic. They are at odds in real life, and the tension manifests in many daily situations. There is therefore a tug of war between one understanding of land ownership that presumes to concentrate most sticks of the bundle in the tight grip of the owner and another understanding that separates out different rights among different rights subjects.

A tug of war is transgression by another name. Some people may, for example, have a right to farm the land but are not free to transact it outside of their kin group. If, all the same, such land rights were to be sold or mortgaged, it is likely to precipitate a conflict of interpretation of the significance of the act, over how many 'sticks' were actually sold or mortgaged, and what elements of the property are now in new hands; all of them or a single twig.

It is tempting to conflate the palpable earthy space with the idea of an entitlement. Hence, people often refer to land transactions as *buying and selling* land. However, this is deceptive and inaccurate. Land is not property. Even if we often refer to land as the 'thing' that is inherited, bought, owned, mortgaged, bequeathed, sold or lost, it is not the land itself that is being transacted but a set of rights to it (Hohfeld 1913). These rights are abstract – mere conceptions of the mind, as Bentham would have it in the epigraph above. What is transacted is, therefore, the *imperfect* bundle of rights, warts and all. A seller sells the imperfect rights she/he has, and the new landholder or house owner will hold the land and house under similar conditions of legal imperfection and possible uncertainty (Lund 2020: 129). In moments of generalized rupture, uncertainty increases and opportunities multiply. This is most likely why some people take the trouble to put *Not For Sale* signs on buildings and land; there is a risk that someone may buy property from someone who is not fully entitled to sell it. The buyer may buy more than the seller can legally or legitimately sell, so to speak. Even time-honoured rights are, therefore, at risk if held by politically weaker groups, and it is clearly still an open question as to what notion of property will predominate in northern Uganda and how distribution of rights will evolve. The push for 'clear' and 'concentrated' rights always has its champions. Whether 'distribution of rights' and 'security for secondary rights-holders' have any effective leg to stand on remains to be seen. The point is that any generalized understanding of what *actually* changes hands is being hammered out in the process, in real time.

'Freehold' and 'bundles of rights' are both eloquent metaphors, but they sound simpler than they actually are. Freehold, unfettered and unencumbered by social obligations, is a fiction and practically an oxymoron. For freehold (or 'any-hold') to work in a social contract, it must be recognized by an authority or society, and the political and contingent nature of any such authority is easy to overlook if we are blinkered by the 'free' in freehold. Similarly, the bundle metaphor can also lead astray our understanding of property. The notion of a bundle may give the impression that we are dealing with multiple fairly equal rights. That is likely to be the exception. More often, some of the 'sticks' in the bundle will be mere slivers, others slender staves, and others yet will be massive beams. They are neither equal in reach, duration or recognition, nor are they always stable or neatly separable.

Rights are immaterial; they are social, political and legal conventions. Consequently, they depend on representations to be seen. Deeds, permits, contracts, surveys, maps and other documents are used to record events, transactions and rights. Documents constitute important reference points for state recognition of a variety of claims. However, away from paperwork, physical markers in the landscape – hedges, fences, trees, ancestral graves and so on – also serve to document historical use and future rights. In situations of post-war displacement and capricious state presence, however, paper documents but a fraction of rights, and physical markers may be destroyed or overwritten by new symbols of claims. Physical proof and representations of rights are scant. This leaves people with oral testimonies of the past to vindicate future claims. In a process of reconstruction, it is no easy task to separate genuine memory from guileless wish. Any institution saddled with the task of adjudication must balance a just view of the past with what will be just in future, but with no recourse to discernible representations of what went before, the job is all the more prospective. Northern Uganda is living through an open moment where the institutional landscape is more in the making than it has been at most other times. The book's attention to land's intimate governance captures the human ingenuity in brokering peace and shows how actors, institutions, rights and representations are produced in the process.

War, violence and displacement evidence that no condition is permanent (Berry 1993). *This Land Is Not For Sale* brings it forth with acute limpidity. Furthermore, just as clear is the fact that the concepts people use to understand property and its transaction are objects of struggle. Actors' identity, institutions' authority, the nature of property and rights and, finally, the representations of all of it are not master concepts removed from the imbroglio of conflict; they each form contested terrains of terminology. The present book demonstrates how analysts of land conflicts must engage a double-barrelled vision to capture what is going on and how people make sense of it.

Christian Lund, Ph.D., is Professor of Development, Resource Management and Governance at University of Copenhagen.

References

Berry, Sara. 1993. *No Condition is Permanent: The Social Dynamics of Agrarian Change in Sub-Saharan Africa*. Madison: University of Wisconsin Press.
Hohfeld, Wesley Newcome. 1913. 'Some Fundamental Legal Conceptions as Applied in Judicial Reasoning', *Yale Law Review* 23(1): 16–59.
Lund, Christian. 2008. *Local Politics and the Dynamics of Property in Africa*. Cambridge: Cambridge University Press.
———. 2016. 'Rule and Rupture: State Formation Through the Production of Property and Citizenship', *Development and Change* 47(6): 1199–228.
———. 2020. *Nine-Tenths of the Law: Enduring Dispossession in Indonesia*. New Haven: Yale University Press.
———. 2022. 'What We Talk About When We Talk About Land', in S. M. Borras and J. C. Franco (eds), *The Oxford Handbook on Land*. Oxford: Oxford University Press.
Mamdani, Mahmood. 2020. *Neither Settler Nor Native: The Making and Unmaking of Permanent Minorities*. Cambridge: Belknap Press.
Moore, Sally Falk. 1978. *Law as Process*. London: Routledge & Kegan Paul.
Pottage, Alain, and Martha Mundy (eds). 2004. *Law, Anthropology, and the Constitution of the Social. Making Persons and Things*. Cambridge: Cambridge University Press.
Rose, Carol M. 1994. *Property and Persuasion: Essays on the History, Theory and Rhetoric of Ownership*. Boulder: Westview Press.
Singer, Joseph William. 2000. *Entitlement: The Paradoxes of Property*. New Haven: Yale University Press.
Ubink, Janine. 2008. *Traditional Authorities in Africa: Resurgence in an Era of Democratisation*. Leiden: Leiden University Press.
Underkuffler, Laura. 2003. *The Idea of Property: Its Meaning and Power*. Oxford: Oxford University Press.

Appendix
Land Legislation and Implementation in Uganda

Anne Mette Kjær

Four main documents constitute the legislative and policy framework on land in Uganda: 1. The constitution of the Republic of Uganda 1995; 2. the Land Act 1998; 3. the 2010 Amendment of the Land Act; and 4. the 2013 Land Policy. The primary purpose of this legislation is to create security of land tenure and to promote well-functioning land markets so as to promote economic development. This appendix highlights key aspects from the legal framework (and briefly addresses some of the main challenges as regards enforcement).

The constitution stipulates that 'Land in Uganda belongs to the citizens of Uganda and shall vest in them in accordance with the land tenure systems provided for in this Constitution' (Chapter 15). This stipulation is in contrast to some other African countries, where all land is government owned. The constitution also says that the government can acquire land if in the public interest. The constitution specifies four types of land tenure systems: Customary; Freehold; Mailo; and Leasehold (Article 237) but does not define any of them. The constitution also stipulates that there shall be Land Tribunals to settle disputes and District Land Boards.

The 1998 Land Act details what each of the four types of tenure entails. *Customary tenure* thus refers to land under customary regulation, usually under communal ownership, owned by groups or persons in perpetuity. *Freehold land* is registered land owned in perpetuity; *Mailo* is a type of land granted to the Baganda by the British in the so-called 1900 Agreement. Mailo land is often owned by someone who does not use it all but lets tenants live on the land. *Leasehold* is a form of tenure 'under which one person, namely the landlord or lessor, grants or is deemed to have granted another person, namely the tenant or lessee, exclusive possession of land usually but not necessarily for a period defined, directly or indirectly, by reference to a specific date of commencement and a specific date of ending'. The rest of the Land Act specifies the processes by which to obtain claims on land; for example, there is a long section on how to get a customary land certificate, how to apply for a freehold title, and how to become recognized as a tenant and/or a bona fide occupant.

The 2010 Land (Amendment) Act has the main purpose of protecting tenants, bona fide occupants and customary landholders' rights to land. More specifically, it narrows down, in a way that is not done in the 1998 Land Act, the circumstances under which citizens can be evicted; for example, if they have not paid their rent. Customary landholders can only be evicted by the decision of a court of law.

The 2013 Land Policy aims to formulate clear policies and thereby seeks to expand and elaborate on the quite general framework in the constitution and the land act. It also seeks to formulate policies on the implementation and enforcement dimensions of land legislation. As stated in the introduction, 'The policy identifies lack of clarity and certainty of land rights in all the tenure regimes to be a critical issue and in this regard, measures are proposed to disentangle the multiple, overlapping and conflicting rights over registered land.' In chapter 5, the Land Policy clarifies land rights administration and outlines strategies to harmonize traditional customary systems with the formal statutory system, and to further decentralize land rights administration to traditional land governance institutions.

Anne Mette Kjær, Ph.D., is Professor at the Department of Political Science, Aarhus University.

Index

access to land, xiii–xiv, 3, 9, 14–16, 20, 51, 104, 106, 111–12, 117, 125–26, 130–34, 145–53, 187, 221, 227
Acholi, ix, xi, 3–7, 11, 15–17, 35, 46, 49, 52, 54, 67, 80–81, 103–4, 106–113, 117–18, 121–22, 124–26, 128, 130–31, 133, 138–46, 148–49, 152, 170–72, 175, 177–78, 206, 208, 214
actor, 2, 4, 13–14, 20, 22, 53, 62, 64–68, 71, 78, 84–86, 152, 189–91, 193, 197–99, 220, 226–27, 230
affine, 70, 148, 152
affinity, 17, 144–45, 148–49
agriculture, 45, 48, 50, 52, 54, 102, 106, 114, 125, 210, 218
agro-business, 20
ambiguity, 10, 105, 107, 110, 127, 197
ancestor, 16, 67, 93, 107–8, 114, 140, 143
anticipation, 176–79, 181
aspiration, x–xi, 165, 176, 178–81
attachment, 9, 17, 49, 113–14, 144–45, 148–153, 226
authority, ix, xi, xiii, 2, 6, 11, 13, 57, 59–60, 62, 64–68, 71, 77–79, 81, 85–86, 105, 109, 111–13, 115–16, 139, 141, 144, 146–47, 162, 167, 173, 185, 187, 189–91, 195–96, 211–12, 217–19, 225, 227–30
autochthony, 147–49, 152, 153n1
autoethnography, xiii, 8, 12, 39, 44, 47

belonging, xiii–xiv, 7, 9, 11–12, 17, 105, 110, 112–13, 138, 144–53, 187
ber bedo, 15, 43, 53, 82, 152
biodiversity, 21, 60, 207, 213
 loss, 210, 221
 richness, 209, 218
 threat, 210
border, 64, 138–39, 204–5, 209–10, 219
 area, 4, 217, 219
borrowing, 47–48, 116, 118, 133, 142, 150, 153, 196–97
boundary, 20–21, 47, 49–50, 65–66, 73–75, 146, 149, 174, 214
 dispute, 11, 20, 22n3, 40–44, 52–53, 59, 66, 75, 77, 82, 87, 108, 138–39, 142–44, 172–73
bridewealth, xii, 32, 70, 75, 87, 94, 102–3, 107, 111, 120, 127, 148, 151, 204
brokerage, 189–90, 194, 197
broker, 19–21, 57–58, 60, 62, 197–99

building, 1, 18–20, 40–41, 46, 48, 50, 53, 166–69, 171, 173, 175, 177–80, 185, 195, 207, 229
    brick building, 175, 178
bundle of rights, xi, 21, 48, 51–52, 63–64, 71, 145, 228–29
buyer, xi, 1–2, 18–19, 34–36, 58, 63, 65–66, 68–69, 147, 168, 180, 229

case study, x, xiii, 218, 221
CBO. *See* community-based organization
certificate of customary ownership, 47
chief, 81–83, 86, 143, 159, 205, 208, 213, 227
    Chief of the Hoe (*see Rwot Kweri*)
    parish chief, 83, 88n2, 142, 169
    sub-county chief, 58, 60, 68, 88n2, 162, 165–66, 170, 203
children, 14–15, 41, 73–75, 85, 87, 102–18, 121–27, 130–31, 133, 142, 150–51, 166, 179–80, 184, 203–4
church, 18–19, 43, 75, 157–63, 170, 172–76
    Anglican church, 157–58, 160–62, 173–74, 180
    Catholic church, 75, 157–62, 173–74, 180
citizenship, 145
civil society organization, 9, 84, 183–87, 190, 195, 197
claim
    claiming land, ix–xiv, 2, 6, 8, 11–21, 22n1, 29, 34–35, 39–45, 47–54, 58, 65, 96, 103, 105–9, 114, 116–17, 123–25, 129–132, 134, 139–140, 143, 146–53, 167, 170, 172–76, 179–80, 196, 214, 225–30, 232
    counterclaim, 129–131, 134
clan, 9–10, 14–15, 17–18, 57–58, 65–66, 70, 74–77, 81–82, 94, 98, 107–108, 111, 113, 117, 120–124, 126–27, 129–30, 132, 148–149, 158, 166, 169, 213, 227
    brother, 120–21, 123–24, 127, 129
    chief, 81
    elder, 9, 65, 74–76, 96, 108, 121–23, 129, 132, 162
    head, 81
    identity, 127
    land, 2, 15, 108, 111
    leader, xi, 57, 70, 123–24, 213
    member, 122–124, 149, 213
    membership, 87
climate change, 190, 210
coexistence, xii, 139, 143, 152
collaboration, x, 10, 78, 86–87, 159, 161–62, 216, 219
collective, xii, 2, 46, 68–69, 71, 115, 128, 179, 189, 212, 227
colonial
    administration, 81, 142
    authority, 144
    era, 107, 162
    government, 45, 143, 192, 207
    period, 3–4, 22n1
    time, 3–4, 18, 80, 142, 192, 207
colonialism, 213
colonialist, 206, 219
commodification, 5–6, 17–18, 87, 171, 220
common good, 173, 210
communal land, 19, 43, 45, 47, 60, 62, 113, 187, 216, 231
community, xi, 15, 18–19, 21, 57–60, 68, 84–85, 94, 98–99, 139–43, 145, 147, 161–63, 165–66, 172–73, 179–80, 184–91, 194–95, 197–99, 211–21
community-based organization, 84
community benefits and costs of conservation, 209, 212, 216–17, 218–221
    conservation justice, 219–21
compensation, 41, 58–60, 63, 70, 165–67, 169, 175, 179, 181, 205–6, 216–17, 219
competition, ix, xiii–xiv, 13, 68, 78, 86–87, 207–9, 211, 215, 221, 227
compromise, 82, 96, 123, 152, 169
conflict, ix, xi–xiv, 2–8, 11–22, 37, 53, 55, 78, 80–87, 109, 111, 116, 121, 124–32, 134, 138–46, 150–51, 161, 163, 170, 174, 177–79, 181, 183, 190, 192, 194–95, 203, 215, 226–28, 230
    ethnic conflict, 138–46, 215
    family conflict, 2, 18–19, 55, 73, 75, 77–79, 86–87, 109, 124, 128, 132
    human-wildlife conflict, 3, 18, 21, 203, 206, 208, 210, 217–18

Index   235

land conflict, ix, xi, xiv, 2–3, 6–8, 11–22, 22n1, 32, 37, 44, 50, 53, 55, 57–58, 66, 69, 73, 77–78, 82–87, 104, 109, 111, 116, 124–26, 129–32, 134, 138–46, 151, 161, 163, 165–66, 170, 174, 177–79, 194, 203, 225, 227–28, 230 (*see also* land: dispute)
   violent conflict, ix, 2, 5–6, 15, 17, 21, 75, 87, 128, 132, 134, 138–46, 183, 192, 195, 211, 225
confusion, 29, 66, 86, 195
connection, 15, 17, 20, 52, 70, 117, 151, 179, 189, 193
consanguinity, 108, 117, 148, 152
conservation, 21, 203, 208–21
   'community-based conservation', 212
   Community-based Natural Resource Management, 211
   'community conservation', 211, 216–220
   fortress conservation, 209–12, 218, 220
   Integrated Conservation and Development Projects, 211
   'new conservation', 211
   protectionist approach (*see* conservation: fortress conservation)
conservation and development
   investment, 212, 216
   tourism, 212, 215–17, 220
conservation and displacement, 212–15, 217, 219, 221
conservation and evictions, 211, 212–14
conservation governance, 220
   community conservation, 211, 216, 218
   community participation in conservation, 212, 220
   conservation conflict, 211, 218, 221
   state-centric top-down approach, 210, 218, 220
Corporate Social Responsibility, 188–89, 196–97
court, 11, 35, 79–80, 82–84, 86–87, 88n3, 124, 168–70, 232
   Local Council Court, 11, 79–80, 82, 84
   Magistrates' court, 11, 13, 79–80, 82, 84, 86–87, 88n2, 96–98
CSO. *See* civil society organization
CSR. *See* Corporate Social Responsibility
cultivating relationships, 16–17, 126, 131–34

cultural capital, 189
customary
   land, 3, 11, 17–19, 22n1, 22n3, 43, 47, 79, 87, 104–5, 107, 115–16, 125, 130, 132–34, 187, 214, 232
   law, xi, 129–30, 132, 134
   ownership, 47
   tenure, 3, 12, 22n3, 44–48, 54, 62–63, 79–80, 109, 113, 115–16, 123, 126, 130–32, 187, 231

daughter, 12, 29, 35, 52, 57–59, 68–70, 75–76, 107–8, 116–17, 120–21, 126, 132
demarcation, 62, 64, 75–76, 142, 191–92, 205, 211, 213
descent, 3, 11, 16, 18, 20, 49, 52, 54, 106–8, 111–13, 115, 140, 144, 148–49, 165–67, 172–73
development, ix–xiv, 2–3, 5–7, 10, 17–22, 41, 45, 52–53, 59, 68, 84, 155, 163, 165–81, 185, 188–99, 206–7, 209–11, 215–20, 231
devolution, 16, 22n1, 109, 153, 220
dialectics of recognition, 227
disagreement, 3, 12, 14, 19, 44, 62–63, 70, 73, 78, 138, 173, 199, 209
disarmament, ix, 6, 190–91, 193
disembedded process, 21, 64–66, 71, 195
dissatisfaction, 58, 68
diversification, 13, 44, 50
diversity, 44, 50, 54, 87, 131
divorce, 14, 108, 120, 125–26, 131, 149
Dodoth, 61, 147, 214–15

education, 15, 19–20, 40, 43, 52, 57, 102, 107, 128, 152, 161–63, 174, 180, 184, 186–87, 189, 192, 198, 203
elder, xiii, 6, 9–11, 16, 57–58, 60, 63, 65–66, 68, 74–76, 96, 102, 104, 108–11, 115–16, 118, 121–26, 129–30, 132, 134, 140–43, 152, 165–66, 169, 183, 187–89, 191, 197, 205–6, 227
elite, 9–10, 19–20, 57, 145–46, 184–99
   capture, 184, 190, 194–95
   local elite, 146, 191, 197–98
embeddedness, xi, xiv, 9, 13–14, 16–17, 22, 44–45, 51–55, 63–66, 68–69, 71, 84, 86, 113, 125–26, 131, 145, 150

embodiment, 13, 62, 64–66, 151
   embodied knowledge, 64–66
encumbrance, 40, 42, 44–45, 51, 167
enmity, 34, 176
entitlement, 51–53, 63–64, 70–71, 108–9, 112, 114, 143, 145–48, 150, 228
   burial entitlement, 114, 149–150
entrustment, 9–10, 16, 18, 20–21, 63–66, 68, 70–71, 113, 115, 171, 180
ethnicity, 14, 17, 138–39, 143–48, 152, 215, 226–27
ethnography, x–xi, xiv, 7
everyday, 2, 13, 22, 94, 117, 133, 152–53, 174, 176
evidence, 10–12, 114, 122–23
extended cases, 7, 170

factory, 185, 188, 196–97
faith-based organization, 84. *See also* church
family land, x, xiii, 15, 48, 50, 66, 78, 105, 108–9, 113, 117, 130, 165, 171, 175, 180
FBO. *See* faith-based organization
fence, 3, 36, 60–64, 70, 206, 229
'fiduciary culture', 9
fieldwork, x, 5, 8, 13, 22n3, 57, 129, 131, 133, 151
filiation, 108, 112, 117
firstcomer, 129–30, 143, 147–48, 152
food
   insecurity, 192, 219
   security, 190
forest, 21, 22n1, 59–62, 65–66, 71, 194, 209–21
   authority, 17, 59–60, 65, 212, 218
forum shopping, 78, 84–85
freehold
   land, 3, 11–12, 22n3, 32, 39, 43, 55, 69, 115, 148, 174, 231
   tenure, 45–46, 48, 52, 62–63, 116
future, 3, 9, 16–18, 20–21, 32, 34, 43, 54, 63, 67, 101, 105–6, 110, 113, 115–16, 121–22, 165, 171–72, 176–78, 180, 229

garden, 11–12, 18, 21, 35, 42–43, 49–50, 53, 70, 74, 76, 95, 107–9, 116, 121, 124, 126, 139, 143, 150, 152, 187, 206–7, 218

gathering, 48. *See also* hunting: hunting and gathering
gender, 6, 16, 106, 120, 125, 129–30, 134, 225–27
   relations, 107, 125–26, 129–30
generation, 16, 101, 104–18, 149
   historical generation, 16, 107, 109–10, 117
gerontocracy, 107, 109, 191–92
gold, 18, 191
good life, 177–78
government representative, 29, 187
grave, 12, 16, 41–44, 49–50, 93, 96–98, 114, 122–24, 130, 150, 152, 167–68, 173, 177–78
grazing, xiii, 4–5, 12, 48–49, 53, 147, 151, 153, 180, 187, 192–93, 209, 215, 228

harmony, 15–17, 53, 63, 82, 142–43, 152, 187, 215, 227, 232
health facility, 18, 20, 170–71, 174
history, 2–3, 6, 9, 16, 21, 49, 64–65, 71, 82, 85, 109–10, 114, 138, 140, 142–43, 158, 172, 174, 184, 191, 212, 225, 228–29
home, 34–37, 73–78, 101–5, 107, 111–12, 114–16, 120–21, 123–26, 131–33, 138–39, 149–51, 203–4, 207–9, 215
homestead, 50, 104, 120–21, 123–24, 208
house, 2, 12, 20, 35, 40, 42, 49, 53, 66, 76, 101, 109, 114, 115, 116, 122, 123, 145, 148, 150, 151, 153, 163, 166, 167, 168, 170, 175, 179, 180, 204, 207, 212, 219, 229, 175
hunting, 5, 12, 49, 133, 193, 205–7, 211, 213, 215–16, 219
   hunting and gathering, xiii, 4, 21, 59, 193, 214–15, 220
   international hunting fraternity, 213
   small-scale hunt, 215
   sport hunt, 216

ideal, 2–3, 6, 8–9, 16, 18–19, 71, 107, 111, 114, 170–71, 174–76, 178–79, 193, 213
identity, 9, 17, 19, 43, 53, 104, 107, 112–12, 127, 152, 186, 199, 215, 220, 225–26, 230

Index 237

IDP camp. *See* Internally Displaced Persons camp
Ik, xi, 4, 13, 57, 59, 61–62, 64–68, 71, 147, 150, 153n2, 198, 209, 214–15, 217–19
imagination, 2–3, 17, 19–20, 22, 153, 155, 172, 176–79, 181, 190, 193–94, 206, 212
indigenousness, 4, 62, 65, 68, 79, 147, 153nn1–2, 188, 195–96, 212
individual, 2–3, 7–8, 14, 18–19, 22, 22n3, 39, 45–47, 60, 62, 65, 67, 113, 115–16, 128, 131, 142–43, 145–46, 148, 172, 179–80, 189, 194, 198, 218
industry, 5, 184, 190–91, 194
informal system, 88
inheritance, xii, 53, 66, 76–77, 85, 115, 123–24
  inherited land, 12, 29, 32, 47, 51, 62, 87, 103, 105, 107, 109, 115, 146, 153, 180, 204, 228
inside-outsider, xiv, 15, 19–21, 145, 183, 188–90, 192–95, 197, 199
institution, 2, 6, 8–11, 13–14, 18–20, 46–47, 53, 60, 62, 65–68, 78–87, 111, 130–31, 147, 165, 170–74, 177, 180, 225–30, 232
  institutional land, 171, 173–74
  institutional multiplicity, 68, 85
intention, 8, 196–97, 199
interment, 149
Internally Displaced Persons camp, xiii, 6, 12, 17–18, 21, 74, 83, 102, 110, 114, 117, 120, 138, 166–67, 170–71, 173, 175, 177–78, 203–5, 207, 214
intimate governance, 2, 14–16, 87, 91, 117, 133, 148, 152, 227, 230
investor, ix, 5–6, 20–21, 57, 65, 68, 181, 183–87, 189, 193, 195–98, 208, 214–16, 219–20
  foreign investor, 13, 57, 65

justice, xi, 10, 79, 82–83, 86, 88, 219–21

Karamoja, ix, xi, 4–7, 13, 17–20, 61, 174, 184–99
Kidepo, 4, 61, 209, 214–15, 217
kinship, ix, xiv, 2, 14, 22, 42, 54, 106, 108, 117, 125–27, 134, 146, 180, 226

labour, 4, 40, 48–49, 108, 130, 148, 151
land
  access, x–xi, xiii–xiv, 3, 9, 13–17, 20, 48, 51–54, 63, 66, 69, 87, 102–4, 106, 108, 111–13, 115, 117–18, 121, 125–26, 130–34, 144–45, 147–53, 187, 195–96, 221, 226–27
  ancestral land, 3, 16–17, 20–21, 42, 47–49, 50, 82, 94–95, 107–109, 111, 113–117, 130, 146, 149, 171, 176, 203, 208, 214
  claim, x, xiii, 12–13, 16–17, 20, 39, 43–44, 48–50, 52–54, 131, 148–50, 152–53, 173–74
  commodification, 5–6, 17–18, 87, 171
  customary land tenure, 3, 79, 126, 130
  demarcation, 64, 75, 191, 205, 211
  dispute, xi, xiii, 2, 14, 50, 54, 66, 74–75, 81, 83, 84, 87, 108, 157, 169, 172–73, 78, 180, 194, 231 (*see also* conflict: land conflict)
  entitlement, 15, 51–53, 63, 86, 108–9, 112–14, 150, 229
  grabbing, 2, 8, 22, 130
  ownership, xiv, 9, 35, 39–41, 45–47, 67, 77, 113, 122–25, 130–131, 167, 174, 180, 187, 195, 228
  reform, 3, 45
  right, 2, 7, 10, 16, 53, 71, 82, 84–85, 125, 129–30, 189, 228, 232
  sale, xi, 1–3, 12–13, 17, 32, 34–35, 39, 44, 47, 54–55, 57–59, 62–71, 83, 105, 111, 115–16, 170–72, 175, 179
  speculation, 78, 87, 177
  tenure, 3, 14, 45–48, 51, 54??, 63, 69, 79, 125–26, 130–32, 134, 231–32
  title, 40, 58, 64, 69, 115
  transaction, ix, xi, xiv, 34, 39, 54, 58–59, 62–66, 69–71, 151, 228
  use, xiii–xiv, 3–4, 6–7, 22, 47–49, 109, 117, 125, 130, 142, 153, 177, 189, 205, 210, 219
landholding, xiii, 3, 7, 9, 12, 21, 43–45, 48, 52, 54, 63, 189
Langi, 4, 17, 138–44, 146, 148, 152
Lango, 140, 142–44, 158
  sub-region, 5, 7, 11, 138–39, 174, 178
large-scale, 2, 5, 8, 20, 22, 22n1, 130, 145
LCC. *See* court: Local Council Court

leasehold, 22n1, 174, 231
legal pluralism, xii, 10, 13, 73, 85–87
legislation, xi, 2–3, 52, 79, 210, 231–32
   National Forestry and Tree Planting Act of 2003, 210, 212, 216
   Uganda Wildlife Act of 2019, 210, 212, 216
   wildlife and forest conservation legislation, 210, 218
legitimacy, 9, 53, 71, 85–86, 146–147, 180, 227, 229
Lela Ogul, 138–43
levirate, 53, 76–77
limestone, 18, 191, 198
Lira, 121, 123, 139–40, 158, 161–62
livelihood, 2, 6, 8, 9, 16, 50, 105–6, 113, 116–17, 118, 132–33, 190, 192–93, 208, 211–12, 215, 218–19, 225
   livelihood strategy, 13, 50, 54, 116, 120, 126, 129, 132–33
Local Council 1
   chairman, 123
   court, 121, 124
Lord's Resistance Army, ix, 6, 17, 94, 111–12, 117, 178, 204, 207
LRA. *See* Lord's Resistance Army
luk, 107, 112

marble, 18, 20, 183–85, 189–91, 194–96, 198
market, 3–4, 13, 17–20, 47, 50, 54, 73, 111, 121, 124, 133, 144, 167, 171, 173, 175, 177, 203
marriage, 2, 11, 15–16, 70, 74, 76–77, 85, 87, 102–3, 106–8, 111, 113–14, 116–17, 122, 125–27, 148–51
maternal uncle, 102–8
mato oput, 35, 144
mediation, ix, xiv, 8, 14, 20, 22, 65–66, 71, 78, 81–86, 142–45, 148–49, 153, 168, 173, 188–89, 191–92, 194, 199
   mediator, 41, 82, 186–87, 191, 195, 197–99
meeting, 12, 17, 29, 32, 34, 36, 41, 43, 58–59, 65–66, 68, 75, 77, 81–83, 94, 98, 102, 110, 121–24, 138, 140, 142–43, 147, 159, 161–62, 165, 168–70, 184–86, 189, 195–96, 203, 206–8
middleman, 2, 20, 57, 65–68, 183–84, 188–92, 198. *See also* brokerage: broker

military, xii, 94, 147
miner, 20, 183–91, 194–96, 198
   artisanal miner, 184–91, 194–96, 198
mineral, 4, 8, 18, 20, 142, 183–84, 188, 191, 194–95, 221
mining, 18, 174, 181, 183–98, 210
   lease, 18, 185, 188, 191
   license, 18, 191, 197
missing link, 15, 127, 129, 152, 186
mobility, 4, 184, 219
money, 3, 17, 32, 34–37, 58–63, 65, 68–69, 81, 104–6, 114–16, 121–22, 128, 142, 167–69, 171, 175, 179–80, 188, 197, 203–5, 217
mother, 12, 14–16, 42, 49, 52, 55, 69, 74, 77, 102–12, 115, 117–18, 122–24, 126, 129–31, 148–52, 178
multiple
   land claims, 39, 44, 48–49
   land ownership, 39–43, 48–49
multiplicity, x, 8, 12–13, 39, 44–45, 47, 50–54, 68, 71, 85–86, 145
multisightedness, 7
multisitedness, 7
Murchison Falls, 4, 18, 203–4, 206, 209, 217, 219

National Forestry Authority, 211–12, 216, 218, 220
national park, xiv, 3–4, 18, 21, 61, 174, 203, 204, 206, 209, 211–19
navigation, 130, 133–134
negotiation, xi, xiii, 2, 10, 12, 18–19, 21, 39, 41, 43, 51–53, 58–59, 62–63, 69, 71, 82, 85, 108, 110, 130–31, 134, 143, 147, 149, 152, 168, 176, 178, 180–81, 191, 199, 206
neighbour, ix, xi, 2, 4, 11, 13–15, 22–23, 40–44, 46, 49, 52, 54, 64, 111, 121, 129–32, 134, 138–39, 145, 149, 152, 158, 168, 215, 219, 220, 228
neighbourliness, 138
nephew problem, 106, 112
NFA. *See* National Forestry Authority
NGO. *See* non-governmental organization
ngom kwaro. *See* land: ancestral land
non-governmental organization, ix, xi, 11, 13, 19–20, 73–76, 79, 82–84, 86–87, 128, 139, 141–42, 174, 186–87, 190, 213, 227

Index

oil, 4, 18, 20, 50, 101, 105, 191, 210
original owner, 13, 58, 68, 123, 147, 198
orphan, 29, 34, 73, 110, 126, 184
outsider, 3–4, 19–20, 43, 59, 67, 105, 127, 177, 187–97, 199
owner, 135
ownership. *See under* land

Pader, 121, 123, 127, 166, 178
   Town, 120, 124, 133
   Town Council, 122, 124
pastoralism, 4, 6, 8, 19, 69, 184, 187, 190–93, 199, 211, 214–15
paternity, 6, 52, 108, 110, 112, 116–17, 149, 226
patrilineage, xiii, 16, 47, 52, 105–8, 111–12, 114, 117, 125–27, 149, 187
   descent, 3, 49
patrilineal fundamentalism, 17, 112, 149
payment, xii, 12, 14, 35, 40, 48, 68, 70, 78, 107, 127, 133, 147, 168, 188
peace, 6, 78, 82, 85, 87, 98, 122–23, 128, 139, 142–43, 152, 178, 193, 207, 213, 226, 230
peri-urban land, 32
perspective, x, 7–8, 12, 51, 59, 62, 65, 70, 82, 107, 176, 195–96
plot, xiii, 1–2, 6, 12, 18–19, 32, 40–41, 44, 48, 52, 57–60, 64–66, 69–71, 98, 115, 124, 128, 132–33, 165, 167–72, 175–80
   plotting, 19, 41, 122, 165, 170, 173, 175–76
plurality, 10, 45, 78, 87
plural legal systems, 9–10
policy, 7, 162, 210, 217, 231–32
politician, 10, 20, 141, 168
politics, 54, 178, 190
'polygraph', 7
population density, ix, 4–5
post-war, 39, 78, 81, 83–84, 133, 179, 226, 229
potential, 3, 17–18, 20, 71, 171, 176, 189–94, 197, 199
poverty, 58, 112, 114, 127, 175, 178, 189, 207–8, 210–211, 214, 219, 225
power, 2, 4, 29, 62, 65–67, 71, 78–79, 81, 83–86, 127–32, 152, 161–62, 174, 176–77, 186–87, 192, 195, 208, 212–13, 218, 220, 227–28

practise, xiii, 15, 17, 145, 149–52
presence, 1, 12, 15, 63, 66, 177, 192–93, 196–97, 209, 229
privatization, 43, 71, 190
property, xii, xivn1, 1, 6, 17, 47, 51, 53, 64, 67, 69, 74, 105, 124–25, 127, 141, 144–45, 148, 151, 162–63, 212, 216, 225–26, 228–30
   right, 17, 46, 51, 69, 84, 129

reburial, 12, 35, 114, 168
recognition, xiv, 10, 22, 47, 64, 66, 112, 114, 151, 166, 176, 219–20, 226–27, 229
refugee, 4, 41, 48, 102, 126, 170, 172–73, 212, 214
   settlement, 48, 172
relation, ix–xii, 2, 4, 9–10, 13–17, 19–20, 22, 36–37, 44, 51–55, 60, 63–71, 85–86, 93, 106–8, 111–14, 117–18, 125–27, 129–134, 144–45, 147–52, 163, 174, 185, 189, 194, 196, 218, 221, 225, 227
research, 1, 3–4, 7–8, 17, 39, 44, 47–48, 52, 79–80, 86, 88, 111, 130–31, 141, 144, 185, 186, 217–18, 228
resolution, 2, 11, 13, 66, 73, 75, 78–79, 81–83, 85–87, 131, 144
   dispute resolution, 13, 75, 78, 81
resource
   curse, 193
   extraction, 189–91, 193–95, 198
revenue
   sharing, 208, 216–20
right
   rights subject, 225–28
   right to land (*See under* land)
road, 18–19, 36, 41, 60, 167–68, 170–71, 175, 178, 183–85, 207, 217
Rwot Kweri, 41, 73–76, 79, 81–83, 85, 142

sales agreement, 32, 35, 39
school, 18–19, 102–3, 157–63, 166–67, 172–77, 179–80, 184, 191–92, 203–4
security, ix, 6, 13, 45, 54, 83, 85, 108, 113, 130, 134, 140, 143, 146, 177, 190, 218–19, 229, 231
sharing, 15, 70, 108, 114, 151, 196–97, 199, 206, 208, 212, 216–20

sign, 1–3, 19, 36, 64, 69, 229
sister, 11, 16, 40, 43, 53, 103, 105, 107, 111–12, 116–17, 120–24, 129, 134, 148, 150, 166, 168, 178–79
small-scale, 2, 102, 121, 130, 133, 214–15
social
  capital, 189
  relation/relationship, xi–xii, 2, 4, 9–10, 13–14, 16–17, 22, 44, 51, 53, 55, 63–64, 66, 70–71, 82, 86, 113, 145, 150, 152
soil, 57, 67, 147, 149, 153, 175, 177
soldier, 62, 77, 123, 166, 172, 179, 183–86, 197, 207
stakeholder, 13, 17, 39, 43, 47, 64, 69, 80–81, 185–89, 191, 195
stealing, 196–97
stewardship, 9, 18, 21, 113, 171
stress, 37, 219
structure, 18, 41–42, 166–67, 175, 179–180
sub-county, 59, 66, 76, 138, 146, 165, 170

temporality, 13, 20, 62, 69–71
tension, xii–xiii, 1, 4, 7–8, 14, 20, 53, 68, 108–9, 111, 116, 126, 134, 138, 144, 146, 171, 189, 191, 215, 228
tenure system, 3, 125–26, 130–31, 231
tourism, 3, 18, 20–21, 174, 207–8, 210, 212, 215–20
town, xiii, 1, 7, 12, 15, 17–18, 20, 32, 40–42, 45, 48, 73, 110, 112, 114, 120–22, 124, 128, 132, 133, 179–80, 184, 186–88, 214
  board, 18–19, 64, 165, 167, 171, 175–76, 178, 181
  council, 18, 76, 88n1, 122, 124, 171, 177, 179
trading centre, 1, 18, 48, 78, 116, 127, 129, 166–68, 170, 173, 203–4, 207–9
traditional authority, 11, 57, 77–78, 81
transaction, ix, xi–xii, xiv, 2, 8, 11–13, 20–21, 34, 39, 45, 47, 54, 57–60, 62–71, 151, 225, 228–30
transformation, 3, 12, 16, 62, 117, 151, 167, 177, 218, 220–21, 225

tree, 12–13, 21, 41–42, 48–50, 57–58, 60, 64–65, 74, 76–77, 109, 123, 143, 167, 175, 178, 184, 210, 212, 213, 215–18, 220–21, 229
trust, xi, xiii–xiv, 1–3, 6–12, 17–18, 20–22, 39, 46, 53–55, 62, 65–69, 71, 75, 78, 81, 85, 104–5, 110, 113, 121, 126–27, 130, 133–34, 141–42, 147, 170, 180–81, 189, 210, 212, 220, 227
  mistrust, xiii–xiv, 2, 6–10, 12–13, 17, 19–22, 54, 69, 71, 110, 117–18, 134, 139–40, 181, 190, 193–97, 199, 219
Turkana, 61, 147

Uganda Wildlife Authority, 18, 204–8, 210–12. 214, 216–20
underground, 187, 192–94
  resources, 4, 18, 21, 153n2, 191–93, 196
urban centre, x, 12, 18–20, 50, 54, 120, 170–72, 174–75, 177–78
urbanization, 170–71, 175
urban plot, xiii, 171
UWA. *See* Uganda Wildlife Authority

value, ix, xii, 3, 9, 17–18, 63, 65, 70–71, 76, 78, 80, 113, 146, 152, 170–71, 176–78, 183, 193–94, 198, 207, 210, 216
virilocality, 16, 107, 125

war, 5–6, 16–17, 34–35, 39–41, 43, 94–95, 110–15, 117, 120–21, 124, 127–29, 133, 171–73, 178, 192, 195, 204, 207, 225–30
  -generation, 110–112, 117
water, xiv, 4, 21, 120–21, 133, 139–40, 147, 177, 193, 196, 205–6, 214–15, 221
wealth, ix, xii, 2, 77, 171, 184, 192–93, 196–97
wild animal, 2, 21, 133, 203–14
witchcraft, xiii, 15, 102, 110
  accusation, 75, 77, 85, 87, 134
  allegation, 17, 82
women, 107–8, 111, 116, 118, 120–21, 125–29
  women's land rights, 125, 128–129, 131

www.ingramcontent.com/pod-product-compliance
Lightning Source LLC
Chambersburg PA
CBHW051535020426
42333CB00016B/1934